A Complete Guide to Lotus Notes® 4.5

Digital Press Editorial Board

Samuel H. Fuller, Chairman
Richard W. Beane
Donald Z. Harbert
William R. Hawe
Richard J. Hollingsworth
William Laing
Richard F. Lary
Alan G. Nemeth
Pauline Nist
Robert M. Supnik

A Complete Guide to Lotus Notes® 4.5

Simon Collin

Digital Press
Boston • Oxford • Johannesburg • Melbourne • New Delhi • Singapore

Copyright © 1997 Simon Collin

All rights reserved.

Digital Press™ is an imprint of Butterworth–Heinemann.

A member of the Reed Elsevier group

All trademarks found herein are property of their respective owners.

No part of this publication may be reproduced, stored in a retrieval system, or transmitted in any form or by any means, electronic, mechanical, photocopying, recording, or otherwise, without the prior written permission of the publisher.

Recognizing the importance of preserving what has been written, Butterworth–Heinemann prints its books on acid-free paper whenever possible.

ISBN 1-55558-175-7

The publisher offers special discounts on bulk orders of this book.
For information, please contact:

Manager of Special Sales
Butterworth–Heinemann
313 Washington Street
Newton, MA 02158–1626
Tel: 617-928-2500
Fax: 617-928-2620

For information on all Digital Press publications available, contact our World Wide Web home page at: http://www.bh.com/dp

Order number: EY-V422E-DP

10 9 8 7 6 5 4 3 2 1

Design and composition by ReadyText, Bath, UK
Printed in the United States of America

Contents

Preface		**ix**
Introduction: an overview of Lotus Notes 4		**1**

1 Quick start to using Notes — 5

About this chapter	5
The Notes main screen – The workspace	6
Sending mail	13
Opening a database	19
Editing documents	28
Using attachments	33
Printing	36
Working with multiple databases	37
Agents	39
Navigators and folders	40
Formatting text	41
Internet integration	42

2 Hardware requirements — 45

About this chapter	45
Server hardware requirements	46
Requirements for workstations	54
Network hardware requirements	55
Links to the outside world	59

3 Operating system software — 63

About this chapter	63
Server software requirements	64
Workstation software requirements	71

4 Networking Notes — 75

About this chapter	75
How Notes views a network	76

5	**Remote access to Notes**	**85**
	About this chapter	85
	An overview of remote access	86
	Setting up remote access	87
	Using Notes remotely	97
	Summary	104

6	**How Notes distributes information**	**107**
	About this chapter	107
	Replication	108
	Setting up database replication	111

7	**How Notes sees the world**	**121**
	About this chapter	121
	The public Name & Address database	122
	Mapping the world with domains	124
	Personal Name & Address database	128
	User groups	130

8	**Managing Notes**	**131**
	About this chapter	131
	Database administration	132
	User administration	140
	Server administration	147
	Administrator administration	156
	Controlling the server	159

9	**Electronic mail and communications**	**167**
	About this chapter	167
	Using Notes mail	168
	Alternative e-mail front-ends	178
	Gateways to other mail systems from Notes	178

10	**Notes and the Internet**	**185**
	About this chapter	185
	The InterNotes suite	186
	Web Navigator	190
	InterNotes Web Publisher	192

	InterNotes News	194
	Domino Web Server	194
	Security and the Internet	194

11 Agents and automation — 197

    About this chapter — 197
    Automating tasks with Agents — 198

12 Creating Notes applications — 203

    About this chapter — 203
    Designing a Database — 204
    Types of database — 204
    How to create a database — 207
    How to create a form — 210
    Designing a form — 215
    Defining fields — 219
    Designing a view — 226
    Navigators — 235
    The final touches — 238
    Database security — 240
    Full-text search index — 241

13 Programming skills — 245

    About this chapter — 245
    Developing applications – the essentials of programming with @-formulas — 246
    Programming examples — 251
    Programming with LotusScript — 254

14 Setting up Notes — 257

    About this chapter — 257
    Setting up users — 258
    Security — 262
    Setting up international support — 274

15 Domino Server — 279

    Introduction — 279
    Domino and InterNotes — 280
    How it works — 281
    System requirements — 282

Installing and running Domino 283
Configuring Domino 284
The user's view of Domino 286
Programming with Domino 287
Security 290

Glossary **293**
Appendix A: @-functions **299**
Appendix B: NOTES.INI variables **307**
Index **311**

Preface

When it was first launched, Lotus Notes provided a completely new type of groupware product. It proved almost impossible to categorize: some reviewers placed it with traditional e-mail products – where it fared well; others placed it up against group calendar and scheduling programs. It is really a product that can do whatever you want it to do. It can manage this because it includes a powerful database programming language that lets you create Notes applications – such as e-mail or scheduling – along with more complex project management applications. In fact, in this new version, Notes now has an e-mail database that looks and works just like the Lotus cc:Mail product many users will be familiar with.

In the latest version of Notes, version 4.5, Lotus has included a wide range of new features. The most important of which is to make Notes Internet-friendly. Notes now includes a feature called InterNotes that provides users with a World Wide Web (WWW) browser and allows managers to set up intranets (WWW sites contained internally, with no potential security risks by accessing remote Internet servers).

One problem for anyone considering creating a distributed database for project management or custom scheduling is the complication of managing the distribution of updates to ensure that everyone has an up-to-date copy. Notes lifts this burden and carries it out for you.

If you have decided that Notes is for you, you need to be an expert on a wide range of subjects. Not only in Notes programming and database management, but also wide-area network links, e-mail design and network connectivity. For most network managers, many of these functions will be new ones that they have not tackled (or had to tackle) before.

Luckily, in this new version of Notes, Lotus has provided all sorts of tools and features that will help new administrators design effective databases and provides a friendlier user front-end to the software.

Who is this book for?

This book is aimed at someone who thinks Notes is for them but needs a friendly guide to show him or her what is needed to run Notes, how to configure the software and hardware elements and how to manage it properly. Add to this instruction on programming in Notes and detailed coverage of networking, accessing the Internet and inter-office wide-area communications make this an essential reference book for any potential Notes manager or supervisor.

I wrote this book to act as a guide for network managers who are trying to come to grips with Notes and the ideas behind distributed groupware. This book covers all the important, and difficult, subjects that any manager will come across. Whether you are installing Notes on a single server and want help on efficient user setup, configuration and management or if you are setting up an intranet or several linked sites and need to know about WAN links, this book will be of help.

The book is arranged progressively: the first chapter is an overview of Notes to provide you with the background information about Notes, the workstation software and interface. Following this is a guide to the hardware that you will need: from server specifications to workstation, Internet links, remote connections and WAN links – all are covered in this chapter. Next is an overview of the software you will need to run Notes on different platforms and any likely problems you will have with network software. Remote access to Notes follows, then a chapter describing how Notes distributes information between multiple servers – and ensures that each database is always up to date.

The next chapters show you how to manage Notes – database, user and server administration that you will need to carry out. How to get the most from Notes' electronic mail feature and tying this in with mail-enabled applications follows. Next is a detailed look at one of the new features of Notes 4.5, the InterNotes WWW browser and Internet connectivity. Finishing up is a chapter on creating a Notes application from programming to design styles.

Throughout the book I have tried to include many tips and tricks that will save you time and effort and help you get the most from Notes. I hope that it helps you provide a reliable and efficient service to your users.

Simon Collin

Introduction: an overview of Lotus Notes 4

What is Notes?

Lotus Notes is an unusual product. Perhaps its most useful description is as a shared information management system – however, that means little to most people. Notes is really a sophisticated database management system with a flexible programming language and excellent data sharing functions.

At the heart of a Notes system is a Notes server. Up until the release of version 3.0 of the software, the server had always been a dedicated PC running OS/2 as its base operating system. Notes ran as an OS/2 task and used OS/2 for low-level network, multitasking and disk management. Now, with the improvements to the Windows range of operating systems, Notes can run under almost any of the major popular operating systems including Windows NT, OS/2, Novell NetWare and Unix.

In short, it no longer requires a dedicated OS/2 server to run Notes, in fact you can even test a system with a couple of users on a server running under Windows 95! However, if you plan to support more than a dozen users, you should budget for a dedicated server and whichever of the 32-bit network operating systems you are familiar with.

The flexibility of Notes comes mainly from its programming language. You can design almost any data-handling application, from a calendar to a contact database; the data storage is managed by the Notes server program.

So far, there's little difference between Notes and any of the many multi-user database software systems available. Where Notes scores is in its ability to communicate and share data with other Notes servers. Notes' main method of distributing data between connected Notes servers is through a process called replication. At scheduled times during the day, each Notes server dials its neighboring servers in the network and the two exchange new updates to their databases. In this way, databases across the servers are kept up to date.

With replication comes the potential for groupware applications. If you have a company spread over several sites or countries, each with its own Notes server, you can be sure that new data entered at one site will be replicated to all the other sites. Making use of this is one of the built-in applications supplied with Notes: Notes Mail, an electronic mail system. In the current version, Notes v4.5, the e-mail database has been developed to provide the look and feel of Lotus' successful cc:Mail product and provides all the features you would expect of e-mail including rules-based intelligence and gateways to other mail systems including the Internet.

Implementing a company-wide groupware system is relatively easy under Notes: since every server has a name, and every user a unique identity, when you install several Notes servers in your company you immediately have a company-wide wide-area network and the databases you develop, including scheduling, contract tracking and e-mail are immediately available to any user.

What can Notes do?

Notes is unlike many other groupware products in that it can carry out just about any groupware function that you program. In its simplest form, Notes is a sophisticated shared database management system with a neat graphical user front-end. The users access a database and a manager (or programmer) can make each individual database look very different.

For example, like other groupware products, Notes comes with a group calendar, a powerful e-mail system and a contacts tracking database. These are all separate Notes databases but each has been made to look like a more familiar application. You could create specialized applications for error reporting, customer order taking, or project management. Alternatively, you can change the existing programs to create your own calendar.

Notes runs on a central server – the Notes server. This is ideally a dedicated server running a network operating system and Notes linked in to your main network and its server.

Notes server was first developed to run on OS/2, and Notes running under OS/2 still provides the most flexible and powerful of all the combinations available. However, you can run Notes as a NetWare NLM on your main Novell NetWare server or you can run Notes on a Windows NT or Unix server.

When you install a single Notes server you are using it as a central, highly configurable groupware product. It comes into its own when you link several Notes servers at different sites. Notes takes care of updating the databases and distributes e-mail across the networks. As an alternative, you can link into another commercial Notes server. This way you can add live news feeds or financial information into your network.

The great advantage is that every user accessing any Notes database will be using the same user front-end and the same button-bar and shortcuts: this user application can run under Windows 3.1, Windows 95 or NT, or OS/2 on a PC or on a Unix station or an Apple Macintosh. The system can cut support calls, since the users are within a consistent interface. It's also easy to pick up and train users: you can access a database by just clicking on one of the large icons.

Lastly, since Notes now has Internet connectivity built-in, together with its own browser, you can easily implement an internal company intranet or you can provide a complete environment for users to access internal data or external data on the Internet from within the same user interface. Notes can also be integrated with other products to enhance a particular facet: for example, it will work with document management software to manage scanned object files, work with other e-mail products including Internet and mainframe-based e-mail or even drive a pager or fax card to add full communications functions to e-mail.

If you need to organize a mass of on-line information or would like to have better access to the data, Notes can provide a very flexible system that will help you get the most from your network investment.

What's new in Notes release 4.5?

The new, latest version of Notes is almost a totally different product from the old system. The functionality and theory has stayed the same, together with the basic programming language and commands, but Lotus has worked hard to improve all the problem areas that were weak in the older version and has included a set of new features for the everyone including the user, manager, designer and programmer.

The first new features you'll see are the user front-end. This now includes a re-designed look and feel that matches other Lotus products including its cc:Mail e-mail software. The Notes front-end provides access to the databases using large buttons, but once inside a database, there are new features everywhere.

It's difficult to decide which is the most useful new feature, so I'll list them in my order of preference! The user's view on a database now lets you set up panes so that a window can be split into different, independent sections. On the left of the screen is usually a pane that shows a outliner's view of the database articles, to the right are panes that display what's in a particular article.

Agents are a sophisticated version of an automated macro that can let users carry out simple programming to make their environment more productive – including adding intelligence to their e-mail so that it'll respond to messages and act accordingly.

Notes also allows users to setup folders within e-mail. Each folder can have sub-folders and can be for a project or for personal mail messages. If you combine this with agents you and your users can create a customized system that will automatically file incoming messages as they arrive.

Still on the subject of e-mail, Notes lets you setup expressive icons within a message. You can have a balloon banner for messages about an office party, or you can tailor the e-mail message to look like a phone-message pad.

Remote users get new features that should help to cut down long connection times when dialing into the server via a modem link. There's now a simple electronic 'form' that remote users can fill in to define when they want replication to take place and which database files to replicate. Another new feature is called pass-through login. This lets you dial into the local office server and access your office server via the server-to-server links. It speeds data transfer and means you can login to Notes just about anywhere.

Lastly, Notes now includes coverage for the Internet. Lotus has included its own WWW browser, called InterNotes, that will display any standard document formatted with HTML commands. You can use Notes to setup an intranet, or you can use the InterNotes feature to give your users access to the Internet itself.

In keeping with this ability to communicate with remote systems, Lotus has greatly improved the links to other mail systems. Notes will now happily exchange mail using any of the major mail standards including Microsoft's MAPI interface used in Microsoft Mail.

In this introduction, I've covered just some of the major new features that are part of this important new release of Notes. Within this book you'll see how to make the most of these features and the many other tricks and re-designed functions that make Notes a more powerful and easier to use environment.

Quick start to using Notes

About this chapter

This chapter takes you through the basic Notes functions, how to access databases and mail together with details showing you how to add, edit, and transfer text between Notes and other applications – quickly and simply. This chapter also introduces the new features including panes, folders and agents – which make release 4.5 of Notes more powerful and easier to use.

If you're new to Notes, use this chapter to become familiar with your new environment. Anyone using Lotus Notes will spend much of their time navigating through the main screen; almost all Notes operations, including supervisor options such as configuring workstations, setting up modem links, and details of data replication, are carried out from the same front-end. The Notes server screen is described in Chapter 8.

The Notes main screen – The workspace

You can run the Notes workstation software on any PC capable of running Microsoft Windows 3.1, 95 or NT, or IBM OS/2. (Accessing Notes from an Apple Macintosh or Unix workstation is almost identical; the subtleties are covered later, in Chapter 3.) The front-end, menus and keystrokes used to drive Notes under both Windows and OS/2 are virtually identical. All versions look and feel the same to the user. Throughout the book I'll be using a Windows 95 workstation, however the differences with other clients are covered in detail both in their own chapters and in tip boxes within the text.

Starting Notes

The Lotus Notes icon

First, find your Notes icon. Notes is normally installed into a Lotus Applications folder under Windows 95 and OS/2 or into a Lotus Notes group in Windows 3.1. To start Notes under Windows 95, click on the Notes icon in the *Start ▸ Programs ▸ Lotus* menu or double-click on the Notes icon in your Windows 3.1 Lotus group.

Tip

You may find it convenient to move the Notes icon into your Windows or OS/2 StartUp folder. This will automatically start Notes when you start Windows. If you don't want to use the Notes front-end all the time, create a shortcut to the Notes icon and right-click on the shortcut icon; select the *Properties ▸ Shortcut* page and change the Run mode to minimized to start the program as a minimized icon. Windows 3.1 users should use the PIF editor for the same function.

The main Notes screen

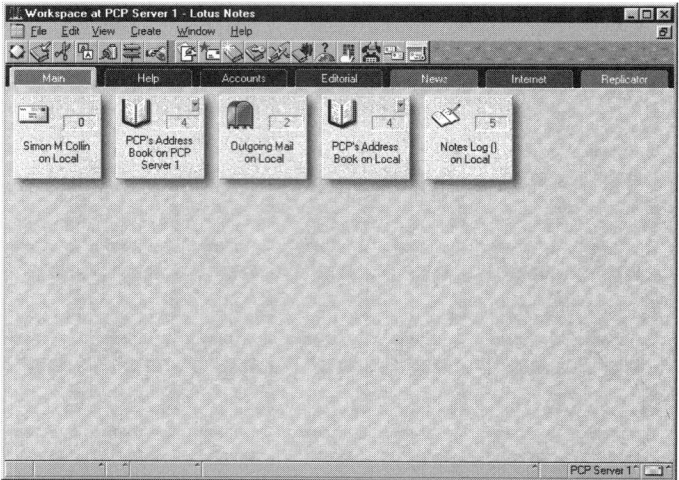

If you have a shortcut to Notes on your Desktop, start the software by double-clicking on the icon. Otherwise, select the *Start ▸ Programs ▸ Lotus ▸ Notes* menu option. The logo screen is displayed for a few seconds, then clears to reveal the main Notes workspace.

Once you start Notes, you will be greeted with a dialog box that pops up to report how many unread messages you have in your active databases (mail messages are also stored within their own database).

To skip this dialog box for the moment, select the Done button. If you want to go through each unread message in every database, select the Next Unread button – but watch out, if you haven't logged in for a few days it could take some time to go through all the new messages!

The Notes workspace follows standard Windows conventions and you can move about using the mouse and left button. Notes 4.5 now uses the right-hand mouse button (in Windows and OS/2) to set the properties of an object. For example, if you are editing text, a right-click will let you set the text formatting attributes.

The workspace is divided into five main areas. Running along the top of the screen is the menu bar – you can access this using [Alt]+[hotkey] conventions of Windows or using a mouse. Below the menu bar is a row of SmartIcons which are similar to SmartIcons in all current Lotus applications. These give you one-click access to the most-frequently used file, editing, search and formatting commands. To make it easier to understand some of the less obvious icon images, Notes now has bubble help to each button; move your pointer over the icon and wait a couple of seconds and a help bubble with a description of the button's function pops up.

The main part of the screen is taken up with six pages; each page has a label tab running along the top. Pages carry large icons that give you access to a Notes database. You can change the text on the page tags, their color, and shuffle the icons between pages to organize your workspace just the way you like it best. To switch between pages, click on the page tag. Although the page tags can have different colors, the background of each page is the same mottled light-grey. When you select a tag, its page is displayed and the tag turns to pale-grey to show that it's active.

Page tags

Stored on each page are your databases icons. Each shows as a descriptive icon and text that is the full title of the database. When first installed, Notes adds a few basic databases into your workspace to help you get started: your personal mail box, an address book, a couple of sample applications and on-line help. To access any database, double-click on its button. Lastly, running along the bottom of the screen is the SmartStatus bar that gives you a one-line summary of your current setup in Notes.

Database icon

SmartStatus bar

The bar is divided up into sections which each carry a different indicator. Running from the far left on the status bar are indicators for:

- disk or network activity
- typeface
- type size
- type style
- status messages
- access level indicator
- location
- access mail database

This status bar also gives you a fast, one-click access to the sections that it displays. For example, if an envelope is displayed in the new mail indicator section (which means you have new mail), you can click once on this section of the status bar to read the mail rather than double-clicking on your mail database. Similarly, if you want to change the font or point size you are using, click once on the status bar section to pop-up a list of available fonts and point sizes.

Access rights in Notes

The access level indicator graphically shows you the access rights you have in the selected database. These rights are stored in an access control list which is maintained by the manager.

If you are a manager of the database (there's normally only one for each database), you are in charge of adding users and defining their

The Notes main screen – The workspace

access rights. To do this, select the database (with a single click from the workspace) and choose *File ▸ Database ▸ Access* menu option.

File ▸ Database ▸ Access Control

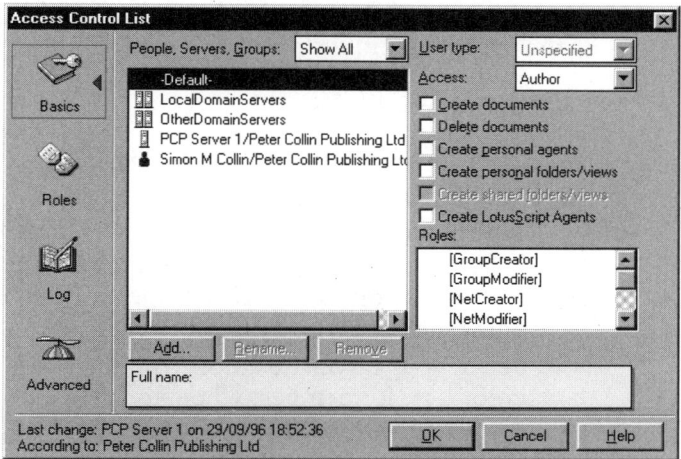

The table below shows the meaning of the symbols representing access control.

Symbol	Status	Rights
Key	Manager	All operations, including deleting database.
Ruler	Designer	Can create, edit views, forms and text.
Pen	Editor	Can create, edit or delete documents.
Pen	Author	Can create and read documents.
Magnifying glass	Reader	Can read documents.
File	Depositor	Can create new documents but cannot read.

The access control window

A list of the users, groups and servers is listed at the top of the box; select a user and his or her access control rights are described by the radio buttons at the bottom of the dialog box. To change a user's access rights, highlight the user's name and click on list-box 'Access'.

Warning — Be careful when changing the access rights of a group or domain – you might inadvertently give users on that server (which might be in another company) full access to your database!

Organizing your workspace

Notes does not try to impose a severe set of rules on every user. You can easily change how your workspace looks, the descriptions and colors of the page tags and the position of the database icons.

Changing page tags

To change the text or color of a page tag:

- Double-click on the tag. A small dialog box pops up and you can type in its description. A quick shortcut with Windows and OS/2 is to move the pointer over the page tag and click on the right mouse button; select the Properties menu option and you can enter the page's text description.
- Select your favourite color from the range of 16 displayed in the color bar. Remember, when you select this page, the tag will be displayed as mottled light-grey (regardless of its base color) to show that it's active.

The tag config box – setting the tag color

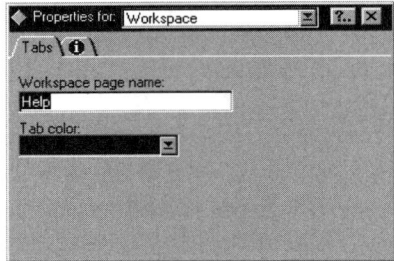

Arranging database icons

You can move icons from one page to another by clicking and dragging the icon onto the new page tag. When you drag the icon to another page tag, the pointer changes to a hand icon.

- To arrange the icons on a page:
  - Click once on the icon and drag it around the page with the mouse button held down.

Moving icons around the workspace

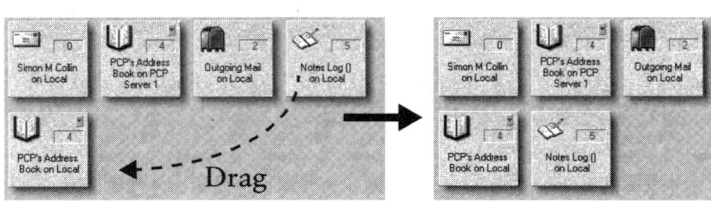

Drag

The Notes main screen – The workspace

Tip The icons can be moved around all over the workspace, but to get back to a neat and tidy workspace select the right mouse button and choose the Arrange Icons menu option to automatically align everything.

- **To delete an icon from a page:**

    Click once on the icon to select it, then press [Del]. A dialog box asks if you're sure this is what you want to do. Remember, you are deleting just the icon, not the entire database!

The delete dialog box

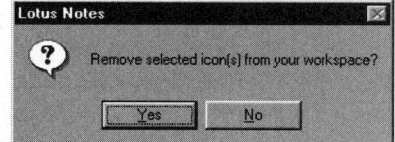

- **To edit the picture on the icon:**

    You can draw your own icon using the graphics editor that's supplied. To start the icon editor is a little cumbersome:

    1. Select the *View ▸ Design* menu option.
    2. Select the Show Design View pane option.
    3. The Design pane is displayed on the left of the screen, select the Other entry from the list and then select the icon entry.
    4. Once you've finished editing, click on the icon in the top left-hand corner of the icon editor window (to the left of the File menu) and choose Close.

View ▸ Design ▸ Other ▸ Icon

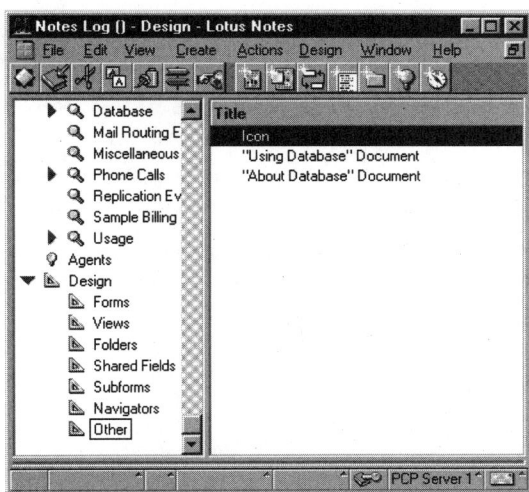

Chapter 1

The icon editor

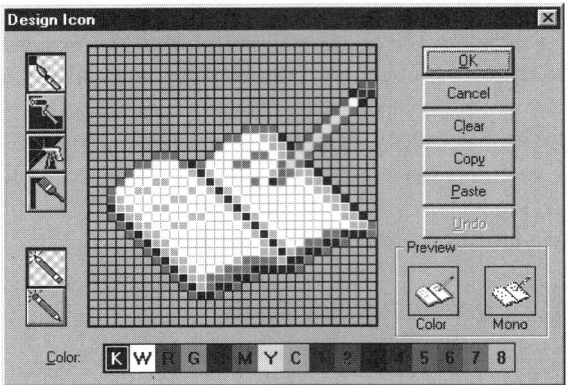

To read in more detail how to manage databases and configure your workspace, see Chapter 8.

Need help?

The Notes help icon

If you need help at any point, press [F1] or click on the help icon in the far right of the SmartIcon bar. The Notes help is actually another database, and can be added to your workspace if you prefer to access it from a database icon.

Summary: the workspace

- Move between pages by selecting the page tag
- Change page tag colors by double-clicking
- Access a database by double-clicking on an icon
- Move database icons by dragging to new pages
- Use the SmartIcon row to speed functions
- Use the right mouse button to access an object's properties
- Check the SmartStatus bar to check for new mail
- Click on the status Bar section to change the option
- Get help from the help database or [F1] key

Sending mail

Mail icon

Notes has a very powerful built in electronic mail system. The program is a little unusual in some respects because it is actually a Notes database. This means that if you don't like a feature, you can always change it by editing the database design! In Notes 4.5, the e-mail database has been totally updated and is now on a par with any of the stand-alone products.

The e-mail front-end has been designed to look and work just like the Lotus cc:Mail software. The Notes e-mail database now includes folders, to help you organise you messages, it provides full drag-and-drop when moving messages or embedding OLE objects in a message and it allows any user to setup intelligent actions that occur in response to new mail messages (for example, filing any message from your boss in the 'Urgent' folder).

Notes' built-in mail

Once you are proficient with the Notes application development language, you can design your own electronic mail system or improve on the system supplied as part of Notes. In Chapter 10, you will see how to make the most of Notes' e-mail program by adding other front-ends or calling from other applications.

The main e-mail database screen

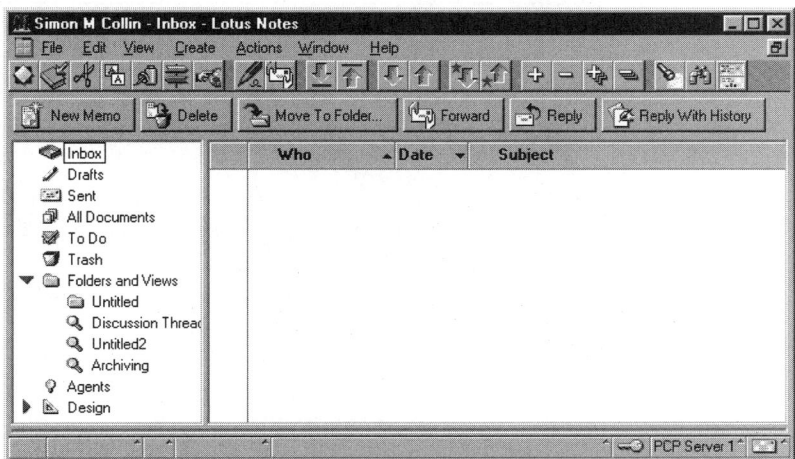

For the moment, I will show you how to use the built-in e-mail database that's part of Notes. When installing Notes, an icon to the e-mail

Chapter 1

database is added to your workspace, together with your Notes user name.

Open up the e-mail feature by selecting the database icon from your workspace. With the e-mail database open, you'll see the left of the screen now displays a pane listing the main folders you have created. These include Inbox, ToDo list, Trash, Sent and more.

Create ▶ Memo

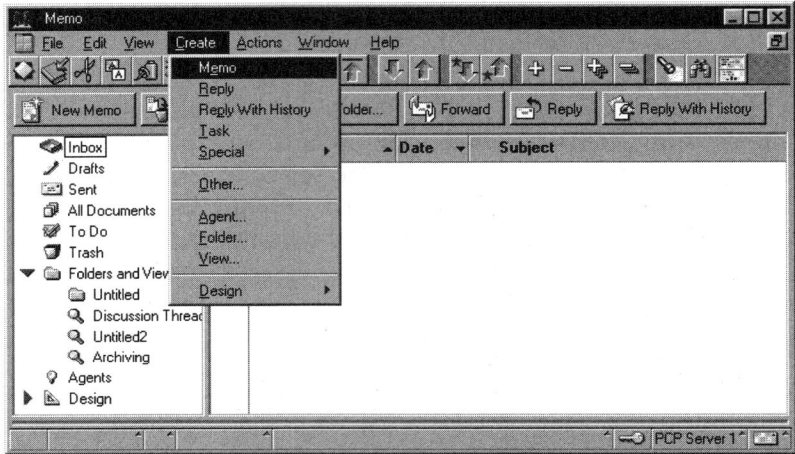

To send a message to another user, select the Create menu. You want to send a message, which Notes calls a Memo, so select the Memo option. The main entry screen for messages replaces the pages of the workplace. As a shortcut, you can click on the New Memo icon in the SmartButton row.

After selecting Create ▶ Memo

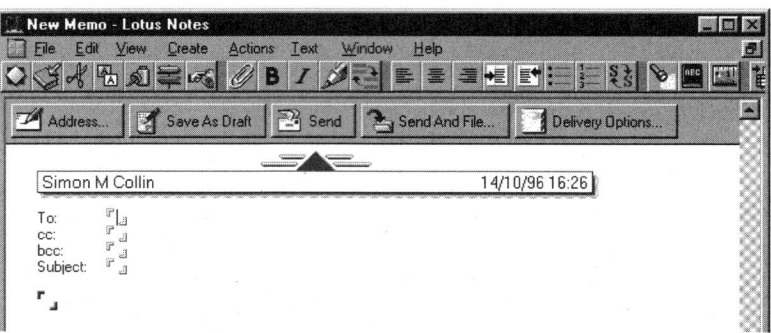

The main Compose screen has a logo in the top corner and just four fields (To:, cc:, bcc:, Subject:) together with space for the body of the message.

The first field is the most important since it contains the address of the person that you want to send the message to. If you know their name, type it in and Notes will try to match this with its address-list database.

If you don't know the recipient's name and correct address, click on the Address button. This displays a new window with a list of all names on the current Notes server. On the left hand side is a list of names, on the right are empty boxes for the To:, cc: and bcc: fields. To pick a name, scroll through the list and click on the name of your recipient. Look at the To: field on the message entry screen and you will notice that it has been filled with the full name and server of the recipient.

Selecting the recipients for your e-mail message

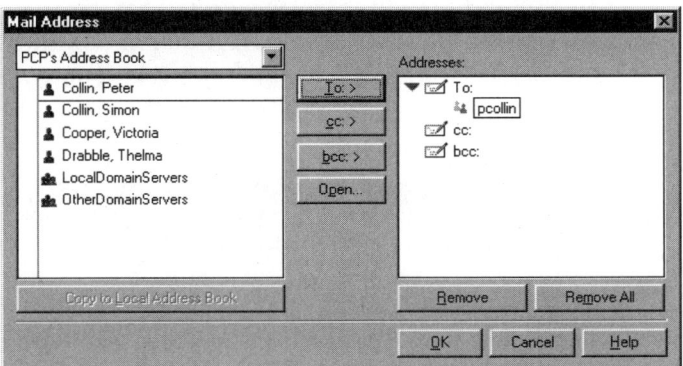

If you want to send the message to several users, click on each of their names. If the user is registered on another server, select the server from the list of names (servers have a different icon) and you will see the registered users on that server.

To send a message to a list of named users, use the cc: (carbon copy) field in the same way as the To: field. Remember, users named in the cc: field will see the list of the other users that received the message. To prevent each user from seeing the list of the other recipients, use the bcc: (which means blind carbon copy) field. Your name and server address are automatically entered within the From: field; so too is the date and time you composed the message. Finally, you can enter subject text that describes the contents of the message.

Message Body

The message itself follows in the main field indicated by the pair of red square brackets in the centre of the entry form. This field is called a RTF (rich text field) and is far more flexible than, say, the To: field which will only accept a recognized user name.

You can type text straight into the main message field, or cut and paste it from another application or you can insert objects directly into the message text. To enter text, move to the message text field and type. You can press [Return] as normal to create a new line. If you want to change the formatting for a particular character or paragraph, highlight the text you want to format and click on the right mouse button to display the font and formatting options.

Attaching Files to a Message

Attaching a file to the message is straightforward: click on the paperclip icon on the SmartIcon toolbar. A dialog box pops up with a list of file on your disk that you can attach to the message.

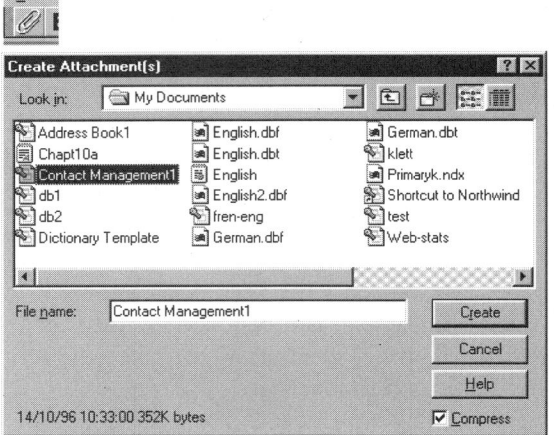

Click on the paperclip icon to attach a file

Adding a File Attachment

To embed an object, such as a spreadsheet or document, use the *Edit ▸ Insert* menu option and choose the Object option.

Mood Stamps

A new feature of Notes 4.5 is the ability to add Mood Stamps to a message. You can choose from a list of Mood stamps by clicking on the Delivery Options button.

Sending mail

*Delivery button
– adding a mood
stamp*

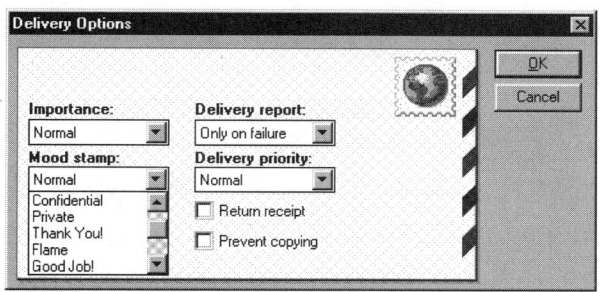

Saving Messages

If you do not finish working on your mail message and want to save it so that you can finish it later, you can store it in the Draft Documents folder of the e-mail database.

*Save message as
a draft*

To save the message without sending it to anyone, click on the Save as Draft button (the second in from the left). To go back to editing the message at a later date, open the Draft Documents folder from the folder pane and double-click on your unfinished message.

Sending a Message

Once you've finished the message and addressed it correctly, you can send it to the named recipients. To do this click on the Send message button on the SmartIcon toolbar (the middle button).

The message will be sent according to the delivery options and a copy stored in the Sent folder of your e-mail database.

If you want to file the message as a record, select the Save and File button in the SmartIcon buttonbar (second from right). This will send the message and let you store the message in a named folder – for example, you could keep copies of all your messages about a particular project in one folder.

Message Delivery

Once you have completed the addressing and message fields, you can choose how you would like to deliver the message; to set the delivery options, click on the Delivery SmartIcon button on the far right of the toolbar. This lists the options that determine how fast the message is delivered and whether there are any reply options.

Chapter 1

Delivery options

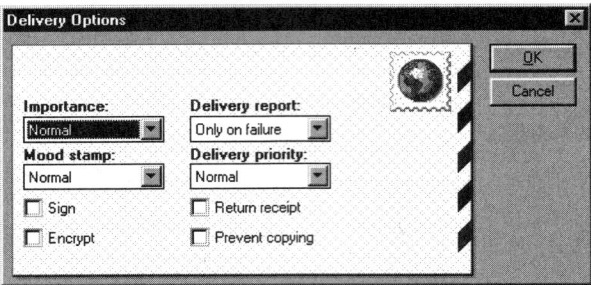

Delivery priority

The Delivery SmartIcon button displays options to determine how urgent your message is – the choices are normal, low and high priority delivery.

- *Normal priority*: will transfer the message when the server next updates the databases.
- *Low priority*: will not send the message until after midnight.
- *High priority delivery*: will transfer the message as soon as possible.

To select the priority, move to the field and press the [Space Bar] to cycle through the options.

Delivery report

The Delivery SmartIcon button also gives you options that indicate if you want a complete report returned describing how the message was sent and when it was read by the recipient.

- *Basic*: means you will receive a report if the message was not delivered.
- *Confirmed*: means you will receive a report if it was, or was not delivered.
- *No report*: will not produce any feedback.

Use the [Space Bar] to cycle through the options.

Receipt report

This will return a message to indicate when the message was opened by the recipient. Use the [Space Bar] to choose either Yes or No. If you have to be certain that the recipient reads your mail, use this option. Lastly, any entries in the Personal Categories field are reflected as new categories and give you the option to define you own categories.

Summary: sending mail
- To send mail, select the New Memo button or *Create ▸ Memo*
- To address a message, use the Address button
- Type the text within the red markers
- To add an attachment, select the Paperclip icon button
- Confirm when a message is read, using Receipt Report
- Add fun to a message with a Mood Stamp!

Opening a database

All information stored by Notes is stored in databases. The databases are stored on a Notes server. Read Chapter 6 for more information on how Notes keeps multiple copies of databases up to date using replication.

Database access using icons

Icons are used as a convenient way to access these databases; database icons can be stored on any of the six pages in your workspace. All the icons on the pages of your workspace access a database. This includes some unusual databases – such as mail and help. The usual way a user will access a database is to use the access icons within their workspace. To start a database, double-click on its icon.

Starting a database by double-clicking its icon

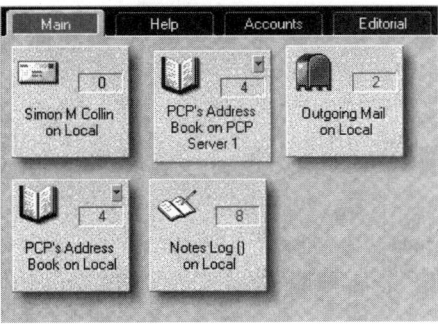

Database access using menu options

An alternative method of opening a database is to use the *File ▸ Database ▸ Open* menu option – a quick shortcut is to press [Ctrl]+[O]. This is normally used only if you don't have an access icon for a database in your workspace.

File ▸ Database ▸ Open Database

Open server selected, databases listed

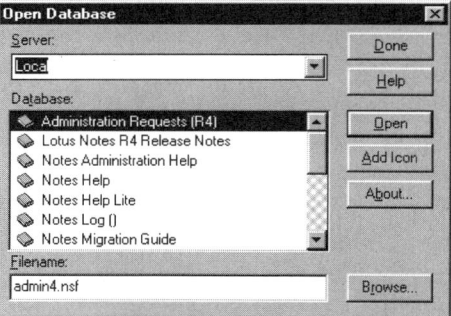

When using the *File ▸ Database ▸ Open* menu option, a dialog box listing available Notes servers is displayed. Highlight and double-click on your local server (or a remote server, if you want to access its local databases). The databases available on the highlighted server are now listed. Double-click on the database that you want to open.

When you double-click on the database, Notes will open the database and give you access. However, once you exit the database, you will have to go through this route of *File ▸ Database ▸ Open* each time you want to access the database – unless you add an icon to your workspace. Click on the Add Icon button and an icon will be added to your workspace providing access to the database.

Opening a database   21

If you want to see a brief summary of the database and what it contains before you open it, move the highlight bar to the database and select the About button.

About button

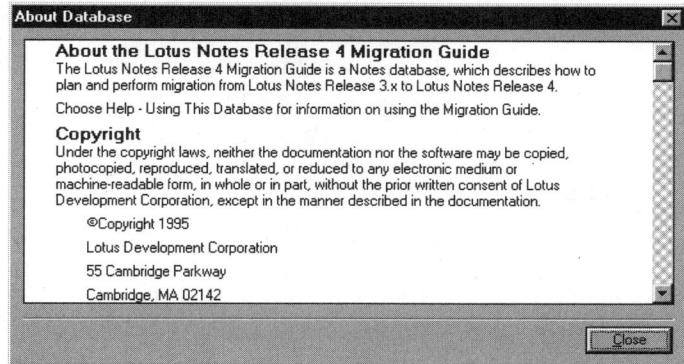

When accessing Notes on a remote computer, you will still see a list of databases and servers available, however, you will not be able to access the databases until you select the Call button which then dials using a modem and logs in. See Chapter 5 for more information on using Notes via a modem link.

How do I use a database?

If, once you have opened the database, you are not sure how to use it, select the *Help ▶ Using...* option. This is a mini on-line guide provided by the designer of the database. To find out who created the database and more about its applications, choose *Help ▶ About* (both of these pages were written by the database's designer, so the amount of information displayed will vary).

Help ▶ About

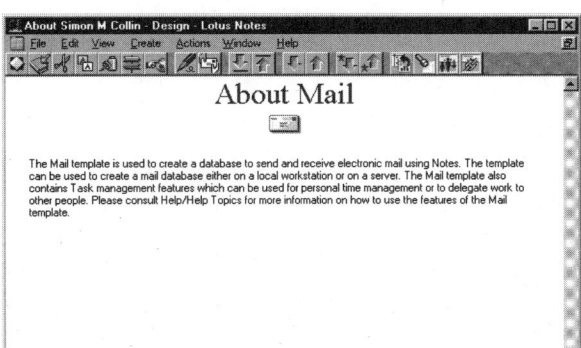

Chapter 1

Viewing the database

Once you have opened the database, either by using an icon or the *File ▸ Open* option, you will be presented with a view of the data stored in this particular database. Since each database looks different, and the way in which the data is presented is determined by the designer, it's difficult to give comprehensive instruction on using databases. However, all work in a similar way and I describe how to maneuver within a database over the next few pages.

Panes and windows

The person who designed the database will also have designed the way in which the data is displayed in separate panes and windows. Each database will often have several different views onto the data, for example to show entries in a contacts database by name, or by company or by client. Generally, the pane running down the left-hand side of the screen is called the contents pane and displays a view of the headings for the articles or categories in the database.

To see the views and panes that the designer has set up for a database, choose the *View ▸ Show* menu option. This menu option is normally equivalent to clicking on an entry in the contents pane shown on the left of the screen.

Example of panes

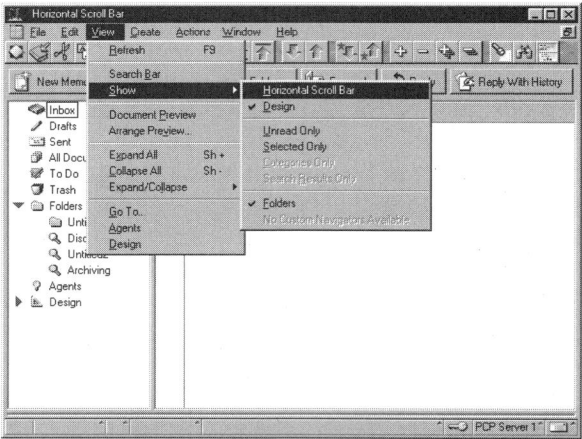

When Notes opens a database for you, you see a particular view of the database. This view lists the main headings for the individual entries or documents that make up a database. For example, if you open the Address Book database you will see a display listing each user – one per

Opening a database

line – with their last name, first name, location and telephone number. This is one view on the data.

Users Address Book list

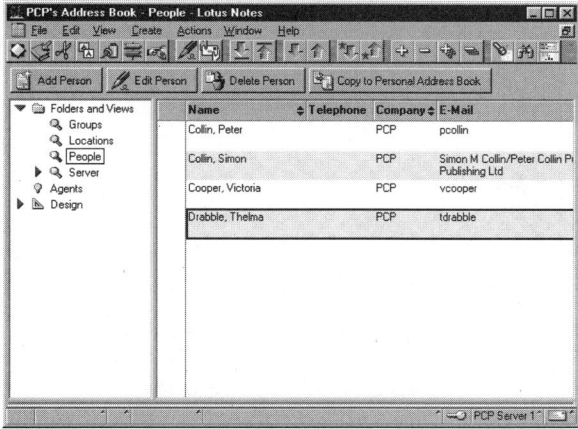

To see more information about a particular user, double-click on his or her name and a second, more detailed view is displayed giving more information about this particular user.

One user detail

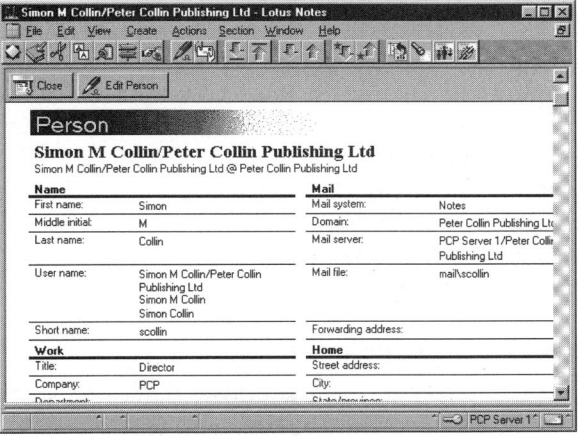

The designer will have created a number of views that he or she thinks will be useful to the user, and allow you to see the same data in different ways. For example, in the Address Book database the first default view when you open the database is a listing of all the users, one per line. To see the other views that are provided, pull down the View menu.

Chapter 1

The View menu

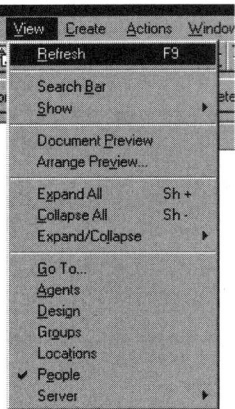

The first half of the options relate to all views, and allow you to show the categories in which the data is organized, or just the entries that you have not read (useful for e-mail), or to zoom in or out in detail.

The bottom half of the menu lists the views that are specific to this database. In the case of the Address Book, there are several that allow you to list users by name, location, server, groups or domains. This, in addition to the default view that lists users by name.

Viewing a document

On the previous page, you've seen how to open a database and view the documents according to their title. To see a particular document in detail, such as a user's complete Address Book entry, double-click on the name and you will open the document. The database's designer determines how the document is formatted when you open it. Some applications might have an image embedded (for example, a catalogue), other might be just text. In this case, there's a mix of data fields. To get back to the initial view of the list of documents, press [Esc].

Changing the panes and windows

The size of the panes and windows that are displayed within a database can be changed to suit the way you work or to display more information. For example the width of the main contents pane that is displayed down the left-hand side of the screen can be changed by dragging the border.

To change the width of the pane, move the pointer over the pane's right-hand border. The pointer changes shape to a crossed arrow symbol. Now hold down the left-hand mouse button and move the mouse to change the width of the pane.

Navigating through documents

If you are using a database in which you want to skip from one document to the next, it's very inconvenient and cumbersome to navigate in the way you've just used – that is, double-clicking to open a document, press [Esc] to return to the main view, then double-click on another document. Notes has a special SmartIcon bar that's just for navigating through documents. To call it up to replace (temporarily) your existing general-purpose tool bar, use the SmartStatus bar:

1. Click on the *File ▸ Tools ▸ SmartIcons*.
2. From the pull-down list, select the most appropriate icon set.

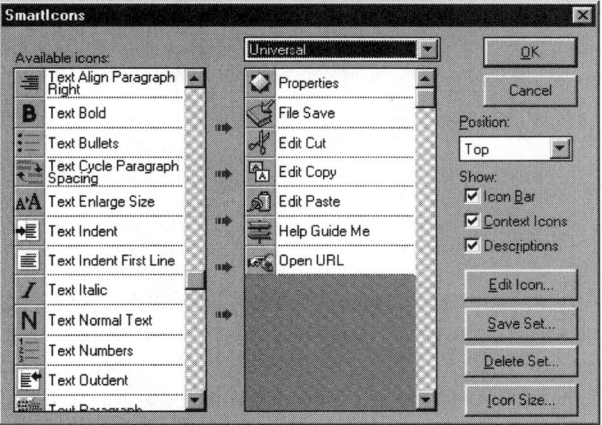

The new SmartIcon bar gives you one-click icons that will move forward or backward by one document, or move between unread or marked documents.

'Categories' organize your data

As you can imagine, if you view all the data with one line per record, you will have a job navigating through the information. What's needed is a way to organize and group related records under sub-headings. Notes does this using Categories. A category itself doesn't contain any data, it has the same purpose as the sub-headings that break up the text in this book.

If you choose *View ▸ Show ▸ Categories Only*, you will not see any of the individual documents in a section, only their headings. It's like an outline view of the contents of the database.

If you open one of the Notes databases that has an organized structure, for example the release notes associated with your particular software, you will see that the default view lists documents in an outline view. Major chapter headings stand flush left, indented next are section headings, then finally the relevant documents (normally displayed in grey, against a color for the headings). The headings are called Categories and you can use them to sift through information in a database.

View the headings within a database

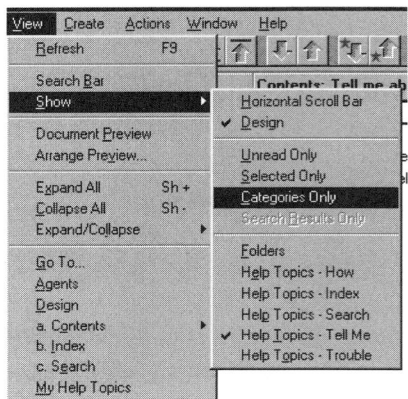

Now that you can expand and compress the outlines that make up a view, you can start to work with the categories and the documents beneath them. To see the documents again, select *View ▸ Show ▸ Categories Only* a second time so that you can see all entries. Now, if you double-click on a category, it will expand to show you the related documents beneath it.

You will find you can skim through a database and narrow your search quickly by using the outline features of categories. It's often easier and more flexible to use categories than using the Notes search engine.

Symbols describe data status

When you look at the data in a view, you might see symbols on the far left grey margin beside some entries. There are a range of symbols that mean different things about this particular entry.

- **star** means you have not read the document
- **trashcan** means the entry is flagged for deletion (it will be permanently deleted when you leave the database)
- **paperclip** means the entry has file attachments
- **tick** means you have marked the document

You can use the extra commands within the View menu, discussed in the last couple of pages, to filter according to some of these symbols. For example, if you want to see a list of all the documents that you have not yet read, select *View ▸ Show ▸ Unread* and those entries with a star beside them are listed.

Tip Remember the special navigation SmartIcon bar you used a few pages ago? It includes buttons to move between documents that have the unread or marked symbol.

Navigating hotspots, buttons and URLs

The current version of Notes allows users to add articles that include extra navigational features. These make navigating between related articles far easier. The new functions that are available include setting up hotspots, buttons and URLs (uniform resource locator).

Double-click on a hotspot to open the URL

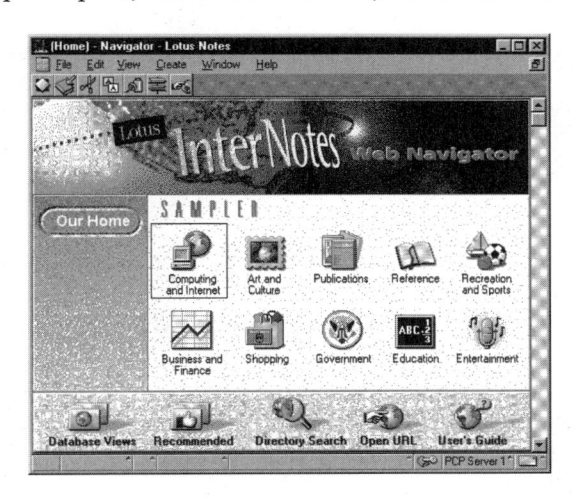

A hotspot to a URL within a document

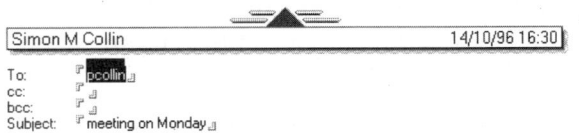

A hotspot defines a section of text or an image as a special area. When the user clicks on the hotspot, Notes carries out a particular action – normally a jump to another article. It's a neat way of linking articles. For example, if you have a database of legal cases, one new case might refer to the case between Smith and the State of Massachusetts of 1978. If this text is setup as a hotspot, when the user clicks on the text it will display the article referring to Smith vs. Massachusetts of 1978.

A button is a similar device to a hotspot, but it inserts a traditional looking Windows button image into an article and allows you to define what happens when a user clicks the button. The actions could include jumping to another article or filling in a field with a calculated result.

Another way of providing a link to another article in the database is to include a link icon. This is a little icon that is inserted into an article; it will move a user to a new article when the user clicks on the icon.

Lastly, it is possible to include URLs within articles. A URL is a unique address to a WWW (World Wide Web) page on the Internet or on a company intranet. For example, if you have a database listing updates to your network, you could include a URL to the Lotus web home page (http://www.lotus.com) that lets a user see the third-party products available for Notes. When a user clicks on a URL, Notes will start its InterNotes WWW browser and will try and connect to the Internet server defined by the administrator.

Editing documents

Now that you can navigate easily between categories and documents, it's time to introduce the Edit mode. When you double-click on a document within a database, Notes opens and displays the document in read-only mode. If you want to add notes to a document or change facts, you have to switch into Edit mode. To do this:

1. Highlight the document you want to edit.
2. Select the right mouse button and the Edit option from the pop-up menu. Alternatively, select *Actions* ▸ *Edit Document*.

You will notice a subtle change to the display now that you are in Edit mode. Each field that you can edit has tiny corner brackets at the top left of the first line and bottom right of the last line of the field.

Document in edit mode

To: ⌐pcollin⌐
cc: ⌐   ⌐
bcc: ⌐   ⌐
Subject: ⌐meeting on Monday⌐

You can use any normal Windows cut and paste edit operations within the fields. The changes to the document are not saved until you exit the document – at which point a dialog box asks if you want to save or discard your changes. If you made a mistake, this is your last chance to discard your changes. Alternatively, if your computer is rather unreliable or you are making a lot of changes, you might want to save the document more frequently. To save the document without exiting, press [Ctrl]+[S].

Adding documents

In many databases, the information is only valuable because everyone can add more or comment on existing data. There are two ways of adding a document to a database: adding a main document or adding a response to a document. These two types of document give a clue to one of the most useful uses for Notes: on-line discussion about a subject. If you want to start a new discussion, perhaps report on a new company that might be worth further investigation as a potential client, you would add a main document. Your colleagues could then read your initial comments about this company. If they find out any further details about this company, they would add these as a response document to your main document. On screen, this looks like a simple outline. The response documents are arranged in date order and indented below their respective main document. The main document shows a count of how many responses it has generated from your colleagues. Main and Response documents will be given different names by the person that designs the database. For example, in our client tracking database, the main document would be a New Client document while a Response document would be called a Followup Information document. To add a new document to a database, use the Create menu. Pull down the menu and you will see a list of available types of document that you can add. In some information-only databases, such as stock pricing, you won't be allowed to add any documents. In other databases, you will have a wide range of possible choices.

Searching for text

Notes has one search engine and two ways of using it. The first, and simplest, is used within a view or document. Select *Edit ▸ Find-Replace* menu option (or use the [Ctrl]+[F] hot-key). A dialog box pops up and you can enter your search string. Radio button options let you select case-sensitive text search and a search within the entire view (remember, this is not necessarily the same as the entire database) or just within the document. After pressing [Ctrl]+[F], the Find dialog box pops up.

After pressing [Ctrl]+[F] to display the Find menu

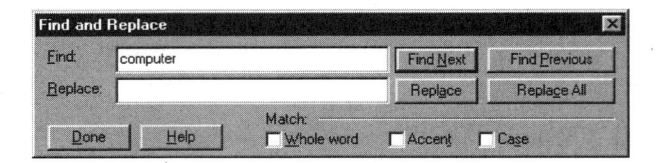

Extended Searches

There is another more powerful way of searching through an entire database or through several marked databases. This second method uses the same search engine but uses a different user interface. Click on the Binocular icon and the main screen develops a new fatter search bar, just below the SmartIcon bar.

The search bar

To search for the word 'book' type it in at the search field in the far left of the search bar. Press [Return] or click on the Search button to start searching. Any documents that have a hit will be marked (and appear with a tick beside them in your view). The search bar has a few more sophisticated tricks up its sleeve. Click on the down-arrow button on the far right of the search bar and it will grow in depth to show new status panels.

Expanded search bar showing new status panels

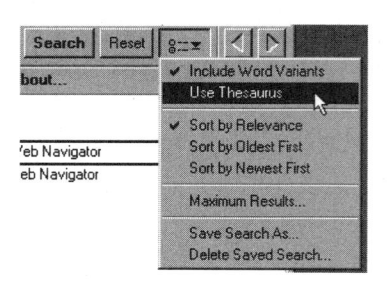

More complex searches can be defined by using the Options buttons on the search bar. Options defines how the results are organized: by date, view or number of hits.

Editing documents

Tip   Remember, since documents that contain a search hit are marked, you can use the View Navigation SmartIcon bar to flip through the marked documents.

Full-text searches

The next step up in advanced searching is to use Notes' full-text search capabilities. To use this, you will have to create an index for the database if one does not already exist (most databases don't have a full-text index). To create the index, select the database from your workspace with a single click and choose the *File ▸ Database ▸ Properties ▸ Full-text* menu option. This displays information on the full-text index if one exists and also lets you create an index. If you select *View ▸ Search* and your database does not have a full-text index, you'll be prompted to create one.

File ▸
Database ▸
Properties ▸
Full-text

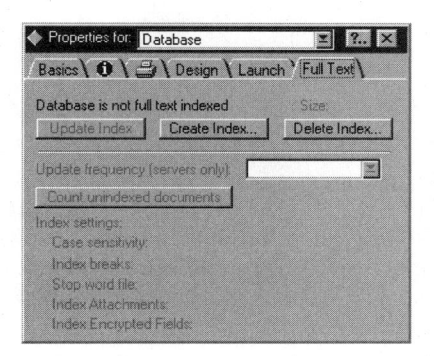

When creating an index, you can specify if you want case-sensitive distinctions, by selecting the check box. In addition, you can remove common words from the index – such as 'and', 'the', etc. – by checking the Stop File check-box (the list of words to exclude are in a file called DEFAULT.STP).

Create Index
dialog box

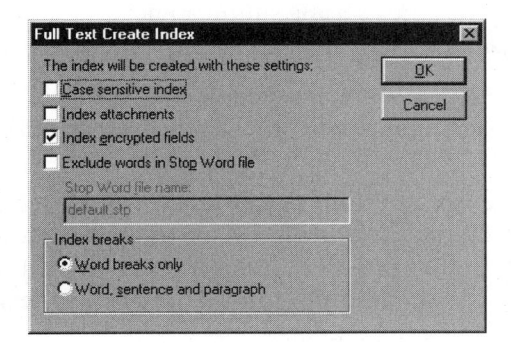

Chapter 1

Notes will now start to work through the documents and create an index for the full-text search engine. Watch out – if your database is big, this could take some time!

Using full-text searches

Once Notes has generated the full-text index, you can use this feature just as you did the basic search function. Select *Edit ▸ Find* or press [Ctrl]+[F] (or click on the torch SmartIcon).

The Search Builder dialog box

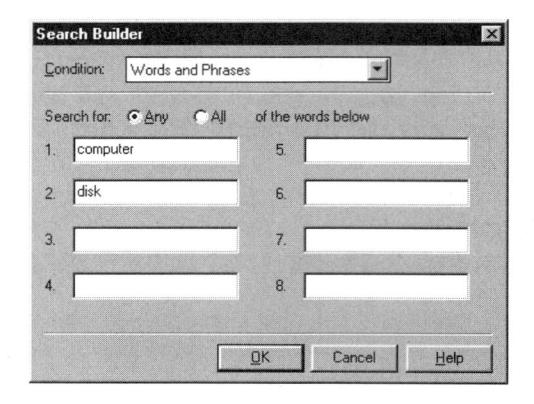

Tip The alternative to the Query Builder, and a quicker system once you are used to logical operators, is to use the search toolbar. Enter the words to search for, in brackets. To create logical searches, use the AND, OR, and NOT operators between words.

To add power to your searches, you can create complex queries that have logical AND, OR and NOT operators by selecting the Add Condition button. Instead of the basic one-line Find window, you are presented with a Query Builder window. You can build up complex searches that find multiple words in a document or near to each other; or hits where words do not occur in a document. The three entry fields are actually the same as using simple logical statements:

- **All of these words:** performs an AND operation on the words
- **One or more of these words:** performs an OR operation
- **Exclude documents with these words:** performs a NOT operation

You can enter multiple words in each field, separated by commas. To start searching, click on the OK button and Notes will trawl through the full-text index (this takes longer to search a database than the simple text searching without a full-text index). A new view is displayed with the matching documents.

Double-click on a document in the view and it's displayed and you are moved to the point where the word occurs (the hit is highlighted with a red border).

A successful search: the hit is highlighted with a border

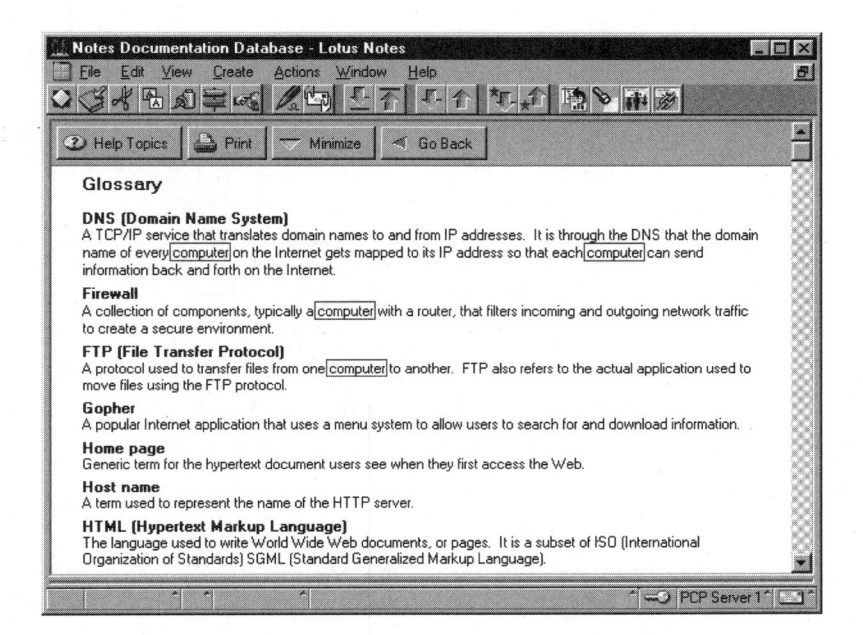

Using attachments

The ability to attach text or data files to a Notes document makes it a useful method of data distribution as well as a convenient way of sending information to other users. You can attach a file (or any Windows object) within any rich text field (RTF) in the document. In the case of a memo message under Notes' e-mail database, the only Rich Text Field is the main body of text, indicated with red corner markers.

Attaching files

To attach a single file to a document, move the pointer into an RTF field and select *File ▸ Attach* or click on the Paperclip icon in the SmartIcon button bar. This pops up a dialog box with files listed on the left and directories on the right. You can move around your disk's contents until you get to the right spot. To select a file, highlight it and click on the OK button.

File ▸ Attach

Selecting a file

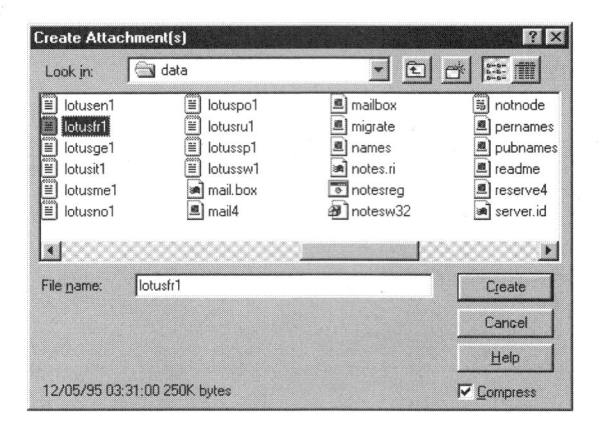

To attach multiple files, hold down the left mouse-button and highlight a range of files – but they must be listed next to each other. You cannot pick and choose odd files from the list – if you want to do this, you will have to include multiple separate single attachments.

Lastly, you can choose to compress the files. This check box is, by default, selected. If you are attaching a ZIP file or any other pre-compressed file, it's not worth wasting time trying to compress it a second time around. However, for graphics files, such as PCX, TIFF or BMP format files, you will save a lot of space and time when transferring the attachments. The attachment appears within the Notes document as a file icon with the file name below.

The File Attachment Information dialog box

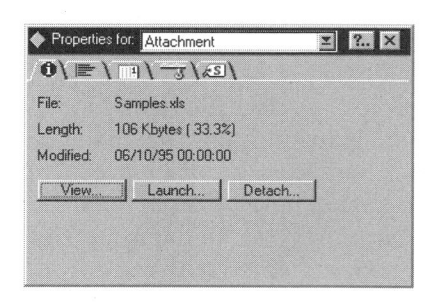

When the recipient opens the document, they will see the icon and can access the attachment by double-clicking on the icon. This pops up a dialog box that gives the file's full name, size and date. You are given the option to remove the file from the Notes document and store it as a normal file on disk, or to launch the application that created the file (assuming the application exists on the recipient's machine).

Within the attachment information dialog box there are page tags for extra features of the attachment – alignment, style and hidden attributes. These let you define how the icon is displayed on the page (you can align it to the text, or centrally, etc.).

For example, if you attach a Microsoft Excel XLS spreadsheet, choose the launch option and Excel will be started with the XLS file. Remember, if you are running Notes on a machine with minimal RAM, you could easily slow everything to a near halt if you try to load another large application along with Notes. You will find that performance improves if you detach the attachment. Then, when you exit Notes, start the application.

Attaching Notes documents

If you want to attach another Notes document, you will need to use a different method. This is because the attachment feature only works with files, and Notes documents are not really files. You can either use the *Actions ▸ Forward* menu option to send the document on to another user (this applies when in mail) or you can select the document text, choose *Edit ▸ Copy* to copy the text to the clipboard, then paste it into a new document. Lastly, you can send a complete Notes database as an attachment, but only if it's on your local hard disk – you cannot send a database that's on the server.

OLE: Adding images and sound

Notes is compatible with Microsoft's Windows OLE specification. This means that you can insert an object into a Rich Text Field within any Notes document. The object can be from any other OLE-compatible application. For example, to add a sound recording of you explaining why you missed the board meeting, record the sound using Microsoft's Sound Recorder (under the Accessories folder) and select the *Edit ▸ Copy* command in Sound Recorder. Now move back to the Notes article and position the pointer in the RTF field in your document and select *Edit ▸ Paste*. Notes inserts the sound object as an icon which you can listen to by double-clicking on the icon.

If any user now double-clicks on the icon, Notes asks Windows to handle this OLE call and the sound file is played back. You could also embed spreadsheet files, bitmap images or any other object that will start the originating application when the reader double-clicks on the icon.

Remember that any OLE-compatible data can be inserted into a Notes RTF field using the simple *Edit ▸ Copy* and *Edit ▸ Paste* menu commands.

A feature of the new version of Notes allows you to include links between two documents. For example, you might include a link to an article that provides background information to a project or to an article that provides further details on a client within a project document. Adding a link to another document is very straightforward. Just like inserting OLE data, you create a link with the *Edit ▸ Copy* and *Edit ▸ Paste* menu commands. To insert a link, move to the document you want to link and select *Edit ▸ Copy as link ▸ Document link*. Now move back to the original document that will contain the link and select the *Edit ▸ Paste* command. Notes inserts a link icon to indicate to users that they can move to another related document if they click on the link icon.

Copying a link to a document

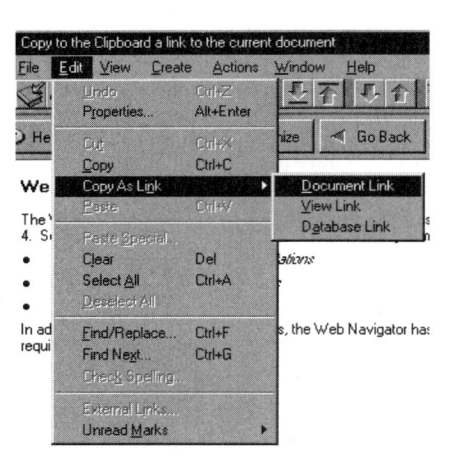

Printing

After locating a useful document, or several related documents, you might want to print them. Although Notes is progressing the cause of the paperless office, it's often more convenient to have printed copy!

Printing a single document or multiple documents works in just the same way. Select a document from a view of the database – or mark several documents – and choose *File ▸ Print* menu option or [Ctrl]+[P] (or click on the Printer SmartIcon). A standard Windows Print dialog box appears letting you define the page range, print quality, number of copies and size of graphic.

In the lower half of the print dialog box are options that relate to multiple documents. You can print each document on a new page, or just print the view (with its one-line document titles) or print the document formatted using a particular form.

File ▸ Print

The Print dialog box

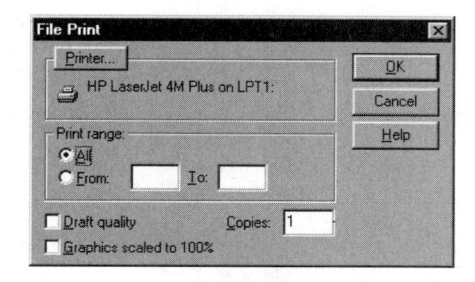

Working with multiple databases

Most Notes users will have several database icons displayed on their workspace: personal mail, an address book, perhaps a company diary and an information database. Each time you start Notes, it will check through all these databases for any documents marked as unread. Before you can reach the main workspace screen, you are presented with a rather abrupt dialog box that asks you what you want to do with these unread documents.

Checking for unread documents

In everyday use, you are probably not too concerned about new, unread messages in the Address Book or diary – as new users are added to the system or other people make their appointments. You do want to know about new, unread mail in your mailbox or new responses to your discussions about your current project. To help manage your workspace, you can select which databases Notes should scan on startup. To remove the unwanted databases from this automatic scanning, choose the *Edit ▸ Unread Marks ▸ Scan Preferred* menu option.

A list of the databases available on your workspace is displayed. You can choose your selection to check for unread by clicking on individual lines. To help you navigate through this list, some entries have a dash each side of the name – these are the different page names within your workspace.

Edit ▸ Unread Marks ▸ Scan Preferred

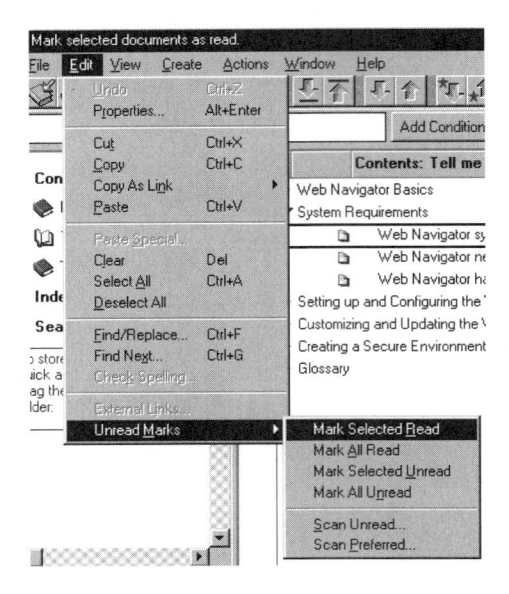

By default, Notes starts this scanner on startup. However, you might not want this option – in which case, deselect the check box below the list of databases. If you want to do a general scan of all unread mail on your new list of preferred databases, choose *Edit ▸ Unread Marks ▸ Scan Unread ▸ Preferred Databases* option.

Scan Unread dialog box

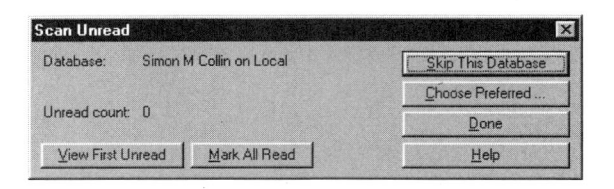

If you click on the Mark All Documents Read button at the bottom of this dialog box, each document unread in the named database will be marked and have a tick displayed next to in the view. Choose the Done button to exit the scanner and return to your workspace.

Agents

Within Notes 4.5 is a new feature called *Agents* that lets you add a degree of rules-based 'intelligence' to your databases. Agents are really automated macros that will run either from the menu, at a particular time or will run in response to an event (such as new mail message arriving). Agents can be programmed using the fill-out Agent creation form in any database to which you have access.

For example, to create an Agent that looks at each new mail message and files them into separate folders according to the subject field, you would do the following:

1. Open the mail database.
2. Select the *Create ▸ Agent* menu option.
3. Enter a name for your Agent in the first field.
4. Select 'if new mail has arrived' from the list of actions that will trigger the agent.
5. Click on the Add Action button at the bottom of the screen to view the possible actions that the agent can carry out on the document (the email message) that has just arrived.

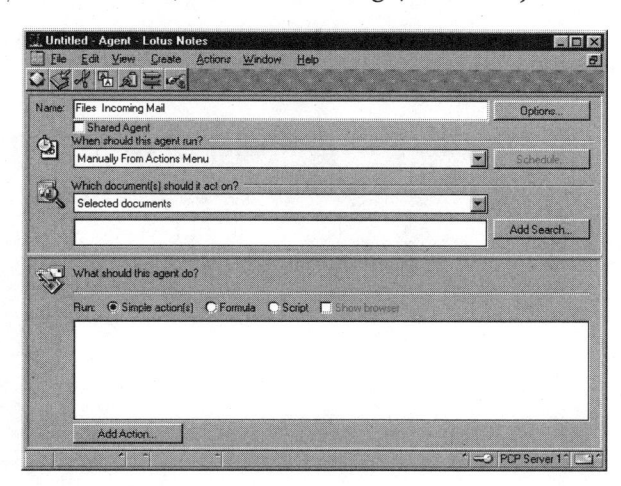

Creating an Agent

6. Select 'Move to Folder' as the simple action for this Agent and highlight the folder into which the mail message should be moved.

Select the desired Action: 'Move to Folder'

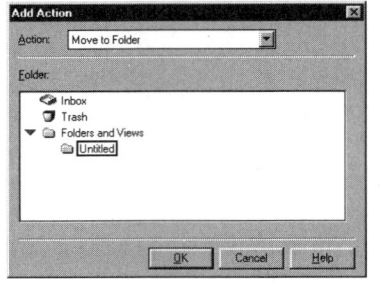

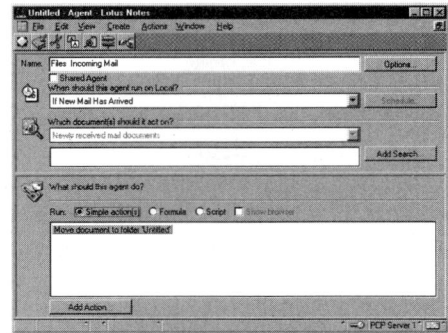

Navigators and folders

One of the new features of Notes 4.5 is the inclusion of special navigator panes within a database view. When you open a database, you'll see a set of icons running down the left-hand side – these are the navigator icons. In some databases, these icons will represent major categories of types of document – for example, in the *File ▸ Replication ▸ Settings* you will see four icons in the Navigator bar describing the main setting groups available. When you click on an icon, the window on the right-hand side changes to show the group of settings.

Navigator icons on the left of view

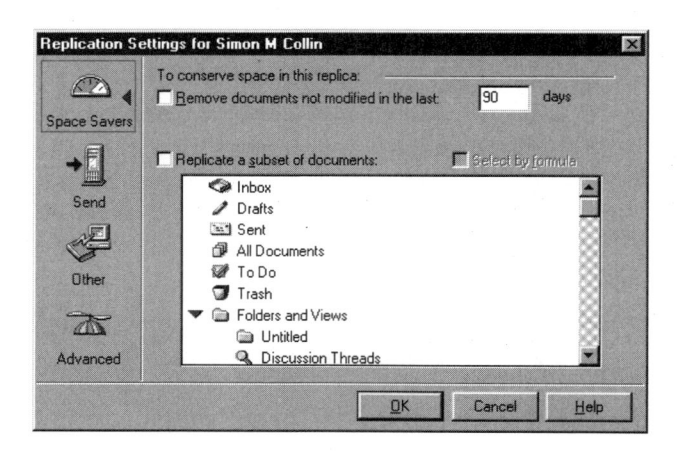

In most databases, the Navigator bar does not have large picture icons, instead it has a tree-structure of folders. These are rather like an outline view of the database and list all the views made available by the designer. For example, if you open the Public Name & Address database you'll see a list of the major setting groups (or views) listed in the navigator bar on the left of the screen. If you click on any folder icon within the Navigator bar, it expands to show the sub-folders or categories within it; click on any sub-folder and you'll see the list of documents displayed on the right-hand side of the screen. Once you are used to this way of displaying structure, it's far easier to navigate than the old View menu command of Notes 3.

Some databases include folders that can contain user-defined documents. For example, the email database lists the folders in the navigator bar to show the in-box, sent, draft and so on. You can drag and drop documents (e-mail messages in this case) into any of these folders.

The Navigator bar is designed by the designer of the database – he or she creates the views and the icons that are displayed. The only changes you can make as a user are to the size of the bar (move the pointer over the vertical separator line and drag the pane to a new width) or, if the designer has allowed it, you can create user folders – as in the e-mail program.

Formatting text

If you are entering text within a rich text field you can format the text to almost any style using the standard formatting tools available under Windows or the GUI you are using. If you are using a Windows workstation, select the text that you want to format and click the right-hand mouse button. This pops up the Properties menu for the text item.

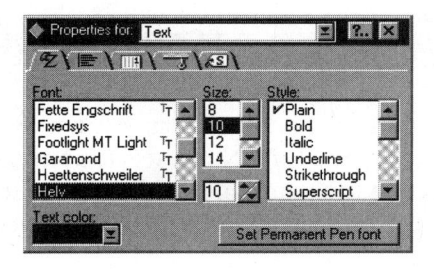

The first menu option 'Text Properties' displays a dialog box that allows you to set the font size, type and color. For fast formatting, use the bold, italic or underline menu options at the bottom of the pop-up menu. If you are not using a two-button mouse, you can access the text property settings from the Action bar buttons along the top of the window.

Internet integration

Notes 4.5 includes full Internet integration – the administrator can setup the Notes server to work as an intranet server, processing World Wide Web pages on an internal basis – or it can act as a gateway to the full Internet.

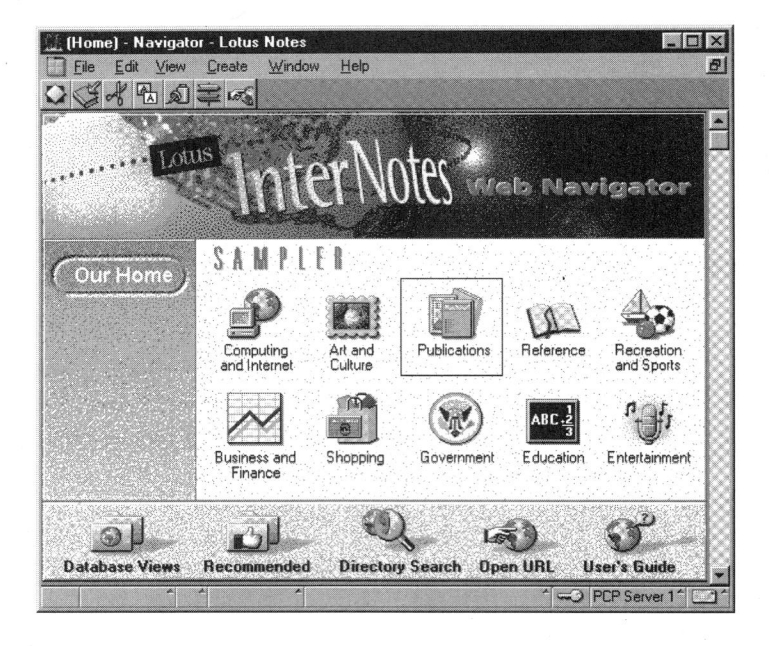

There are two parts to adding Internet functionality to your Notes system. You must setup the InterNotes server software for both internal intranets and to access the external Internet. Users see the browser software that displays graphical WWW pages – this too has to be installed separately.

Once the software has been installed on the server and workstation (see Chapter 10), you can access WWW pages by clicking on a URL (uniform resource locator) within a document or by entering the URL manually. To enter a URL manually, click on the World icon in the Action bar. A URL is an address to the WWW page and tells the InterNotes server where to find the page – it's entered in the format:

http://www.*servername*

For example, to access the Lotus home page on the Internet, you would enter the URL http://www.lotus.com.

2
Hardware requirements

About this chapter

Setting up a new Notes server is relatively straightforward if you do a little planning. In this chapter, the hardware requirements of a Notes system are discussed. Coupled with the choice of operating system on which Notes will run (discussed in Chapter 3), you also have the choice of hardware platform on which to run the Notes server application. If you are installing a new, dedicated Notes server then you will need to specify a new server PC, while if you're running Notes for NetWare on your existing NetWare network server or Notes for Unix on a Unix server then you need only boost the server's RAM and hard disk capacity.

In this chapter, we'll start by looking at the basic hardware requirements for a Notes Server; this is followed by the extra network requirements – network adapter cards, and options for a high-speed backbone linking several Notes servers. Lastly, there's a section covering communications hardware including modems and ISDN links that'll let your Notes server communicate with the outside world.

Server hardware requirements

There are three ways of running a Notes server. The first is to run it on a non-dedicated server – Notes Windows Server runs in the background under Windows 95 or Windows NT – in which the workstation is also used by a normal user. This is only suited to small networks with less than 10 users. There are problems: if the workstation crashes, it's likely the Notes server will also crash.

The peer-to-peer Windows setup

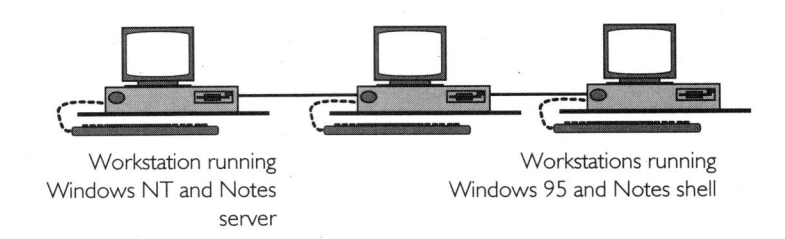

Workstation running Windows NT and Notes server

Workstations running Windows 95 and Notes shell

For larger networks it is normal practice to have the second option: a dedicated PC that is running the Notes server application. The Notes server application runs on top of OS/2, Windows NT, Windows 95 or Unix and is connected as part of a network. The third option uses the newest versions of Notes that are installed on top of an existing Novell NetWare network operating system running on the main network server.

Client–server OS/2 and Notes setup

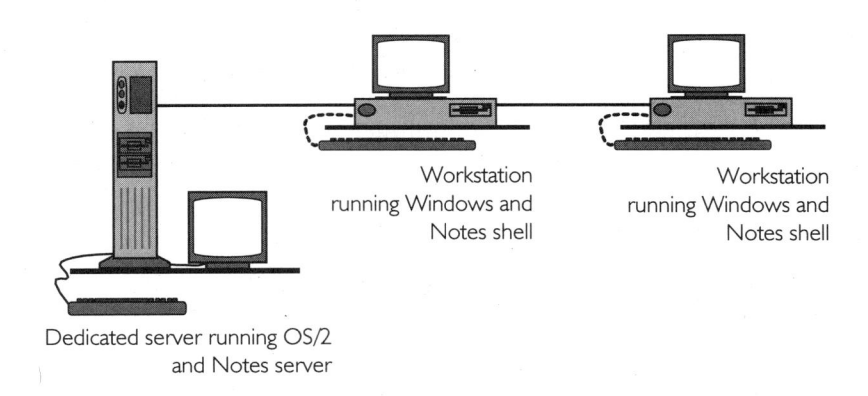

Dedicated server running OS/2 and Notes server

Workstation running Windows and Notes shell

Workstation running Windows and Notes shell

Whether the Notes server is supporting tens or hundreds of users it will be transferring a vast amount of data to and from the disk. In order to get the best from your Notes server you should examine how you want to use Notes and how many users are likely to depend on it.

When installing Notes on a NetWare server, you will need to expand the server's RAM and disk capacity or your users will notice a drop in performance. If you are installing on a dedicated server, you will need to make the right choice for the server hardware. This chapter looks at the types of server upgrade and server hardware that are available and assesses the best for Notes.

The Notes server requirements

The bulk of this chapter covers the requirements for additional products that connect to your Notes server – such as backup drives, modems, and network adapters. To actually run, Notes needs only straightforward basic server hardware. You need a server with at least an 80486, but a Pentium processor is preferred. If you are using a multi-processor server you should contact Lotus for details of the license agreements required to install Notes on multiple processors and the hardware platforms supported.

For a NetWare server you should install at least 24Mb RAM, for an OS/2 server at least 24Mb and for a Windows server 16Mb. The hard disk should be as big as you can afford! Realistically, take 1Gb as a minimum. With these minimums set, the rest of this chapter covers the options available to get the most from this hardware.

Server architecture

Notes will run on just about any hardware that will run Windows NT or OS/2. Under Unix, Notes supports the HP-9000 server, Sun SPARC servers, IBM RISC/6000 series server hardware or any platform that supports Novell NetWare. Multiprocessor support is implicit if the operating system can handle more than one processor.

The most flexible hardware platform, and the one which can cause most problems due to the number of choices available, is the PC platform used for Windows, OS/2 or NetWare servers. When choosing your PC server one of the first options is the bus architecture: the five choices are ISA, EISA, MCA, PCI local bus and proprietary bus.

The least efficient bus for a server is the ISA (Industry Standard Architecture) bus; this 16-bit bus was used in the earliest PC/ATs carries data in 16-bit chunks and its speed is normally 8 or 10MHz. The data-carrying ability of an ISA bus is limited by the bus speed and word size. On an ISA bus, all peripherals talk to the central processor through the bus and the data transfer of all the peripherals is controlled by the CPU. With 32-bit CPUs, such as the 80386 and 80486, the 16-bit ISA bus acts as a bottleneck and limits the speed at which data can be transferred to and from the CPU, which cuts data transfer rate considerably.

To widen the bottleneck of an ISA bus, two new bus architectures were developed. A group of manufacturers developed EISA (Extended ISA) while IBM introduced its MCA (Microchannel Architecture) design. Both buses are 32-bit and allow a feature called bus-mastering, but EISA has gained the greater market share by virtue of backwards compatibility. Old ISA cards can still be used in an EISA bus PC. For a server, this is of little consequence since you should always fit 32-bit cards to take advantage of the 32-bit bus.

Bus-mastering gives more control to the adapter. An adapter can take over control of the bus from the CPU and pass data directly to system RAM without requiring control from the CPU nor adding to its workload.

You should not use anything less than either an EISA or MCA-bussed PC as your server. EISA has the advantage in data-carrying capacity: the bus operates at up to 33MHz and uses 32-bit words. You will also find that there's a greater range of EISA adapters than MCA cards which gives you more choice.

Most PCs designed as servers will include some form of local bus architecture. The most common form of interface is called PCI (Peripheral Connect Interface). This provides a direct link between an intelligent adapter and the main memory. If you want to provide the cleanest channel that offers high speed data transfer, a PCI network adapter is one of the best solutions.

The final option is to choose a server computer that uses a proprietary bus. These are normally included in servers that support multiple processors. Often, the manufacturer combines the proprietary bus between the CPU and main peripherals (such as video and network cards) but also fits an EISA adapter for compatibility.

The server processor

Your Notes server will have to cope with high data-throughput which places a particular strain on the network adapter, the bus and the hard disk. The processor in a server is modestly used in comparison to the traffic that the storage system has to cope with. This means that you should pay more attention to a fast hard disk and as much RAM as you can afford.

How much RAM do I need?

With many network operating system, there's a formula that you can use to calculate the amount of RAM you will need to fit in the PC. Systems like NetWare use any spare RAM as cache memory. As an example of the different effects of RAM fitted to a server, a Pentium-based server loaded with 20 users running NetWare 4 performs very differently when it has 16, 24 or 32Mb of system RAM. By halving the system RAM, performance in Mbit/s of throughput was reduced to a third.

Operating system memory requirements

Operating System	Server RAM requirements
OS/2	48Mb
Novell NetWare	48Mb
Windows NT	48Mb
Unix	64Mb

What type of disk controller?

If you want to improve your server's performance in one easy step, forget the processor, look instead at the bottlenecks that form around the I/O system – particularly the network adapter and the hard disk system.

Notes is a very disk-intensive application – it's really a database management application and so it feels the effects of a slow disk system more than, say, a shared application that is loaded once then run from the local workstation. The most flexible type of disk interface that can also provide good rate of data transfer is SCSI (Small Computer System Interface). SCSI is now in version two, SCSI-2 which improves its control and performance. Most SCSI controllers currently on the market are also compatible with the newer SCSI-2 standards.

Watch out for workstations being sold as 'servers' that have a standard IDE drive common in most workstations. An IDE drive is cheap and neat and you can easily get drives greater than 1Gb in capacity.

ESDI is a drive standard to avoid. It's being phased out of production and is expensive and slow.

SCSI can transfer data at 5Mb/s, SCSI-2 can work at the same rate but it can also work in two high-speed modes. SCSI-2 Fast doubles the data rate to 10Mb/s while SCSI-2 Wide adds a second data path boosting the standard 8-bit wide data path up to either 16 or 32-bits (depending on the implementation) giving Wide a maximum transfer rate of 40Mb/s.

Disk cacheing

A disk cache uses fast memory and logic to try to keep the data for the next request in cache memory. This effectively gives the processor faster access to the data when it needs it. There are problems: disk data cannot be accessed byte by byte. Instead, it must be accessed one whole sector at a time (typically 512 bytes). To be of any practical use, the smallest chunk of data that a disk cache has to deal with, called the line size, has to be several times greater than a sector.

A second problem for a disk cache is timing. Unlike RAM caches, there are different retrieval speeds for different data locations on a disk. The speed at which data you request is delivered depends how far the read head has had to move and where, in relation to it, the last access was located.

Lastly, coherence or synchronization can be catastrophic if not properly addressed. If the contents of the disk do not match the contents of the cache then security can be compromised, especially if your PC crashes before the cache has had time to update the disk. If you make a change to the FAT, and you switch off your PC before this is passed on to the disk, you could risk a totally corrupted drive.

Delaying write operations is the basis of write-back cacheing; it gathers together a number of write operations destined for the same sector or track and sends them as one packet. This optimizes disk write head movement, but unless precautions are taken, it's not as secure as a write-through operation which sends on all write operations as they are received.

Delaying write requests can cause problems when trying to maintain coherence. In Unix systems, it's common to run the Sync command before shutting down the operating system. This ensures any cached data is written to disk. Software and hardware cacheing methods under DOS should trap the reset interrupt. By clearing up tidily before allowing a [Ctrl]+[Alt]+[Del] to work, they prevent disk corruption.

Write requests can be consolidated into groups addressed to the same disk sector to minimize disk head movement. In much the same way, disk reads can be minimized by using a read-ahead method. Instead of just reading in the 512-byte sector from disk, read-ahead caches pull in data from the subsequent sector. The assumption is that the application will want to look at the next sector in the future, and when it does, the cache can deliver data straight from RAM rather than waiting for disk.

If you are considering adding a cacheing controller, check first that it won't adversely affect the performance of your operating system.

Odd though this may seem, the performance of some network operating systems – particularly NetWare – can drop dramatically if you add a hardware disk cacheing controller. The reason is that NetWare uses any spare RAM as a very efficient software cache and orders read and writes effectively in software. Add a hardware cache controller that's trying to do the same thing and it will be redundant and could even work against the software and reduce performance. Instead, you should buy a fast, non-cacheing disk controller and more RAM.

Where to place the server

If your Notes server goes down, how badly will this affect the users? Do they depend upon it? If so, you should try to keep the server out of harm's way. If you have a room for your network server or wiring closet, place the Notes server there. Not only will your Notes server be out of the way of accidental physical damage – such as someone switching it off by mistake or knocking it, but you can link it to your LAN server's UPS.

Backup hardware

The one component of your Notes server that is statistically most likely to fail is its hard disk. Most hard disks in servers have around a 4–5% chance of failing in a year; to get around this risk, you need to install a backup device. There are a range of devices that you can fit to backup your Notes databases, in the next section I cover the main options.

One of the cheapest methods is tape storage. At the low end are tape drives using QIC (¼-inch cassette) tapes which are very robust and can store from around 80Mb. One big advantage is that DC2000 drives can be plugged straight into the server's floppy controller. Their disadvantage is a slow rate of data transfer; around 2.5Mb per minute is typical. DC600 cassettes store more than a DC2000 tape on a physically larger tape but the drives are more expensive and need a SCSI adapter. One advantage is a better speed of data transfer at up to 10Mb per minute.

The current standard backup tape is a DAT drives that can pack much more data on to tiny 4mm tapes. DATs can carry a nominal capacity of 1.3Gb but using data compression software or hardware, many manufacturers claim up to 5Gb can be saved on to a DAT. A development on this is the Data/DAT that allow random access, like a normal hard disk.

Another popular technology is optical disks – WORM (write once, read many) technology or CD-R. CD-R creates CD-ROM discs but can be limited for backups since its discs can only have data written to them once, which is good for archiving or data distribution but not so good for weekly backups.

Siting the backup device

Once you have your backup hardware, where do you fit it? This isn't such a silly question since there are three options, and each depend on your requirements. The first uses a backup device on a workstation (normally the supervisor's PC). With this method, no load is presented to your Notes server but the data being backed up streams across the network, clogging up the available bandwidth and slowing all other network operations. It does mean that you can insert a tape, start the backup, and remove the tape without leaving your desk.

The second method is server based. The drive and software run on a server. This provides the maximum speed of transfer for server-based data and allows any user with rights to the software, to initiate their own back up. This is probably the best solution for a Notes server since there's little to be backed up from users' workstations – you need only to backup the server-based databases. The third option is to use a dedicated backup server. This can be any old PC that removes the load from the main file server. Like the first option, the backup data streams across the network to this secondary server and fills available bandwidth.

Disk mirroring

If you are concerned about providing a fast recovery service to your Notes users, one solution would be to install disk mirroring. Mirroring makes an exact duplicate of a disk on another hard disk. It's a cheaper, but less secure way of protecting data than disk duplexing – with a mirrored drive, the disk controller card remains common to the multiple drives.

Disk duplexing is one of the best ways of protecting your data. Not only is the data written on to multiple disk drives, but each drive is controlled by separate controllers. If one drive or controller fails, the second subsystem is still operational. Some disk controllers include disk duplexing and disk mirroring as part of their feature list, although the most common setup uses multiple SCSI drives.

- ### RAID disk arrays

An alternative way of increasing a server's fault tolerance is to use a disk array. RAID (redundant array of inexpensive disks) is currently a common addition to many dedicated server PCs. The different levels of RAID allow you to implement data stripping (that is, spreading blocks of data across different drives) together with mirroring and duplexing. RAID also provides facilities for error correction. In this case, one of the drives in the disk array is dedicated as a parity drive and stored data is spread across the remaining drives. If one drive fails, the parity bit allows the stored data to be re-constructed.

Uninterruptible power supplies

An essential component to keep your Notes server running when the power fails is a UPS. If you already have a UPS for your main network server, check the new power requirements of the second server and any communications equipment that is running from Notes (such as hubs, gateways and modems) that also need to be kept powered. There are several types of power problem that a UPS should cover:

- **Brownouts:** these are a short-term decrease in the electrical supply's voltage level. These are the common power problem, and account for over 80% of all electrical problems. Brownouts are normally caused by the power company lowering the voltage in an area to compensate for extraordinary power demands. Brownouts do not necessarily cause the computer to shut off, instead they will be sneaky and cause the PC to reset or a keyboard to lock-up or a drive error.
- **Spikes:** a spike is an instantaneous increase in the voltage level on a power supply. Spikes are normally caused by a lightning strike, damaged cabling or faulty equipment. As you can imagine, a sudden voltage spike, several times the normal mains voltage level, can damage the components in your computer. Less than 10% of electrical problems are spikes – but they can effectively damage the hardware as well as causing data corruption. Surges are similar to spikes, but less abrupt and of a lower voltage level – they cause less damage than a spike unless sustained for a long period of time. Blackouts are a total loss of power. Blackouts occur rarely and are often due to storms or lightning. Like spikes, blackouts account for around 5% of problems.
- **Electrical noise:** 'noise' is caused by EMI (electromagnetic interference) and RFI (radio frequency interference) and disrupts and distorts the normally smooth sine wave of an electrical supply. Large electrical devices, especially motors, generators and other computers that are not properly shielded can generate noise on the main supply. The effect of noise is to cause small, single-bit errors in data, either in RAM or on disk, which can corrupt a program or data file.

- **UPS power ratings**

    The most obvious feature of a UPS that needs to be checked when you buy it is its power capacity. If there's a blackout, would it supply your Notes server for long enough to provide an orderly shutdown? Second, is it capable of communicating with your server to let the server know it's operating from its battery and to initiate an orderly shutdown? There's little point in buying a UPS that cannot provide enough power to support your computer, but it's not always easy to work this out. The power of a UPS is measured in V–A (volt–amps). Computer equipment, in contrast, is rated in watts.

    The calculation is watts = volts × amps

    The rating of a UPS, in V–A, does not take into account the power factor of a device. This power factor is a number, between 0 and 1, that indicates the amount of useful energy that's used by a device. For example, a light-bulb has a power factor of 1 – it's a rare case. Most computer equipment has a rating of around 0.7. Because of this, the V–A rating of a UPS is always larger or equal to the watt rating of the computer equipment it's supplying. To calculate the size of UPS you need to power a server and monitor, look at the labels on the back of each. These will normally either give the power rating of the equipment in watts or the amps drawn.

    UPS power calculations:

    Computer + Monitor amps = 3 amps
    AC Voltage = 240 volts
    Total watts = 720 watts (3 × 240)
    Power factor = 0.7
    UPS V–A rating required = 504 VA

Requirements for workstations

So far in this chapter I have covered at length the requirements for a Notes server. In contrast, the workstations used to access Notes need only a minimum specification in order to work correctly. The Notes workstation software is modest in its hard disk requirements (around 3Mb) and leaves most of the hard work to the server software.

For PC workstations

PC workstations can run the Notes software under either OS/2 or Windows. Both GUIs provide very similar functions and their requirements are near identical: a minimum requirement in line with the GUI being used. This means an 80486 or preferably a Pentium based PC and at least 8Mb of RAM (although 16Mb is recommended).

Add to this a minimum of a 400Mb hard disk (Windows alone can take up around 30Mb of this) and you are set. If you are running a shared version of Windows that's pulled off the central network server, you can have a smaller disk. It is possible to run Windows and Notes from a diskless workstation, which boots up from a ROM on the network adapter card and downloads a Windows or DOS disk image from the server – refer to your network operating system to configure this.

For Macintosh workstations

The Macintosh Notes workstation software has been improved dramatically and is now stable and works well. It presents a similar front-end to the Windows product with the same functionality, if not always in the same way. If you are still running System 6, try to upgrade to System 7 or you could well encounter more problems (there are problems with System 6 and some OS/2 2.1 servers). For even better connectivity functions, go for the latest version – System 7.5. The disk requirements are modest, again just around 3Mb and the processor requirements are less demanding than the PC version – you can run Notes from a PowerBook or a PowerPC.

Network hardware requirements

One factor that can affect the performance of your Notes server is the efficiency of the network adapter card. Not just in its ability to send data to and from the server to the workstations, but to pass data to and from main memory and the CPU. There are four ways used by adapter cards to transfer data to memory, which are covered below.

Shared memory is a technique in which the network adapter card is fitted with a buffer memory that can be accessed by the server's processor. The processor can read or write data to the on-board shared buffer memory at full speed; high-speed RAM chips are used so that no wait states are required from the processor. Shared memory cards are generally the most expensive, and near the top in speed – with only bus-mastering coming first. Its only real problem is the possibility of memory conflicts with other peripherals.

Programmed I/O provides adapters with an efficient way of transferring data in which the adapter has an on-board processor which transfers data to a pre-defined area of the computer's main memory; the computer's processor does the same. Each time either processor has written new data to the area of memory, it signals to the other processor that data is available.

Another method of data transfer is using DMA (direct memory access). In this scheme, the server is fitted with a DMA controller chip that takes over the bus and directs data from the network card to an assigned area of system memory. The main server CPU can, in the meantime, get on with other tasks making DMA very efficient. The problem tends to be a limitation of the DMA controller chip which in high-speed servers can be running much more slowly than the CPU.

The fastest method of transferring data is to use bus-mastering. In this, instead of the server's processor being interrupted each time that a transfer is happening, the solution is to modify the bus to allow other processors, in addition to the main CPU, to take control of the bus. This is what bus-mastering does: the network adapter has its own processor which can transfer data from the network adapter to the main system RAM without having to interrupt the central processor. Only the MCA, EISA and Local Bus buses can cope with bus-mastering.

PCI local bus

This provides a direct link between the adapter and the computer's main memory. Most server and high-performance workstation PCs feature PCI connectors. You need to buy a PCI adapter (there's no cross-standard with, say ISA). However, although more expensive than other adapters, PCI peripherals provide the best way of adding high-speed data transfer devices to your computer. Typically, PCI is used for high-throughput network adapters or graphics adapters.

Network connections – the software

When setting up a new Notes server it is likely that you will have to carry out some network connectivity. Perhaps to connect a small network to your main Notes network to give more users access to Notes or to provide a feed from a remote data source (such as a database manager, mainframe or mini on a different LAN). The simplest job is to connect two similar LANs: you can use a repeater to boost the signal across the gap between the buildings. This will work when the two LANs are the same (two Ethernet or Token Ring), but won't work if they are different. Some devices can be used to connect different transmission types, but normally need a similar protocol, such as IPX or NetBIOS, running on each.

Once you have to start linking networks that are separated by miles rather than a building, your problems increase. If the two sites are relatively close, within a couple of kilometers, it might still be practical to try to cross this using standard LAN transmission methods – notably by using a fiber-optic cable link. This is immune to electrical interference, offers good weather resistance and is capable of running to 100km without a repeater. The cost of installing adapters at each end is often no more than a couple of high-speed modems or ISDN links, but the problem is getting permission to lay the cable.

For more remote sites, often the most logical method of connection to a similar remote device is to use a modem. Remote bridges, routers and gateways will connect to a modem and link, via the standard telephone network, to any other device around the world. Typically, you can expect data rates of 28,800bps (bits per second), although current high-speed modems with carrier rates of 36,600bps will transmit data at around 60Kbps using advanced data-compression techniques. An alternative is ISDN which can transmit 64Kbps, but requires a specially installed phone line (see later in this chapter for more information on modems and ISDN).

Network connections – the hardware

When linking networks to create a multi-server installation you will have to look at hardware to provide the network connectivity. For some simple jobs, such as swapping mail messages, you could rely on a modem link between servers, but for large data transfers – often required during a Notes replication process – you will need to find a higher bandwidth product. In the following section I describe some of the options available if you are linking networks together.

Repeaters

The simplest method of connecting together two similar LANs is to use a repeater device. This works at the physical layer in the ISO seven-layer model and only provides signal regeneration; as an electrical signal passes along any length of cable it is attenuated (the level goes down) and noise is introduced. A repeater removes the noise from the incoming signal, regenerates the pulse and re-transmits it – they are often used to extend the length of a LAN segment which would otherwise reach the limits of the media. Repeaters can be used to link two identical networks. The one problem with repeaters is that since their sole function is to form a link between two LANs, everything that comes along is passed across. This can immediately double the load on each LAN.

Bridges

Repeaters are very basic in processing power and are unable to link different types of network. A bridge adds processing power and can read the destination address contained in each packet's header data. It compares this to its internal address list and, based on this, either sends the packet across the link or keeps the packet local. Effectively, bridges work at the MAC level of the data-link layer within the ISO model and are often called MAC-layer bridges. All a user sees is the benefits of a newly extended network with remote resources now available. From a supervisor's viewpoint, bridges won't load either LAN unnecessarily.

A bridge can also allow you to link two different media types. You could, for example, use one to link an Ethernet LAN to a Token Ring LAN – as long as the protocol used is the same on each side. Specialized bridges will link two totally different LANs, and can cope with different protocols at each end. They strip out the data packet from the incoming frame and insert it into an appropriate frame in different protocol that's running over the second LAN.

Routers

Routers work in a very similar way to bridges and can be used to extend a network by linking together LANs. They also incorporate more processing power to provide an added function: to pick the best route for a particular message. Typically, a router might have several delivery routes available – each with a different cost and speed of delivery. According to the size and urgency of the packet to be delivered, the router can select the best route for it. Routers provide connection service at the network layer of the ISO model (one layer higher than a bridge).

A router can take more intelligent decisions than a bridge, but because of this tends to be slower. A router can also be used to connect LANs that are running different protocols or transmission methods. Routers are often used when connecting LANs over a long distance – either over a leased line, ISDN, X.25 or asynchronous modem link. Since the price of these inter-network links is expensive you would use a router to make more efficient use of the link than a bridge.

Links to the outside world

When setting up a wide-area network, or one that stretches between two buildings, you will have to consider the options available for remote connections. This section is not just for power administrators with hundreds of users to support; you might just want to set up a remote node from someone's home giving them full access to the network.

The subject of remote connections can be split into two. The first covers the hardware available: modems and transceivers. The second covers the transmission medium: satellite, microwave, telephone or leased line.

If you have two LANs in neighboring buildings, then the job of connecting them is relatively easy if they are similar LANs. A repeater can be used to boost the signal across the gap between the buildings. This will work fine for two identical networks (two Ethernet or Token Ring), but hits a problem if they are different. Some bridges, as described above, can be used to connect different transmission types, but normally need a similar protocol, such as IPX or NetBIOS, running on each.

The problems start when the distance to be spanned between the LANs increases. It becomes very expensive to try to provide a direct link between the two LANs at the speed of a transmission method such as Ethernet (10Mbps). Expense dictates that you will normally have to try to find a low-cost, practical method of spanning the two networks.

If the sites are relatively close, within a couple of kilometers, it might still be practical to try to cross this using standard LAN transmission methods – notably by using a fiber-optic cable link. This is immune to electrical interference, offers good weather resistance and is capable of running to 100km without a repeater. The cost of installing adapters at each end is often prohibitive for standard workstations, but could be bearable in this situation. The main problem in this case is getting the permission to lay the fiber between the buildings.

For more remote sites, often the most logical method connection to a similar remote device is to use a modem. Remote bridges, routers and gateways will connect to a modem and link, via the standard telephone network, to any other device around the world. Typically, you can expect data rates between 28.8Kbps and 36.6Kbps for current high-speed modems – which will transmit data at around 60Kbps using advanced data-compression techniques.

Modems

One of the most convenient ways of connecting a remote user to your central office is to use a modem link – it's also one of the cheapest ways of linking two distant networks, or providing the physical link in a gateway to a commercial e-mail service. The trend in modem technology is towards ever higher speed rates of data transmission with the norm now 28,800bps over a standard telephone line. Since these are asynchronous modems working on a normal telephone line, there's no need to lay down a leased line or special hardware if all you need is to transfer mail between two medium sized e-mail networks. If you want higher rates of data transfer, ISDN provides a cheap and very reliable option offering up to 128,000bps. You need a special ISDN adapter and telephone line, but the phone calls cost no more than a normal telephone call. The next advance since the launch of ISDN is ATM and both are covered later in this chapter.

There is a vast range of different types of modem available, together with a great range of standards for data transmission. If you are considering adding a modem to give your e-mail setup access to the outside world, this section will guide you through the main options available.

Providing a fax option

One useful addition to any e-mail system is a fax gateway. This will let your users send faxes from within their mail package. The user composes their mail message as usual, then sends it to the fax gateway; the gateway software strips out the telephone number, converts the message (and any attachments) into a graphic file, and transmits the fax. This is a particularly simple add-on function especially since many high-speed modems now also include a fax option for very little extra cost. The ability to receive faxes is less important and far less practicable. The faxes have to be stored as large bitmap files, then passed through OCR software, and re-addressed to the correct recipient as a mail message. Unless yours is a model office, it's far simpler to have a normal fax machine for receiving faxes!

If you are using a Windows-based e-mail system, you could drive a fax card by installing it as another printer; Windows 95, Windows NT and even Windows for Workgroups all have this support built-in. To send the fax, the mail is printed to the fax modem. This doesn't make a neat solution, and it can be difficult to share a local fax card. Some networking software, such as Windows, includes fax modem sharing capabilities, and lets you send MS-Mail messages to the local fax server. Alternatively, you will have to use fax gateway software – available for almost all the main e-mail systems including cc:Mail, Microsoft Mail and BeyondMail. To control the fax modem there are several different standards covering the method of sending commands. The main two standards are extensions to the Hayes AT command set called Class 1 and 2. In addition, Intel has its own standard, called CAS, that is supported by some fax modem manufacturers and software developers.

ISDN

ISDN (Integrated Services Digital Network) offers high-speed, virtually error-free data transmissions with little extra equipment and all at the cost of a normal phone call. An ISDN adapter costs around twice the cost of a modem and, apart from paying for a new ISDN connection to the office nothing else is required.

The main advantage of ISDN is that it provides a digital transmission line that can support data rates up to 64Kbps, but these lines are not available everywhere – it depends on the phone company. If you are thinking of setting up a WAN or need to link two offices on a regular basis, or to exchange a lot of mail, you should put ISDN at the top of your list. One of the great advantages of ISDN is that it provides instant connection to the remote system – there's no delay for dialing or connection. This makes an ISDN link ideal for connecting two remote servers or for connection to the Internet (but check your service provider has ISDN support).

There are two types of service you can buy from your phone company. The first, Basic Rate Interface (BRI) service, combines two 'B' channels – each transmitting digitized data, voice, text, images or video at 64,000bps – with one 'D' channel used for signaling information at 16,000bps. The second is called Primary Rate Interface (PRI) service, and offers 23 'B' channels plus one 'D' channel. Users are charged only for time on-line, not by the amount of data sent or received.

The most common installation is the Basic Rate Interface, with two 64,000bps channels. It might seem strange to have two separate channels, but some adapters can run these in parallel to provide an effective throughput of 128Kbps. With data compression, this can easily equal a transfer rate of 400Kbps.

One problem with ISDN is its image. It is shadowed by a strange cloud that turns buyers off at the very mention of its name. To get around this, some vendors (such as AT&T in the USA) have even renamed it (AT&T is now calling it SDS IS!). However, ISDN has now really taken off in the US and Europe. There are cheap ISDN adapters that are little more than the price of a good modem and connection fees to an ISDN telephone network have also been cut. With instant connection and high-speed data transfer, it's an ideal product for company e-mail links to the Internet or for e-mail links between buildings or offices.

3

Operating system software

About this chapter

In this chapter we look at the operating system software requirements of Lotus Notes. Notes is comprised of two components: the server software and the workstation software used to access the databases. The users' workstations need to run the Notes workstation software in addition to the network workstation shell.

The Notes server software is an application and runs on top of an operating system. In addition, your network uses a network operating system.

You can run the Notes server program either on a central dedicated server or on a shared workstation. The latter is really only useful for a test-run before committing fully to Notes. Using Windows 95 as a simple server and Notes provides a simple test bed for ideas, but will not support more than a few users.

Server software requirements

Notes is effectively a complex database management system operating efficiently with a client–server architecture. This means that the server has to run efficiently and be able to handle the data throughput that Notes will generate. In version 4.5, Lotus has worked hard to improve the routines that manage the three main activities of a Notes server: indexing, routing and replication. The server software has been improved to cut down the load on a server during these tasks and can improve performance by up to 30% over a similar Notes 3 server.

Notes will run on a range of operating systems within a network. In some cases it needs its own dedicated server, while in its Windows version, you can try out Notes easily with little extra hardware requirements. Notes will run on server software with either single processor or multiple processor technology, including server platforms such as the Sun Microsystems Ultra 3000 server with six processors.

Traditionally, Lotus has used the OS/2 operating system as a platform for the Notes server – this was the first operating system that Notes server could operate under and still accounts for over 90% of the Notes server market. However, in Notes 4.5 there are many changes to the server software that mean OS/2 is not necessarily the best server operating system choice for your company.

However, whichever operating system you choose, tests have shown that changing from the Notes 3 server software up to Notes 4.5 can increase your server's user capacity by between three and four times. As an example, *PC Magazine's* ZD Labs ran tests on Notes servers loaded with 300 workstations representing the equivalent load of between 900–1500 users. In fact, the ZD Labs results found that there was little degradation in performance when using any of the possible server operating systems – with the exception of OS/2! It found that the same server hardware could easily cope with the 300 workstation load during mail routing or indexing; again, the only operating system that showed cracks was OS/2.

I'll cover the pros and cons of each operating system in the next few pages, however it's worth keeping an open mind when choosing a server platform for Notes rather than picking the traditional OS/2 platform. The Notes server software displays just a simple command-line prompt at which the administrator can type in server commands (see Chapter 8 for more details). Apart from this minimal user interface, reminiscent of DOS, the Notes server application works as a database management and access control system and relies to a considerable extent on the speed and efficiency of the underlying operating system.

One of the most important factors that affects the performance of Notes is the speed of the server's processor rather than the size of the RAM. For this reason, the recent multiprocessor server platforms are particularly attractive and the new versions of NetWare SMP and multiprocessor OS/2 WARP server bring these two operating systems level with Solaris and Windows NT SMP.

The last feature that will affect the way your Notes server runs is the provision for network protocols supported by the NOS. Although the vast majority of Notes servers are connected to NetWare file and print servers using Novell's IPX/SPX protocol, it's safe to bet that TCP/IP will catch up fast given Notes' position as an intranet server and its close links to the Internet. When choosing a server platform for Notes 4.5 it's important that you consider all of these factors and assess how they will impact your installation.

IBM OS/2

OS/2 was the first server platform for Lotus Notes and is by far the most popular platform with over 90% of the installed base. It's also probably the most reliable, given its history and the opportunity to iron out any bugs, and is certainly the most flexible of any of the platforms supporting every Notes feature and more protocol stacks than any of the operating systems. Notes will run on either the new IBM OS/2 WARP 3 Server or the OS/2 WARP Connect and IBM LAN Server combination.

Typical OS/2 installation

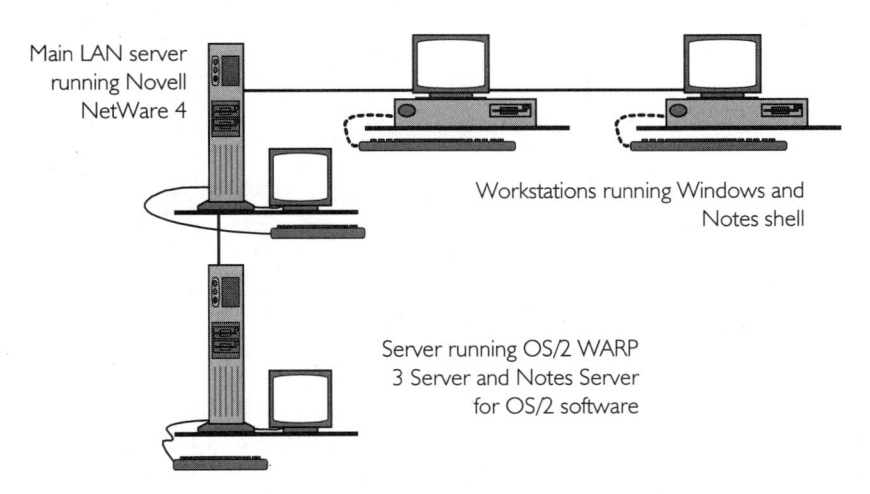

Main LAN server running Novell NetWare 4

Workstations running Windows and Notes shell

Server running OS/2 WARP 3 Server and Notes Server for OS/2 software

Setup

Notes Server for OS/2 is straightforward to install directly on the OS/2 server and can be managed from a Presentation Manager front end or from a remote workstation. It's very smooth to migrate up from Notes Server 3 for OS/2 to Notes 4.5 and installing the NetWare client is easier to setup under OS/2 WARP than under previous versions of OS/2. And the best part of switching to Notes 4.5 on OS/2 WARP is the improvement in performance; with the multiprocessor version of OS/2 WARP available, this platform provides an easy installation, simple upgrade and good performance.

Compatibility

Currently, Notes running on an OS/2 server is the only server platform that will support all the types of workstation listed below (OS/2, Windows, Macintosh and Unix). Notes Server for OS/2 is still the only software in the pack that will support all of the following protocols: TCP/IP, IPX/SPX and NetBIOS.

Microsoft Windows 95

Notes Server will not officially run under Windows 95 – but in practice there's no problem! As such, although it's of no practical use as an enterprise-wide Notes server, it is an excellent way of trying out Notes without incurring any costs for extra hardware. This turns any existing Windows 95 workstation into a Notes server – that can be connected to your existing network using standard Windows network drivers and can support several users – although it's hardly able to support an entire corporation!

Windows 95 installation

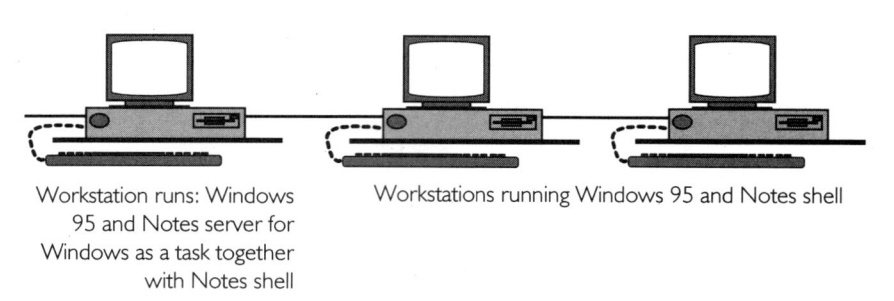

Workstation runs: Windows 95 and Notes server for Windows as a task together with Notes shell

Workstations running Windows 95 and Notes shell

The Notes server application will run on any PC with 32-bit Windows either 95 or NT (Windows NT is covered later). Lotus does not really recommend using Windows 95 as the server operating system, but it's a useful work-around if you want to benchtest a new configuration or check suitability. In addition, you can also use the server as a workstation – although this will dramatically slow down the response to other users.

Microsoft Windows NT

The combination of Notes Server for NT and Windows NT Server provide an excellent platform for new Notes sites and is nearly as flexible as the OS/2 platform when judging migration paths. The only snag with Windows NT is its poor NetWare integration which can cause performance problems – this is a Windows driver problem rather than any reflection on Notes and will only be of consequence if you have to connect to a NetWare server using the Novell IPX/SPX protocol. If you are setting up a new Notes server and have the luxury of changing the protocol, you would be wise to stick with the Windows NetBIOS (called NetBEUI) or TCP/IP, but for the majority of existing sites which have to connect to existing NetWare servers you should stick with SPX.

Windows NT is very simple to install and with its current version 4, it has the look and feel of Windows 95. Once NT is up and running, you'll need to install connectivity to your NetWare server (I'm assuming you're the majority and have an office NetWare server for file and print sharing) – this means installing the NetWare protocol stack and the gateway software supplied with NT.

Installing Notes onto the server is very straightforward. Once in place, there are two ways to run the server software: either as an application or as a Windows service. The advantage of the latter is that this means the Notes server will automatically start and stop as the NT server is brought up and down.

One of the down sides of the Notes for NT server is that it is very loosely integrated with NT itself. Notes Server does not use NT for any user management and there's no way of easily transferring existing network user information from the NT Registry to Notes users. However, if you're also working with a central NetWare server (which does allow user data to be imported into Notes Server) there's no such problem.

Windows NT is an excellent server platform in terms of usability. There's the familiar Windows 95 user interface and network tools and it supports most of the current protocol sets – the only weakness being SPX. Finally, Windows NT SMP support provides a simple upgrade path for any manager that wants to use a server platforms such as the Compaq ProLiant server with two processors.

Novell NetWare 4.1

With previous version of Notes there came the option to run Notes Server as a task on the central office server that ran Novell NetWare. This idea continues with Notes 4.5 which has been released as an NLM to run on the NetWare 4.1 platform. This means that you can install it on to your existing office NetWare server and run Notes without any other server hardware. This is ideal if you have an existing network and want to install Notes without having to buy and manage an extra server or you are wary of setting up gateways and managing a mix of protocols over your network.

Although billed as Notes Server for NetWare 4.1, the Notes NLM will work correctly with NetWare 3.12, 4.01 or 4.1. The Notes NLMs work in the same way as any other NLM for a NetWare server; the NetWare operating system is not a full pre-emptive multitasking operating system (as are OS/2, NT and Solaris). This means that it's up to the application (Notes) to relinquish processor control when asked. NetWare cannot force the application to do much, so if you have a badly written or rogue NLM loaded at the same time as the Notes NLM you might find performance drops to nothing. NetWare 4 gets around this problem with better control over the memory and time allocation, but in order to provide compatibility with NetWare 3.12, Notes 4.5 Server does not use these modes.

There are a few problems when installing Notes 4.5 onto the NetWare 4.1 server. The main thing is simply how awkward the install process is when compared to Windows NT or OS/2. Notes for NetWare has to be installed from a remote workstation onto the server; this is no different from many other NLMs that run on a NetWare server, but Notes 4.5 will only install correctly from a workstation running Windows 3.1 (95, NT and OS/2 are not correctly supported).

Managing the Notes server is carried out from a remote workstation. You can carry out all the usual basic NetWare commands – such as Monitor under NW 3.12 – and load and remove the application or tweak drivers from the menu-driven and command line NetWare server interface. However, for anyone that's used NetWare this will not be a problem and is just as fast as a more visually appealing Windows front-end.

The advantage of running the Notes Server software on your existing NetWare server is a central server platform that you already know how to manage. It's not as neat a package either during installation or administration as Notes for Windows or OS/2, but it is effective, fast and provides support for SMP and, naturally, IPX/SPX protocols.

Novell Netware installation

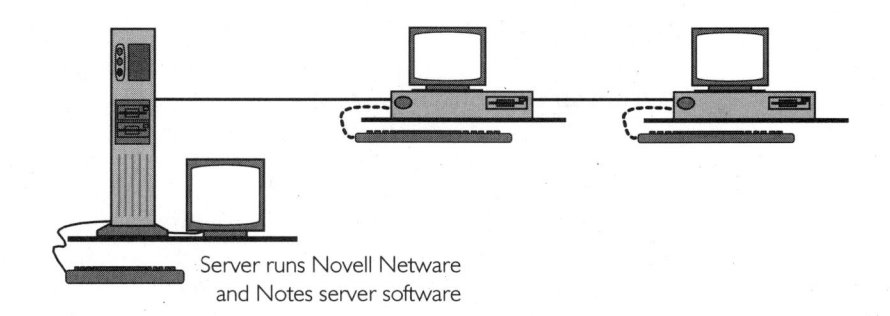

Server runs Novell Netware and Notes server software

Notes for NetWare will run on any PC server that is running Novell NetWare 3.12 or 4.*x*. The server software installs easily, but you have to install from a workstation, rather than directly onto the server (however, this is common with all NetWare NLM applications). Once installed, you use the standard NetWare system tools (such as Syscon) to setup the users and to export the user list to a text file, ready to import into Notes.

Notes for Unix

One of the best ways to support two thousand users is to setup Notes on a Unix platform. And one of the neatest versions of Notes for Unix runs on the Solaris operating system. This server software has been totally re-written since the first attempt in Notes 3 and now, with Sun Microsystems' new Ultra series of multiprocessor servers, it provides an excellent route for company-wide Notes servers supporting several thousand users. Other similar products running under Unix include Notes for IBM AIX and Notes for HP UX. Both of these are very impressive products, but the Solaris solution has the advantage of the Sun hardware.

To setup and run a multiprocessor version of Notes under Solaris you will need Solaris 2.51 and compatible Sun hardware – both of which are very new.

Installation of Notes onto the Solaris, or other Unix operating systems, is straightforward but does require a good knowledge of Unix. If you are setting up a new Notes installation to work with an existing office server running, for example, NetWare, then you will need to budget for Unix expertise and the expense of the Unix platform hardware (which is more powerful and expensive than PC products).

The Notes–Unix solution is ideal if you need to support thousands of users and is the only combination that can comfortably provide the processing power to do this. However, you will need a budget large enough to accommodate the expensive Unix hardware and you will need to re-train or hire Unix expertise, especially if you are migrating from an OS/2 or NetWare site.

Choosing the right server software

Choosing which version of Notes to use with your installation can determine how efficiently your Notes and network run. For example, if you have experimented with a test group of five users supported under the Notes for Windows, you cannot expect the same software to support hundreds of users. Similarly, if you want to see what Notes can do for you, then it's unlikely that you have spare budget to buy a new Sun server and install Notes for Solaris. Instead, your choice is likely to be greatly determined by the existing hardware and software setup.

Running Notes on its own, a dedicated server will provide the best performance for your users – but there's the cost of the server, operating system and the extra time to manage this server. However, if you're expecting a reasonable traffic load from more than 50 users, you should really consider a dedicated server solution.

From a practical point of view, Notes for OS/2 has been around the longest and so is likely to have the least number of bugs! It also provides the most flexible and wide-ranging support of any of the operating systems. Notes for NetWare lets you add Notes to your network with little extra expense – although you would be advised to boost your server's RAM. Novell NetWare 3.12 uses server memory efficiently: any spare memory is used as cache memory, which directly effects the throughput on a busy server.

One warning when running Notes on any version of NetWare below 4.0: if one NLM server program crashes, it's very likely that the whole server will crash. So if you have a custom-written NetWare program, make quite sure that it's well written and won't try to grab too much memory or other system resources. This isn't a problem with NetWare 4.0 or OS/2 since each task that's running is protected from the others. If one OS/2 utility program crashes, the other tasks just keep running.

Notes for Windows NT provides one of the neatest environments to manage the server, but there are potential performance problems if you connect to a NetWare server. Lastly, Notes for Unix provides just about the most powerful system – if you can afford installation and running costs.

Workstation software requirements

In order to access Notes, each workstation needs to run a copy of the workstation software. In contrast to the command-line interface of the server software that will only be used by an administrator, the work station software provides a friendly graphical front-end to Notes. Each database is displayed as a large icon which can be arranged on different pages of the Notes desktop environment.

The Notes workstation application was originally written for the Microsoft Windows GUI environment, but it's now available on a range of different operating systems for the PC and on Unix and Apple Macintosh computers.

Microsoft Windows 3.1

The Notes workstation software can run on any PC that is running Microsoft Windows 3.0 or higher (although you should try to use Windows 3.1 or higher). The Windows interface works equally well for a network connection to the server or via a remote modem link.

Once the user is connected to the Notes server, he/she can use most normal Windows functions, including cut-and-paste between Notes and other applications (or the other way around if the database has a rich text field into which you can paste graphics or text).

Microsoft Windows 95/NT

The current 32-bit versions of Windows (95 and NT) are both designed for use on workstations (NT/AS runs as a server operating system). They differ from earlier versions of Windows in that they are the complete operating system – they do not rely on DOS to manage the low-level PC hardware.

Windows 95 is a very stable product that includes excellent networking functionality. It can support multiple protocol stacks and is easy to setup. Straight from the box, Win95 includes protocols to connect a workstation to almost any standard server, including Microsoft, Novell, Banyan and Unix servers.

There are several management features within Windows 95, such as User Profiles and System Policies, which allow a supervisor to define the way in which each workstation looks and works and allows you to limit what a user can do. It also allows roaming users on the network – a user can log in on any workstation and they will see their own, customized Desktop appear.

Windows 95 was originally supposed to improve on the performance of Windows 3.1 while still using the same amount of RAM. In reality, you will need a minimum of 8Mb of RAM and an 80486 processor, but this can be unbearably slow – you would be better off with a Pentium processor and 16Mb of RAM.

Notes runs with no problems under Windows 95. You can even install the Notes server software under Windows 95 – although this would only be for experimental setups! Lotus has included new mail gateway features to link its standard mail system – VIM – with the rival from Microsoft – MAPI.

The new Notes 4.5 programming features allow you to make the most of OLE 2 (with the Notes/FX 2 feature) and you can interrogate standard Windows database packages using the ODBC extensions to LotusScript.

IBM OS/2

The Notes workstation software will run under OS/2. The software presents a graphical front-end that's very similar in look and feel to the Windows software. Notes workstation for OS/2 will run on IBM OS/2 WARP 3.

Unix

The Lotus Notes workstation software is available in a version that will run on Unix workstations. This gives the user most of the same functions that are on the standard Windows user interface – with two notable exceptions. Notes for Unix cannot support DDE links (which are used to update data from another application) nor can it support OLE objects (such as embedded WAV sound files). To try to get around these problems, Lotus has developed another version of OLE called LEL (link embed to launch) which can support embedded objects on a Unix workstation.

At present, the workstation software will run on HP/UX, Sun Solaris, SCO Unix and IBM AIX platforms.

Apple Macintosh

Most large companies need to integrate their Apple Macintosh workstations into the main mass of PCs in order to keep the Mac users up to date or add them to an e-mail system. Just as with many other large PC applications, Notes took some time to get running reliably on a Macintosh. It can now run on any Macintosh with System 7 or higher installed and presents a similar graphical front-end to the desktop seen by a Windows or OS/2 user (although some option boxes and check boxes are different, the look and feel is very similar).

To support an Apple Macintosh Notes workstation make sure that the Notes server has an entry for the AppleTalk protocol in the Configuration field of the Server document in the Public Name & Address database. You will also need the AppleTalk zone name when you bind the server name to the protocol.

4
Networking Notes

About this chapter

Notes transfers information to and from users' workstations via your network. The protocols used to packet this data will depend on the network operating system that you're using: for example, OS/2 LAN Requester normally uses NetBEUI (a form of NetBIOS), while Novell NetWare uses its own IPX/SPX protocol. Each network operating system has its own default standard for the protocol that it would like you to use, but almost all can support other protocols – a necessity when interconnecting networks.

How Notes views a network

Notes software communicates over the network using network ports. These are software switches that tell Notes which driver, protocol and adapter to use when routing traffic over the network. There are two types of network port: a LAN port for LAN communications that works with the Notes adapter drivers and LAN protocols. The second port is a COM port used for communications via a modem or X.25 wide area network.

Notes network traffic

As your users make more use of the Notes databases, you will begin to see an increase in the traffic on the network. This does, of course, depend on the other applications that you use; Notes is a rather efficient client–server application designed to minimize the traffic on the network. However, if your users were previously only using the network for shared printing, you will see a marked increase in traffic. If, previously, all the users accessed a central store of shared files, then since the traffic will already be high, it's unlikely that Notes will make too much of a difference.

Notes supports a wide range of networks, but the choice becomes very limited with the newer versions of Notes. For example, the list of networks supported by Notes running on an OS/2 server is as follows:

- AppleTalk
- Banyan VINES
- NetBIOS
- NetWare SPX on OS/2
- TCP/IP
- Lotus Notes Connect for SNA

This means that if your existing network is running on one of these operating systems or protocols, you can install an extra Notes OS/2 server and your users will be able to access Notes via the existing network.

Not all the server platforms are as flexible as OS/2 with support for protocols – see Chapter 3 for details on the protocols each operating supports and the advantages of each platform.

In the Notes client–server model, when a user accesses or searches a database, he or she is issuing a single command to the database engine (which is running on the server); the engine searches the server-based database and sends back the answer. There's very little traffic generated. The alternative model used by older or badly designed applications would see considerably more traffic: a user would run his or her local database application which would access the centrally-stored, shared database file. The database file would have to be transferred over the network to the workstation where the application is running before it can be searched. This is taking rather an extreme view, but it illustrates the simplicity of client–server and its low impact on network traffic.

Client–server model

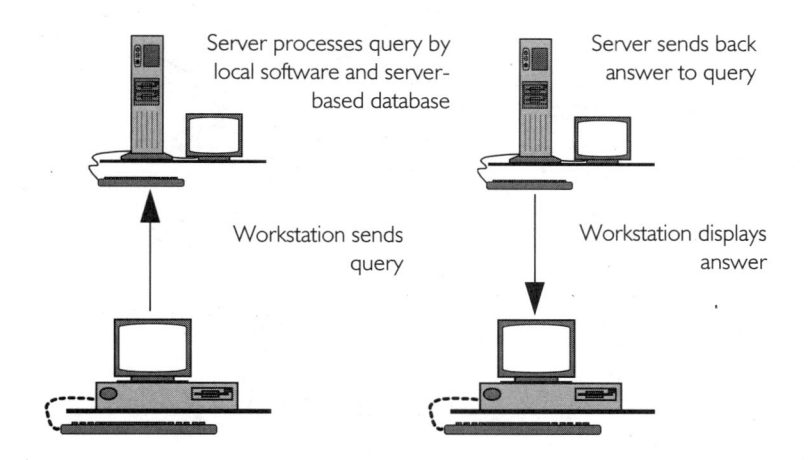

Server processes query by local software and server-based database

Server sends back answer to query

Workstation sends query

Workstation displays answer

If you find that your network is beginning to run out of bandwidth because of high traffic, there are a number of solutions that can help. The first is split the network into different segments. If you are using an Ethernet network, which is bus-based in architecture, you would normally have one end of the cable ending at your file server, the other end at the last workstation. With, say, 50 users you are dividing the available bandwidth of Ethernet, 10Mbits/s, by 50. Why not split the network into two segments of 25 users each; install a second Ethernet card in your server and you will effectively double the available bandwidth for a low cost. To do this, make sure that your network server operating system is capable of supporting several cards and routing between them (all of the 32-bit operating systems supported by Notes, including Windows NT, NetWare and OS/2 can support multiple cards).

When connecting several Notes servers together, perhaps you have several in your office building, you might consider a separate high-performance backbone for the network. An example might be to install a 100Mbps Ethernet or FDDI network connecting just the servers (the Notes and central LAN servers) together. You could, for the ultimate performance, create a backbone with ATM that offers a minimum of 155Mbps. The users would then connect to their home server over a standard Ethernet, 10Base-T or Token Ring link. (See later in this chapter for more details of connecting different network hardware.)

Backbone connecting servers

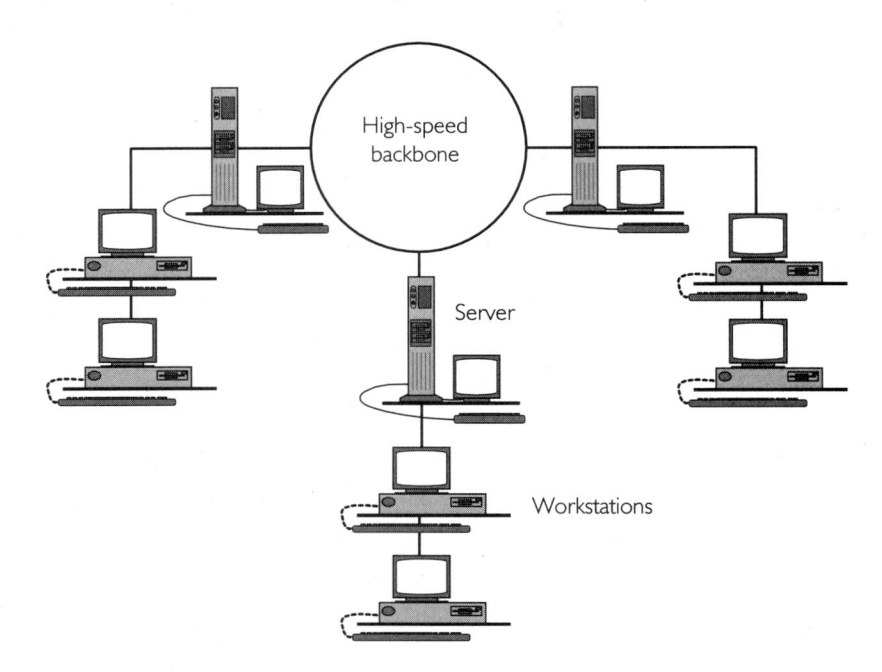

Network protocols

Notes supports a range of network protocols that cover the major standards used by most of the network operating systems. When setting up your current office network you might have considered the different types of protocol available with the network operating system, or you might have settled for the default protocol. Installing a new version of Notes provides a good opportunity to evaluate the network protocols you are using and to make any changes that could affect performance. For example, it's possible to have one protocol for communications between Notes servers – which have particular demands – and a different protocol for communications between server and workstations – which have a different set of requirements.

AppleTalk, Banyan VINES and NetBIOS are all convenient protocols that are well supported and easy to use, and provide good general-purpose protocols even if they are not efficient.

Novell's SPX/SPX II is well suited to high-speed links thanks to a larger packet size and is a good choice between servers.

TCP/IP includes extra fields in the packet that make it an excellent choice for data that has to be routed around multiple networks. It's a good choice for wide area links and any connections to the Internet (which is based on TCP/IP).

NetBEUI (the extended version of NetBIOS) is good for small, self-contained networks. It provides good performance, but cannot be routed so is of little use for wide area communications.

As you can see, there's no ideal solution. However, there are no rules that say you cannot mix protocols to get the best for different tasks!

Network shells

Any information that is received or sent by Notes passes through layers of network applications before it actually gets sent along the wire. Many of these error-checking and packaging routines are within the network shell program that often also contains the network protocol code.

For example, on a workstation that connects to a Novell NetWare network you need to load the driver for the network card then the protocol stack (which is normally IPX) then the redirector software.

The software interface for network cards has, to a degree, been standardized with Novell using its ODI interface and Microsoft sticking to its NDIS system. Both provide a standard interface for the network software to control the network adapter card.

Under DOS, the protocol stack is loaded as a TSR (terminate, stay resident) program. For example, under NetWare you would run IPX.COM which loads the TSR into memory. Lastly, the redirector is loaded – also as a TSR – and this controls the path of data to and from shared rather than local drives. To get the latest network shells for your operating system, look on CompuServe or other on-line services which have support areas. Notes is not fussy about which version of the network shell you're using; some take up more memory than others, each new version normally fixes a minor bug in a previous release – so try to use the latest releases.

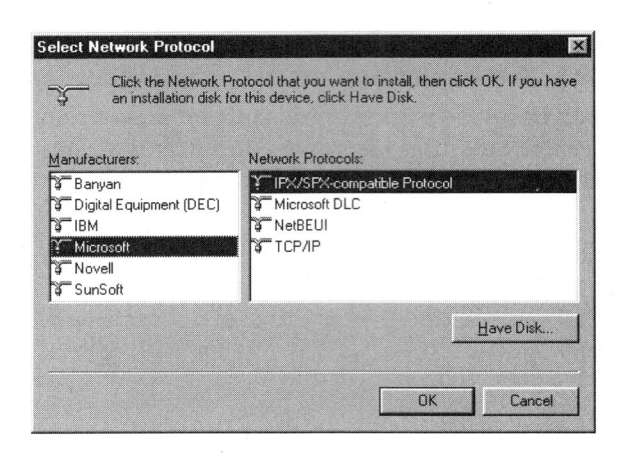

Under Windows, the protocol stack is loaded and managed by Windows itself. Windows 95 can support multiple protocol stacks and so a Windows workstation can connect to multiple servers running different operating systems – for example, the protocol stacks to connect a Windows 95 workstation to a NetWare server and an OS/2 server are provided with Windows.

Connecting platforms

When you are trying to link together your workstations into your Notes LAN you will probably come across various different platforms – each with its own connectivity problems. Similarly, if you need to link your Notes server to another network server you are likely to strike against different network operating systems. Although Notes often runs on an OS/2 server, it's quite likely you would want to connect to a LAN server running Novell's NetWare (which still has the biggest market share).

Straight from the box, NetWare 4 uses its own IPX (Inter Packet Exchange) protocol. Novell includes a software router which can bridge different protocols. NetWare 4 also includes support for connectivity to TCP/IP and AppleTalk protocols.

The next most likely protocol for establishing links is the TCP/IP protocol. This is used predominantly in Unix-based networks and normally runs over an Ethernet transmission hardware. The big advantage of TCP/IP is that software drivers are available for hundreds of different computers from IBM mainframes down. It is also the protocol used for communications over the Internet and if you have a direct internet link you'll need to provide at least server support for TCP/IP. Most PC-based

NOSes, such as NetWare and Windows 95/NT, include options to handle TCP/IP traffic.

NetBIOS comes next, simply because it is supported by almost every network operating system in some form or other. It's mostly used by DOS-based peer-to-peer network operating systems such as Artisoft's LANtastic and by the server-based NOS, LAN Manager. Windows NT uses an enhanced version of the basic NetBIOS protocol, called NetBEIU.

The Macintosh provides the next protocol, AppleTalk. AppleTalk is normally integrated at the server by adding in support for the protocol: Novell NetWare 4 includes built-in support for Macs with an internal AppleTalk protocol. The Notes protocol drivers used to communicate between the Notes server and workstation software provides AppleTalk support for NT and OS/2 servers. Similar products are available for Microsoft's Windows NT and Banyan's VINES. Because of this centralized solution, changing the capability of the server rather than the workstation, it's actually easier to integrate Macs into a PC environment than many other computers.

If you are working the other way around (that is, have mostly Macintosh computers and want to integrate a few PC workstations) then you will probably be running the AppleTalk protocol already. The OS/2 and NT server versions of Notes can both support AppleTalk and there are third-party protocol products that allow Windows workstations to work within an AppleTalk network.

Connecting Macintoshes

To connect a Mac to a PC-based server you need to ensure that your network operating system is capable of storing Mac-length file names. Both the OS/2 and Windows NT Notes server software versions can support the AppleTalk protocol and Macintosh workstations. For example, if you want to link a Mac to a NetWare server you need to setup NetWare to provide AppleTalk and make sure that your workstations are running AppleShare and, preferably, have System 7 installed.

The Notes Server software must also be configured to support the AppleTalk protocol and the AppleTalk zones for the servers and workstations. To add AppleTalk to the list of supported protocols, select the *File ▸ Tools ▸ User Preferences* menu option and choose the Ports icon in the navigator. Add AppleTalk to the list of supported protocols in the communications ports field at the top of the window.

Connecting OS/2 platforms

If you have an OS/2 server, there's no problem connecting OS/2 workstations. Problems only creep in if you want to connect workstations running OS/2 to Novell NetWare servers. You need to install the NetWare requester for OS/2 on the workstations and the server. (This is also the software required to link an OS/2 server to a NetWare server – such as a OS/2 Notes server to a central NetWare LAN server.)

Connecting PCs to multiple LANs

There are two situations in which you will need to connect a computer to two different network operating systems: if you are using a dedicated Notes server running OS/2 and a main NetWare LAN server or if your Notes server needs to connect to another network – perhaps for a data transfer or to be accessible by other users. Your users' workstations will also need to be able to connect to multiple network operating systems. To do this, Novell uses its Open Data-Link Interface (ODI) system which adds support for multiple protocols and multiple adapters within a single PC. Microsoft uses its popular NDIS (network driver interface specification) standard that does a similar job in defining the software interface between driver and hardware.

Using ODI, you can easily connect to different networks that use other protocols from NetWare's default IPX/SPX. Adding support for AppleTalk or TCP/IP is easy and you don't have to add multiple network adapters to the PC to do this. Because ODI is a fixed specification, any drivers that conform to the ODI requirements will work with any ODI workstation, and protocols can be added without rebooting the PC each time.

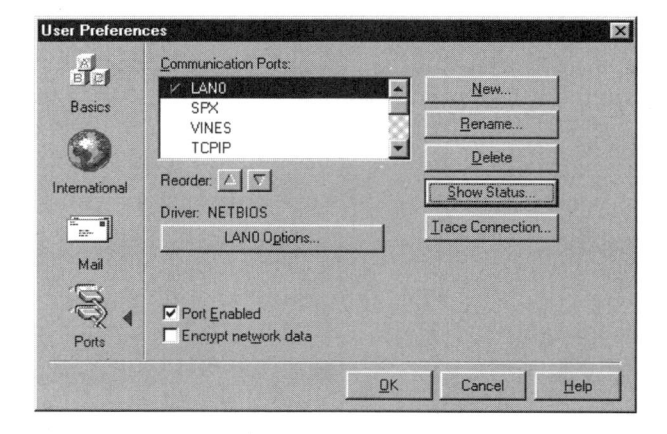

Monitoring protocol activity

One way of tracking down any problems or errors is have a regular look at the log file kept by the Notes server. The Notes Log.NSF file records any network errors and warnings and provides useful warning about impending problems.

Tip To check the status of a network port and that both the adapter and driver are working correctly, select the *File ▸ Tools ▸ User Preferences ▸ Ports ▸ Show* Status menu option on a workstation or type in the Show Port <name> on the server console.

5

Remote access to Notes

About this chapter

One of the functions built into Notes is the ability to support remote access; you can access Notes when you're away from your office by using a modem link from a laptop or home PC to the Notes server. Notes 4.5 improves on this functionality with a set of new features that make it easier to work remotely. Remote links are now easier to manage, more efficient and more secure.

Remote links let you send and receive e-mail messages and access any Notes database – you can do just the same as if you were connected on the LAN. In practice, there are two ways in which remote access can be used. The first is by users who are based in the office but travel and still have to keep in touch. One day they'll be the in the office using Notes from their desktop, the next day they'll phone in from the laptop and expect to have the same functionality. These users require network and remote access. The second set of users are homeworkers: they'll only ever be remote users and will never come into the office to use Notes. Although Notes supports remote access, and it's easy to configure, you'll have to make a number of administrative decisions before you let any remote user log in. This chapter describes how to configure the server and the workstations for remote access; the problems connection time during data transfer (you want to try and avoid users downloading a 20Mb file over a slow telephone line). Lastly, there are security issues – how to make Notes easy to access but difficult for hackers? Notes 4.5 includes a set of new, improved features that are specifically aimed at remote users. This chapter explains how to use the new features and also covers the hardware – normally a modem – that links remote user to server. However, for more information on general communications hardware, refer back to Chapter 2

An overview of remote access

When connected to a Notes server over a LAN there's no question about how you work – the connection to the server isn't charged for connection time and the rate of data transfer is fast. It's very different when you log in over a phone line. The cost of connection time for the phone line can soon become expensive and the rate of data transfer is slow. There are two methods of connecting to a Notes server and exchanging information:

- interactive connection, and
- database exchange.

Interactive connection

The first method is to work as if you were connected via a network – it's called an *interactive connection*. The remote workstation need only have Windows and the Notes access software installed; the user calls the server, logs in and can then use the remote databases stored on the server. Any changes or new entries to the databases are reflected immediately and the user is notified of any new e-mail messages as they arrive. As mentioned, this method mimics a network connection. No expense is spared to provide the user with a real-time environment. There's little overhead for the workstation and it's easy to set up and configure, however it is expensive in phone use and the performance will be tens of times slower than a workstation connected via a network link.

Database exchange

The alternative to interactive connection is called *database exchange*. This is a far more practical way of working for most remote users: it's cheaper and faster but doesn't offer real-time response and takes more effort to set up. In a database exchange system, the remote workstation is initially configured with local copies (a replica) of the databases the user will be using. Since this can mean transferring tens of megabytes from the server to the workstation, it's most conveniently done by temporarily attaching the workstation to the network. The remote user works on the local replicas of the databases so changes are instant. To reflect your local changes with the server-based database, you have to dial into the server and allow the exchange of new or edited documents between your replica and the original database. At the same time as your changes are transferred, so the changes made by other users are exchanged. E-mail can also exchanged – after all, it's another database – so any mail you've created is sent and any new mail is collected. (There are a number of options relating to e-mail exchange for remote users, which are covered later in this chapter.) Once the new document exchange is over, you can disconnect and carry on working on the newly updated local databases.

There are disadvantages to this method of database exchange. First, it's not ideal when working with very large databases because they have to be stored locally; if you're using a database that's used a lot, you might find that the document exchange takes a long time – pushing up the phone bill. Last, of course, the information is always a little out of date. However, the response time is much faster when you're working on a local database and the telephone calls are kept to a minimum.

Replication

Replication is one of the main features of Notes – it's the process by which any changes to one database are reflected in other copies of the same database stored on other servers or on a remote workstation. When you dial into a server, the changes to your local database will be replicated on the server-based database.

Notes 4 includes a new Replicator Workpage that makes it easy for any user to setup and configure the schedule for replication. For example, you could setup your laptop to automatically dial into the local Notes server to carry out replication changes twice a day. Alternatively, you can use the same Workpage to indicate the order of importance for replication: for example, the mail diary database should be replicated first, and then the project database and lastly the contracts database.

The Replicator Workpage displays icons for all the databases that you want to replicate. You can move the icons up and down the list to indicate the order in which they are replicated and it's to setup automatic schedules.

Setting up remote access

Before you start reconfiguring your Notes server and workstation, you should decide on the type of remote server access (or topology) that your users will find most useful. There are two ways of setting up your server topology:

- Use replicas of databases on each remote server that the user will access. Since the user can only access one server at a time, create a replica of each database he or she is likely to use on each server he or she is likely to connect to.
- Setup the remote server as a *passthru server*. This is a new feature of Notes 4.5 that allows a user to dial into one Notes server and immediately have access to any other Notes server on the network.

Passthru – the stepping stone between servers

Notes 4.5 now includes a new feature called *passthru*. This feature is of immense benefit for any company that has more than one server. Passthru allows workstations and servers to connect, via the passthru server, to another server that does not share a common protocol. This might sound rather complex, but it's illustrated with three possible scenarios:

1. If you have three servers that are connected on the LAN, one of which is setup for remote use, you can set this remote server up as a passthru server so that a remote user can have access to the other servers that are not setup for remote use.
2. As an alternative, you can use a passthru server to work as the 'translator' between two servers that don't share a common protocol. For example, if one server is running NetBIOS, another is running TCP/IP they cannot communicate. However, you can setup a third server with both NetBIOS and TCP/IP running as a passthru server. The two servers can now communicate via the passthru server.
3. The third example is to use the passthru server to connect a workstation and a server that do not share common protocols. For example, if you have a workstation that only supports TCP/IP and it needs to connect to a server that only runs NetBIOS, you could setup a passthru server that supports both protocols. The workstation would connect to the TCP/IP server via the passthru server.

Setting up Passthru

Before you can use the passthru features, you need to setup all the workstations and servers that will be involved in the passthru connection. This can be a rather long job, but once done it will give you and your users greater freedom when connecting to multiple servers.

Setting up remote access 89

1. First, define the topology for the network – how will servers communicate via the passthru server and what type of workstation will be able to use the passthru server via what communications device.
2. Setup the passthru server (you can have more than one passthru server) to define which other servers and workstations are allowed access to the passthru server.
3. Setup the destination server to describe which other servers and users will be allowed access via the passthru link.
4. Setup any workstations that will access the passthru server.

The Passthru Topology

The first step is to design the way in which your network uses a passthru server. For example, should you have a server dedicated to the job of routing passthru connections?

Setting up a Passthru server

To setup a server as a passthru server is very straightforward. You only need to tell the server the names of the users that can use the feature and the name of the servers to which the users can connect.

The step-by-step process is as follows:

1. From the Notes workstation program, select *File ▶ Tools ▶ Server Administration*.
2. Select Servers and choose the Servers View option
3. Highlight the server that will be the passthru server and open its Server document from the list.
4. Select the Restrictions and move to the Route through field. In this field, enter the names of any server, groups and users who will be allowed to use this server.
5. Move to the Destinations allowed field and enter the names of the servers that the passthru server is allowed to contact on behalf of any incoming requests. (If the destination server is accessed via a remote link, you'll also need to create a Connections document for each.)
6. Save the Server document.

Chapter 5

Highlight the server you want to setup as a passthru server

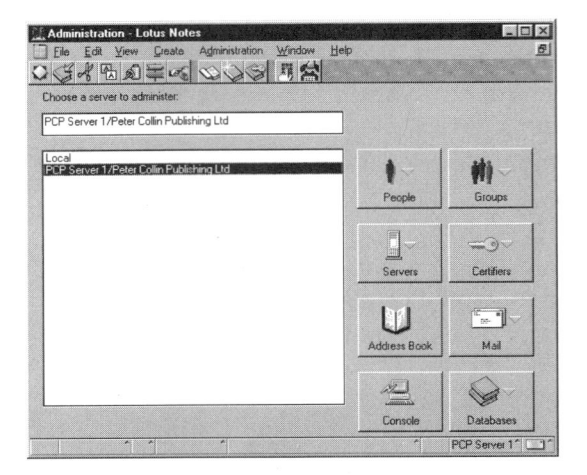

The server's document lets you set the 'Route through' field to define passthru

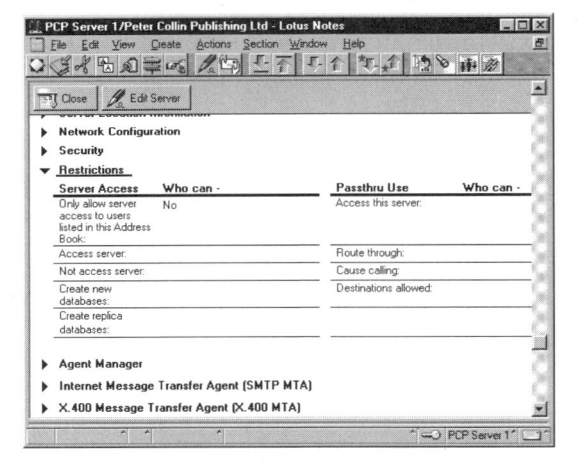

Setting up a Destination Server

Now that the passthru server knows the names of the destination servers it can access, you need to configure these destination servers to accept data from a passthru server. Again, this is not particularly complex:

1. From the Notes workstation program, select *File ▸ Tools ▸ Server Administration*.
2. Select Servers and choose the Servers View option.
3. Highlight the name of the current destination server and open its Server document from the list.
4. Select Restrictions and move to the Passthru Use section and move to the Access this server field. In this field, enter the

Setting up remote access

names of any server, groups and users who will be allowed to use this server. If you want to allow any user to access this server, enter a '*'.

5. Save the Server document.

Configure the destination server to allow user access

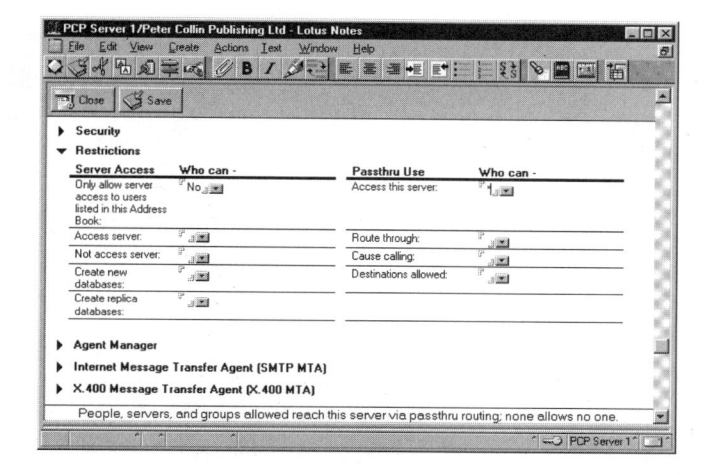

Setting up a Workstation to use a Passthru Server

The final step, now that you have setup both the passthru server and the destination servers, is to setup the workstations that will be able to dial into the passthru server to gain access to the destination servers. To setup the workstation, create a passthru Connection document for the main passthru server in the workstation's Personal Address Book.

If your installation is big enough to warrant multiple passthru servers, these can be defined in the Locations setup field of the passthru Connection document (the user can then choose the correct passthru server by selecting his current location with *File ▸ Mobile ▸ Choose Current Location*).

File ▸ Mobile ▸ Choose Current Location

Server requirements

Once you have decided on the topology you'll use for your remote server, you need to make sure that you have all the software and hardware that you will need for both the server and workstation.

For the server:

- You will need a modem; however, you might find that a multiple serial card is useful if you want to support a number of remote users. Notes can drive up to 16 serial ports, each with a modem attached.
- If you use a server access list, make sure the user is granted server access.

For the workstation:

- Each workstation will need a certified user ID file on a floppy disk; the user needs the server's full name, organization name and access telephone number.
- A modem, ISDN device or other remote network connection.
- You will need to make sure your new users are covered within your user license.

The server

To set up a Notes server before you can dial in from a remote workstation is a simple job for the administrator. Notes server communicates with any communication device via its own XPC drivers – these are installed automatically and you don't need to do anything more to setup Notes. Make sure that you have a modem and free serial port (or a multi-port serial card if you want to support multiple modems.) There are just two steps: configuring the serial port and setting up the modem.

Configuring a serial port

Before the Notes server can use a modem, you must configure the server's serial port. (If you have already configured the serial port during the initial Server Setup process when installing Notes, you can skip the following section). To add support for a serial port, you must add a new port to the Notes configuration.

Setting up remote access

First, shut down the Notes server. Now, start the Notes workstation program and select *File ▸ Tools ▸ User Preferences,* and choose the Ports option.

File ▸ Tools ▸ User Preferences ▸ Ports setup dialog box

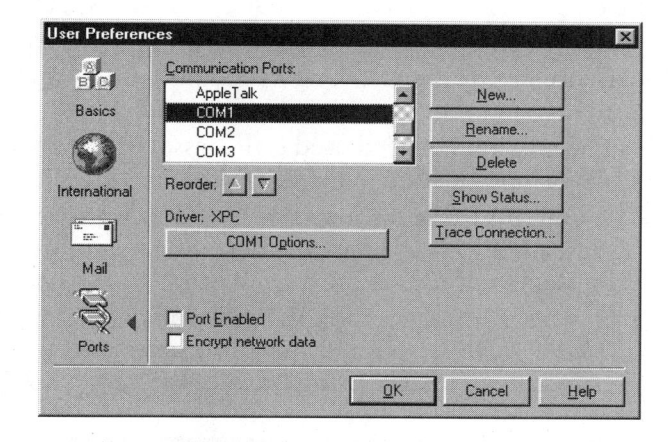

The Port Setup dialog box (above) lists the available ports on the server – including the network adapter. Move the highlight bar to the serial port you want to use for the modem connection and select the check box Enable Port. If you are using a multiple serial card, you might have to add the serial port – select the Add Port button.

Tip To ensure that data transmission cannot be read, even if it's intercepted, check the Encrypt Network Data check box for the serial port. This slightly reduces the data throughput, but will ensure any data transmitted is encrypted. This option is detected and automatically enabled by the workstation.

Configuring the modem

With the new serial enabled, as per the previous section, you can now configure Notes for the type of modem connected to the port. This is carried out from the same Port Setup dialog box used for the serial port (selected via *File ▸ Tools ▸ User Preferences ▸ Ports*).

Highlight the serial port that's connected to the modem and select the Additional Setup button. This displays a detailed dialog box that describes the type and specification of the modem.

The main configuration for the modem is determined from the modem type list at the top of the window. This list is actually a list of .MDM modem setup files – these describe the type and spec of a particular modem. The full name of the MDM file for the selected modem is displayed just below the scrolling list. If your modem is not listed,

Chapter 5

choose one of the auto-configure Hayes-modem-compatible settings (there are two: one for modems with V42, one for those without).

The more general modem configuration settings are selected using the range of radio buttons. These are obvious, but there are a few tips that you should bear in mind:

- If you are trying to debug a modem fault, it might be helpful to switch on modem speaker to check the tones.
- The maximum speed used is the lesser of the one selected on this screen and the one in the .MDM file.
- If you are using an interactive connection, you might want to increase the *Hang up if idle for* setting to allow them to read long messages without being logged off.
- If you are suffering a lot of data errors, make sure that *Hardware flow control* is selected on both this screen and the modem – especially if you are using transfer rates above 14,400bps.

File ▸ Tools ▸ User Preferences ▸ Ports

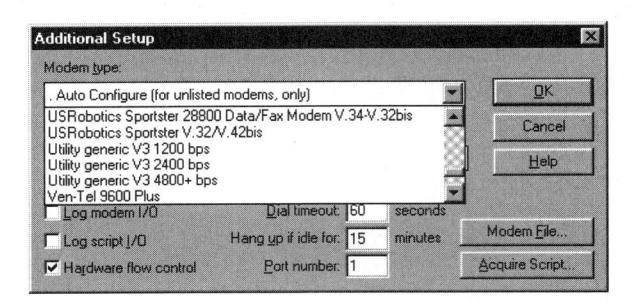

Once you are happy with the configuration, select OK to save the settings. You can now restart the server; it's now ready to receive calls from remote users.

- **Confirming Server Comms Port Status**

To check that the server has been correctly setup, enter the following command at the server command screen: 'show port *name*' (where *name* is the comms port – for example 'COM1'). The server will display the status of the port.

The remote workstation

To configure a workstation for remote access to a server follow a similar path to the server configuration. If this is a new installation of the Notes workstation software, you are given the choice of type of workstation: choosing Dialup (Laptop) Workstation enables the COM1

Setting up remote access

serial port and disables the LAN0 network port for you. However, if you are converting an existing LAN workstation to remote access or want to use a laptop for both remote and network access, you will need to change the network port settings.

If you need to work both from a modem and a network link, Notes will switch between the two automatically. However, you might be plagued by Dial server now? messages even when connected via the network – if so, you should temporarily disable the COM1 serial port.

Configuring the serial port

Start the Notes workstation program and select the *File ▸ Tools ▸ User Preferences* menu option and choose the Ports option.

File ▸ Tools ▸ User Preferences ▸ Ports Setup dialog box

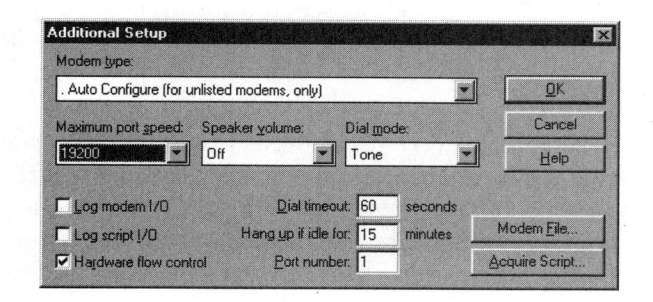

The Ports Setup dialog box lists the available ports on the server – including the network adapter. Move the highlight bar to the serial port that's connected to the modem (remember, on a laptop COM1 is often the mouse port) and check the Enable Port check box. (If you selected the Encrypt Network Data option in the server setup, check the Secure Channel box in this dialog box.) Finally, select the Configure Modem button to set up the modem (above).

Configuring the modem

The setup modem dialog is very similar to the server's modem setup screen. At the top is a list of the available, pre-configured modems. If your modem is Hayes-compatible but isn't listed, choose the auto-configure option (either the Hayes-compatible V32 or non-V32 types); Notes interrogates the modem to find out what sort of device it is.

Note If your modem isn't listed, and it's not a Hayes-compatible, you might have to create and edit a new .MDM configuration file for the modem. This is best done by using the sample TEMPLATE.MDM file as a basis. Click on the Edit button within the Setup Modem dialog to edit the file.

Chapter 5

■ Confirming Workstation Comms Ports Status

You can check the status of the comms port via the Notes workstation software. Select the *File ▸ Tools ▸ User Preferences ▸ Ports* option. From the list of ports, choose the one you want to check (for example, COM1) and click on the Show Status button to view the port's current status. The information you'll see displayed includes the amount of data transferred via the port, the number errors detected and the speed of the data transmission.

Workstation software configuration

Now that the serial port and modem hardware has been defined and configured, you need to set up the workstation software to connect to the remote server. In practice, this means creating a remote connection document within the local Name and Address book. You will need a connection document for each remote server or for the one passthru server if you are using passthru.

To create a new remote connection document, start the workstation software and open your personal Name and Address Book. To check that there are no previously defined connections, select the *View ▸ Connections* menu option; this will also list the connections defined if you are using your workstation both on a LAN and for remote access.

To create a new remote connection, open the Personal Address Book database and select the *Create ▸ Server Connection* menu option. This displays a remote connection form ready for you to fill in with the server's name, user name and access number. This form also defines some basic replication rules for the remote connection.

Creating a new Server Connection within the Personal Address Book

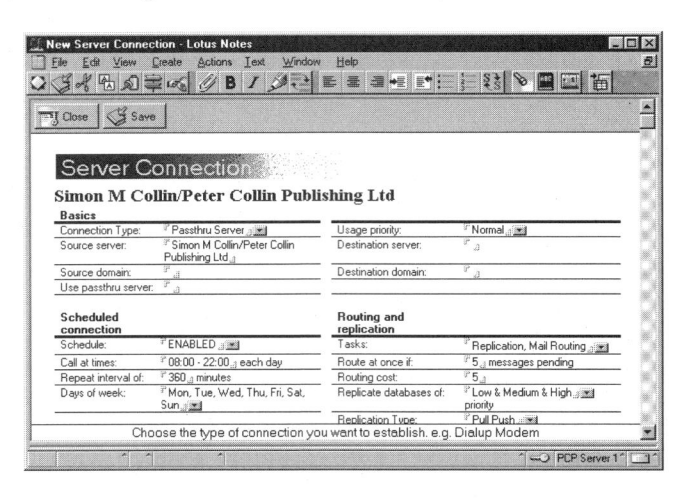

Fill in any of the main details that are missing including the server's name and domain and its telephone number. The scheduled calling section can be ignored – its settings are used for server-to-server calls and won't normally effect the remote access from a workstation. Select the serial port previously configured and connected to the modem.

If you are connecting to a passthru server, set the Type of Connection field to Passthru.

Tip When entering the telephone number, if you need to include a pause, use a comma; each comma will provide a one-second pause. When dialing out from an office switchboard, you often need to pause after dialing '9' to get an outside line before the dial tone is heard.

Registering a remote user

If the user is new to the Notes server, you will need to define the user's certified ID, user name and password. This tells Notes where to look for the ID and password (either locally or on the server) and confirms the ID to the remote server; this is established from the license disk. The certified user ID data is stored in the Name and Address book for that particular user.

When the user first logs into the server from a newly installed remote workstation, the workstation will retrieve the user's ID file from the Name and Address database.

Using Notes remotely

At the beginning of this chapter, two methods of remote access were described: database exchange and interactive connection. Most users will set up the database exchange configuration, in which replicas of the databases are stored locally on the workstation and any changes are exchanged when the workstation is next connected to the server.

Mail and a remote access workstation

There's one problem with database exchange: how to cope with e-mail. When you compose an electronic memo, Notes would normally send it immediately. If you're a remote user it becomes wasteful and slow to dial up the server, log in and exchange documents for each single e-mail. If you've set up database exchange, this is exactly what you are trying to avoid. To make sure that any electronic mail you compose is stored locally then exchanged when connected to the server, you will need to configure the workstation preferences.

To make sure that any new mail you compose is stored locally, you must set the Hold Mail option. Messages are then stored in the Outgoing Mail database (called MAIL.BOX) until the document exchange. If you exit Notes without having connected to the server and exchanged mail, you will be prompted with a message You have outgoing mail. Do you want to transfer it now? If you answer yes, Notes will dial the server and exchange mail. If you answer no, the mail remains safe in the MAIL.BOX database until you next exchange.

Select the *Options ▸ Preferences* dialog box. One of the run-time options is Hold Mail, which you should select if you are planning to use database exchange. If you are installing the Notes workstation software and selected a Dialup (Laptop) Workstation, Notes will have automatically selected the Hold Mail option.

Warning   If you use your workstation both for remote and network access – e.g. a laptop – then you might run into problems with the name of your mail file. When you switch Hold Mail off – when you connect to the LAN, Notes will look for your server-based mail file named at the bottom of the Options Preferences screen. If the directory path and mail filename of your server mail database is not exactly the same as the workstation file, Notes might not be able to find the correct file and will generate a new file. Try to keep both files the same: e.g. \MAIL\SCOLLIN.NSF on both server and workstation.

Configuring remote access mail

The previous section describes the problems of exchanging new mail documents on a remote workstation and how to get around this. However, once you have set the Hold Mail option, you must configure the workstation Notes software to use a local Mail database rather than the server-based mail. If you are only using an interactive connection, there's no need to follow these steps, since you will still be using the server-based mail database.

To setup your mail database for remote use, you'll need to configure the replication settings for the database. To do this, highlight the mail icon on your workspace and press the right mouse button. From the menu, select Replication Settings.

The Navigator on the right displays the categories of settings. Select the Send icon to configure the way the mail database documents are exchanged.

Using Notes remotely

There are just three basic options for mail replication:

- **Do not send deletions made in this replica...** If you want to delete local messages, but want to preserve the integrity of your server-based mail file.
- **Do not send changes in document title & catalog...** Does not replicate simple changes in document titles
- **Do not send changes in local security properties...** This allows you to secure your laptop with different settings to the server-based files.

If you are using cc:Mail or any other VIM-compliant e-mail package rather than the Notes mail system, you can specify the software from this dialog box.

Lastly, to ensure that you are correctly set up to use workstation-based mail, you must also check in the Location setup which defines the domain and time zone Notes – along with the type of mail used. Select the *File ▸ Mobile ▸ Locations* menu option. Edit the Location document:

Check that the mail file Location is set to local

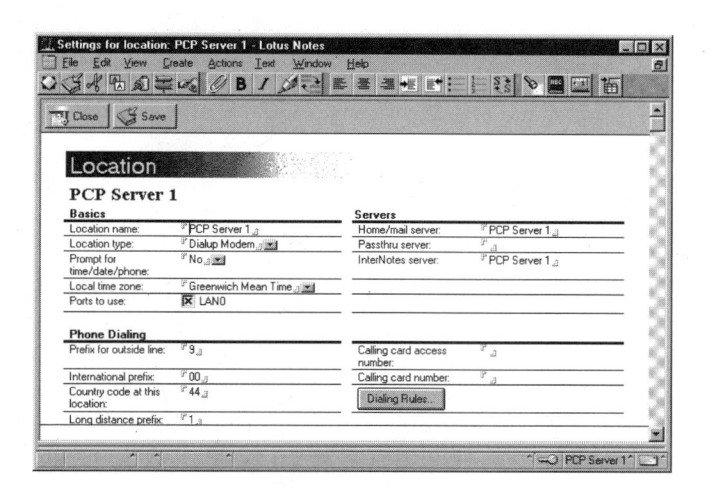

You are now set up to use a local mail database. The following section guides you through using database exchange to replicate your other databases and exchange documents.

Remote access: the database exchange method

The most practical and commonly used way of setting up remote access to Notes is to implement a Database Exchange system. This method is cheaper and faster than an interactive connection, but doesn't offer real-time response and takes more effort to set up. In a database exchange system, the remote workstation is initially configured with local copies (a replica) of the databases the user will be using. This replica can be either a complete replica or a partial replica.

Creating a replica icon of a database

Before you can connect to the server and carry out a database exchange for the first time, you must first create replica icons for each database you will want to access on the server. This process does nothing more than create an empty database shell, but you must do it before you exchange documents with any remote database for the first time. If you installed the Notes workstation software and specified that this was a Dialup (Laptop) Workstation, Notes will have automatically created a replica icon for your mail database.

Select the File ▸ Replication ▸ New Replica menu option

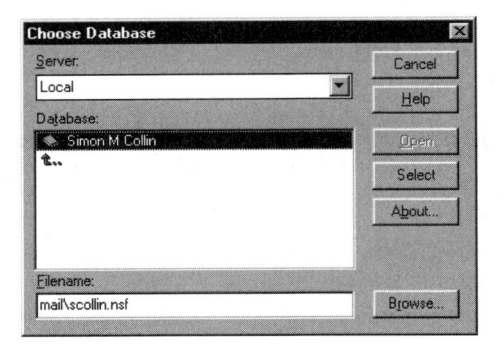

In the Original Database section of the dialog box, click on the down arrow to see a list of the available servers and select the server where the database is stored. Type in the name and path of the database (omit the first backslash) on the server. In the New Replica section of the dialog box, type in the name you want the local replica database to be called – the file server will normally be Local. Click on the Select button to display the settings for the new Replication document.

At the bottom of the dialog box is the Replicate Access Control List check-box that defines whether to replicate the Access Control List for this database from the server. Make sure that this is selected. If you do not replicate the ACL, you will effectively be a Manager, which won't effect how you use the database locally, but might prevent you from being able to exchange new documents with the server.

You can also limit the size of files that are replicated: click on the size limit button to limit the documents that are copied over during the replication to those created within a period of time.

Select the OK button to create an empty database and place an icon in your workplace – when you dial into the server to exchange documents, the database will be filled up. You must repeat this process to create a new replica icon for each database that you want to use.

Copying a complete database

If you are using a laptop that is sometimes connected to the network, sometimes used as a remote access workstation, you can save yourself a long phone call and a lot of bother by using the Database Copy command to copy databases from the server on to your laptop's hard disk while you are connected to the LAN (although this will create a complete replica, not a partial replica). To do this, highlight the database icon and choose *File ▸ Database ▸ New Copy*, select to copy Forms, Views, Documents and ACL and, finally, when you select the OK button a copy of the database will be made on to your local disk.

Configuring replication for a database

Once you have created replica icons using the method outlined above, you can start to decide how these replicas should operate. For example, setting up a partial replica of a database saves a lot of transfer time and means the local database will be smaller – saving hard disk space. You can also define that documents older than a certain age should be automatically deleted; in addition, you can define whether these deletions should be reflected in the main server-based database. Lastly, you can temporarily remove a database from the document exchange process (for example, if you are in a hurry or want to cut the phone-bill to a minimum). To configure all these options, highlight the database icon on the workspace and click on the right mouse button. Choose the Replication Settings menu option.

From the dialog box that's displayed, choose the Send icon in the Navigator bar and select the 'Do not replicate deletions to replicas of this database' check box. This ensures that documents that you delete from this database are not deleted from other databases. You should select this option if you want to make sure that you don't accidentally delete documents from the server-based database.

Select the Other icon from the Navigator and click on 'Temporarily disable replication of this database'. This will remove this database from any exchange operations. This is useful if you think your copy might be corrupt or if you want to cut down on connect time.

Select the Space Savers icon from the Navigtator and click on 'Remove documents not modified in the last ... days' This will delete and purge documents created before the cutoff date set in this line.

Note   If you select Clear from the history display this deletes the replication history and ensures that the next exchange is a complete replica rather than an incremental update. This is rarely needed, but can be useful if documents appear corrupt. It will increase the time taken to transfer the data.

Setting access control levels

If you do not have the correct access control level setting for a particular database, you could find that you cannot exchange documents. For example, if you are at designer level, you can transfer to the server-based file, but the server will not send your local workstation any documents.

Setting the Access Control Level

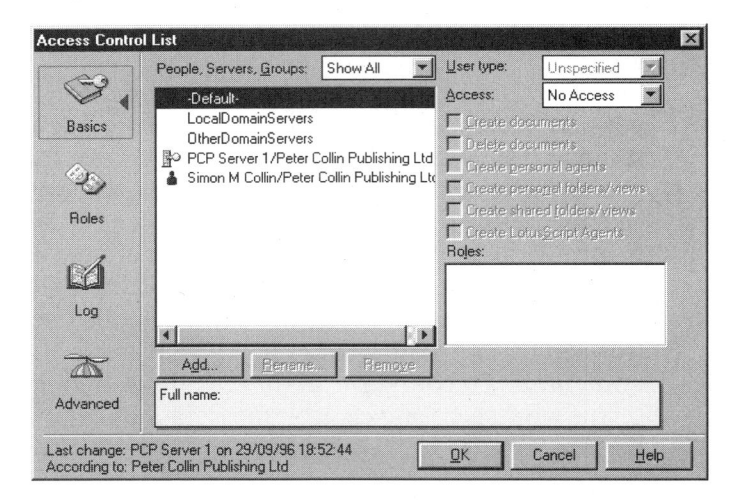

In order to carry out correct exchange, you must be set to manager level. To check if you have the correct access level and, if necessary, change this, do the following:

1. Highlight the database.
2. Select the *File ▶ Database ▶ Access Control* menu option.
3. Enter the admin password, if requested.
4. Select your user name from the scroll list of People, Servers, Groups.

Using Notes remotely

5. Select the Manager option from the Access pull-down list on the right hand side of the window.
6. Select the OK button and Notes will change the ACL settings.

Repeat these steps for all the replica databases on your system.

Database exchange with the server

You should now have configured the serial port, modem and replica icons for the databases you want to replicate. The previous section described how to limit the replication to particular documents. Now, finally, you can dial the server and actually exchange documents.

Highlight the database you want to replicate, then choose the *File ▸ Replicate* menu option. This displays the Replicate dialog box. You've got two options – either replicate now (in the background) or replicate with options. If you choose the first option and select OK, Notes will automatically dial the server and replicate the selected database. If you choose the 'Replicate with Options' selection you can override the configured replication settings for this database.

Managing the Replicator Page

You will notice that your workplace has a page tag on the far right labeled Replicator. This contains the Replicator Page settings for all replications that have been setup (including the automatically configured mail replication). Once you start to configure the replication it's far easier to move straight to this page rather than changing the individual database settings. Not only can you see clearly which replications are due to take place and when.

To view the replication page, click on the Replicator page tag on your workspace. The first icon on the page is the timer settings – which links to the Location document in your Public Address Book. Beneath this are entries for each database that will be replicated, together with any settings they have for document compression and deletion.

Calling a server manually

You can dial a server manually, rather than allowing Notes to use the Remote Connection Document to automatically dial the server. To do this, select the *File ▸ Mobile ▸ Call Server* menu option.

Select the server from the list and enter its telephone number and any dialing prefix. If you are calling from a hotel room, or have to go through an operator, click on the manual dial button. Notes prompts you to manually dial the number; when you hear the answer whistle from the server's modem, click on OK and let Notes take over.

Remote access: the interactive connection method

As described at the beginning of this chapter, there are two methods of working remotely. We've covered the first and most commonly used setup – Database Exchange. However, in some situations, the second method might prove preferable.

This interactive connection method has none of the complicated setup that's just taken several pages to describe. There's no problem with the mail file nor replication worries. Instead, you are linked directly to the server via a phone link instead of a network link, but you are using the server-based databases. This means changes to documents by you or other users take immediate effect, you are notified instantly mail is received, but it's expensive in connection time and doesn't allow any other remote user on – unless you install multiple modems at the server. In practice, interactive connection is only useful if you have to work with a database that's too big to store locally.

Connecting to the server

You should have set up the server and workstation to support a serial port and modem. Once this is done, you can call the server by selecting the *File ▸ Mobile ▸ Call Server* menu option.

Select the server name from the list and enter its telephone number. Choose Auto dial to let Notes dial for you or the Manual dial button if you need to go through an operator. Once you are connected, you can use Notes just as if you were connected to the network.

Tip Try to save documents as often as practical. Remote links are not as reliable as a network link and you could lose your working document if the connection breaks.

Summary

Using Notes from a remote workstation can bring tremendous benefits. Traveling reps need no longer feel out of touch – they can still receive e-mail and take part in any database. The costs are minimal – just a modem at each end – and the software already supports this feature, so there's no need to buy any extra utility. Once you have configured the replication methods for the Database Exchange system, which is an initially time-consuming task, you can leave the users to work on their own.

6

How Notes distributes information

About this chapter

Notes can distribute information between users in three basic ways. The first is the simplest: by sending documents between users with its electronic mail functions.

Second, users can all access a database stored on one central server. Third, a database can be replicated over many interconnected servers and the information shared by users on different networks.

The first option is no different from any other e-mail system, such as Lotus cc:Mail, Beyond Mail or Microsoft Mail. The second is similar to any database application where the main data file is stored on a central server's hard drive and all users can access the data and add to it. It's the third option, replicating databases across multiple servers, that differentiates Notes from other e-mail or shared database applications.

Replication

Replication ensures that all users on a global network will be able to access the latest version of the database. If a user makes a change to the data on one site, Notes will (if correctly set up) reflect the change in the data stored on the other servers.

As a concept, replication is easy to understand. In practice, if you don't configure the replication function correctly, you could find changes to data lag days behind or that your WAN links are permanently busy transferring data changes.

Note   Notes 4.5 improves on its performance when replicating databases by reducing the size of the elements replicated. Now, Notes 4.5 will replicate the individual fields within a changed document, rather than entire document. This will cut the transmission time – particularly important to remote users.

Replication starts by transferring a database from one server to another. At this starting point, the two databases are identical. If a user makes a change to a document on one database, the replication engine will reflect this by updating the database on the second server. For correct data integrity, replication must also work if two users both try to make changes to the same document; both changes must be reflected in each database. Notes' replication engine is powerful enough to resolve complex update arguments, such as this.

It's up to the system manager – or the database manager – to configure how a particular database should be replicated. You have to decide whether to sacrifice communications charges to ensure all databases are up to date, or whether to replicate only certain parts (or even only certain documents) within a database to save on connection time.

Replicating between servers is one use of Notes, but it's also common to replicate a database between a server and a client workstation. If, for example, you have salesmen out visiting clients during the day, they will add data to their local copy of Notes. At night, they will dial in to the server and replicate the changes.

It's worth pointing out that replication, although a useful feature for many applications, is not much use when it comes to transactional applications. The Notes replication engine will ensure that all databases contain the same data, but it takes time – and in some cases it might be hours or days before all new data is exchanged. If you're running a ticket reservation system then you need to know availability instantly – so Notes would not be much use in these applications. If, as mentioned previously, you have salesmen with laptops, Notes would be a good central system with which to collate and update sales leads.

Problems when replicating

One problem with Notes when compared with many multi-user databases is that Notes does not support record locking. This means that if two users open the same document on the same server the last person to save his document will be the one recorded and previous changes will be overwritten.

When replicating databases, this sort of conflict will crop up time and again – but when replicating, Notes is more capable of dealing with the problem. If two users both try to save edited versions of a document on two separate servers, Notes will have a job matching these updates when it tries to replicate the changes across both servers. It solves this problem by checking to see which document has the most changes. This it then calls the Main document. The second document, with fewer changes, is called a response document and is filed under the Main document.

A second problem could occur if one user updates a document on one server, while another user deletes the entire document. In this case, Notes will delete the document during replication (although this feature can be turned off from the settings option window).

Replicating databases and mail messages

Notes has two types of data that it can transfer when it's updating another server. The first is to ensure that all databases are up to date. The second is to deliver any mail messages addressed to the server. The database update process is called *replication*, while the mail delivery is called mail *routing*. In some cases, these processes both take place at the same time, controlled by the same settings. In other installations, you will find that you need to configure Notes to correctly replicate databases and route mail.

Controlling replication and routing

In order to replicate a database or route mail to another server, you have to tell Notes how and when to carry out these data transfers. All the information that describes the when, what and how to update databases on other servers is stored in Connection Documents which are part of the public Name & Address book.

Deciding which server should call the others in a group is a difficult choice, since there are many options. Let's get the first, and easiest, one out of the way. If you have an installation with just one server and several remote users (who dial in each evening) then you don't have to do anything on the server. The replication is set up on the workstations and initiated manually by the user. (A more detailed explanation on setting up remote users is described in Chapter 5.)

If you have two or more servers in your system, you will have to start making decisions. If there are just two servers, then the best solution is to setup one to call and replicate its databases on to the other regularly during the day. There's no point having each server call and replicate to the other, since this wastes connection time, so only one replication connection document is needed on one of the servers. However, both servers should have connection documents for mail routing to the other server.

If you have more than two servers, you have a choice. One solution is that each server has connection documents to call all the other servers in the group and replicate and route mail accordingly. This is fine for three or four servers, but any more than this and your servers will spend their entire time transferring data to other servers. This setup is called a push–pull configuration since each server is both calling and being called. Lastly, if you have a large installation with more than four servers, you will find it more efficient to set up a central hub server that services all the other servers.

Large WANs could benefit from a central hub server

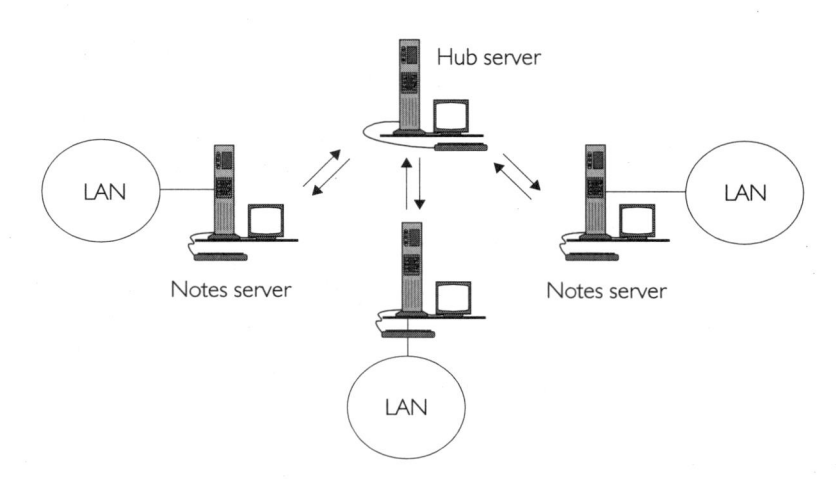

In this case, users never actually log on to the hub server. Instead, it spends its time calling the other servers, one at a time, and replicating and routing mail between each. The node servers use the hub to carry all the data between them. It's an efficient way of managing replication on a large scale and, since none of the hub servers is set up to call any other system except for the hub (when high priority mail has to be transferred) the connections are orderly and no server is missed. It's worth noting that Notes carries out replication instructions according to the Connection Document schedule. If you have a hub setup and give the same time and period in each Connection Documents to each node, then Notes will carry them out in alphabetical order of node name.

Setting the schedule time to be the same for all nodes might seem odd, but actually provides a fair and equal service. For example, if one server took too long replicating, it could knock out the next in line by over-running into its scheduled time with the result that some servers might not be replicated.

Each node server needs at least one mail routing connection document back to the hub. The hub needs replication and routing connection documents out to each node.

Summary

- One server has replication started manually from remote workstations.
- Two servers should be setup with only one calling the other for replication, but both calling each other for mail routing.
- Three or four servers should each call the others in the group.
- More than four servers will find the previous setup takes too much connection time and should use a central hub.

Setting up database replication

As just mentioned, database replication does not happen by itself. At least it does, but first you have to tell Notes how and when to do it. Once these details are entered in the Connections Document, Notes will happily carry out database replication according to its schedule. In some cases, you might want to override the schedule – for example, if a particular high-priority document is spotted, or if the database goes past a threshold number of new documents.

To create a database replication connection document

This step-by-step procedure will generate a connection document that will be used to replicate information between databases on two servers that are connected to the same LAN.

1. First, open the public Name & Address Book database on the server.
2. Choose *Server ▸ Connections*.
3. Click on the Add Connection button to create a new Connection document (or edit an existing one).
4. Select the Connection Type field and enter Local Area Network.
5. Select the Source field and enter the name of the calling server
6. Select the Destination field and enter the name of the answering server.
7. In the Use the Port field, enter the comms port that will be used (for example LAN0).
8. Setup the scheduling information for the time and frequency of the replication.

Setting routing and replication scheduling for a server

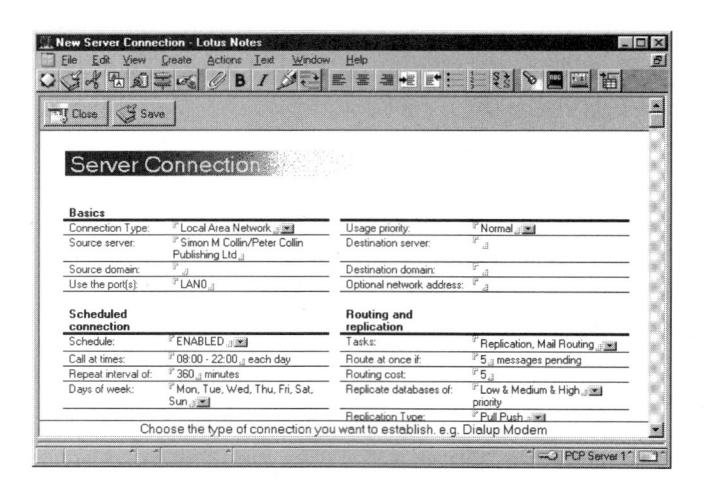

Fill in the information fields with the database to be called, the port to call through (normally LAN0 – COM1 will be described later and is used for a remote server). Next, set up the schedule to call the server. Typically, you would replicate every hour; see the end of this chapter for more details on scheduling.

Under the tasks field, select Replication. The options for this are Replication or Mail Routing or both. It is more flexible to set up connection documents for the different types of data transfer, but awkward to manage. Most supervisors will set up combined replication and mail routing within one connection document. You could, however, set up one connection document for Mail Routing that specifies a scheduled call every three hours, while a replication connection document might need a connection once per hour.

Dealing with remote servers

To replicate a database on a remote server that is linked by modem, you will need to create a remote connection document – it's very similar to the above.

Creating a replication setting for a database on a remote server

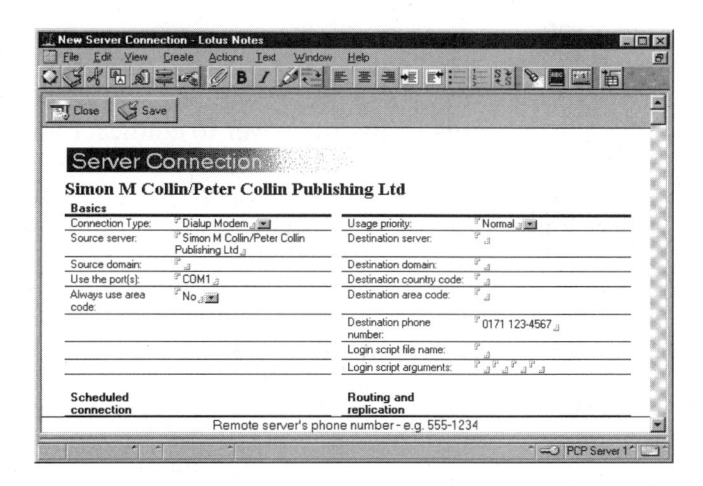

1. First, open the public Name & Address Book database on the server.
2. Choose *Server ▸ Connections*.
3. Click on the Add Connection button to create a new Connection document (or edit an existing one).
4. Select the Connection Type field and enter Dial up Modem.
5. Select the Source field and enter the name of the calling server.
6. Select the Source domain field and enter the domain of the calling server.
7. Select the Destination field and enter the name of the answering server.
8. Select the Destination domain field and enter the domain of the answering server.

9. Enter the dial up telephone number for the destination server.
10. In the Use the Port field, enter the comms port that will be used (for example COM1).
11. Setup the scheduling information for the time and frequency of the replication.

Fill in the information fields with the server to be called and the port to call through (which is normally COM1). Enter the telephone number to access the remote server. Next, set up the schedule to call the server. Typically, you would replicate every hour; see the end of this chapter for more details on scheduling. Since this connection is going to cost you money per minute of connection time over the public telephone system, it's best to try to minimize this. You could make slight adjustments to the frequency of the calls, or move the time of calls to an off-peak rate.

Replicating with a Passthru Server

If you have setup a passthru server to connect two or more servers (see Chapter 5), then you can setup a replication process to work via the passthru server – it uses exactly the steps as specified above, but simply specify a passthru server as the destination in the Connection document. The passthru server will then manage the link to the final destination server.

Note   If the remote server has several access ports or access telephone numbers, you can include more than one number in the Dial Phone Number field – separate each with a semicolon. If the first is busy or doesn't answer Notes will try the next in the list.

Rules for replication

The replication of a database is governed by a whole set of different rules.

What will replicate?

Access level	ACL	Design & Formulas	Edited documents	New documents
Manager	Y	Y	Y	Y
Designed		Y	Y	Y
Editor			Y	Y
Author				Y
Reader				N
Depositor				N

Setting up database replication

The first is the connection document that sets out the automatic replication. The second is the ACL (Access Control Level) described in Chapter 11. The ACL comes into play when a user asks to replicate a database (perhaps they are bringing their laptop up to date). The user level (which is indicated in the far right of the SmartStatus bar at the bottom of your workspace) determines what will replicate across to your workstation.

Individual database settings

Each database can have a number of settings configured to work with the general connections document. These settings are displayed in a dialog box when you select *File ▸ Replication ▸ Settings* (you must first be in, or highlight the database).

Settings for a replication that allows individual sections or folders to be replicated

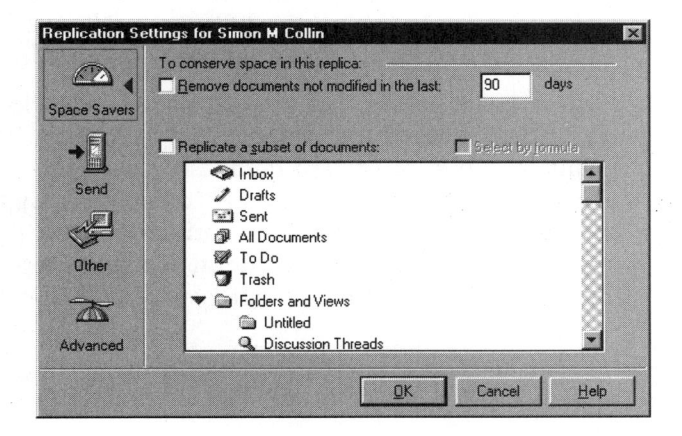

You'll see the database's replication settings with a navigator bar to the left displaying the main categories of settings. These are arranged as follows:

Space Savers: Allows you remove documents that have not been modified in the last '*x*' days

- *Remove documents saved more than ... days ago.* Works with the first option to delete documents saved before the cutoff date.

- *Selective replication.* To give you more control when replicating large databases, Notes includes the ability to select certain documents according to a formula. Click on the 'Replicate a Subset' check-box and again on the 'Selective' check-box. A programming field is displayed below these check boxes and you can enter a selection formula within this selection field. To see a list of all the available @-functions that you can use to select documents, click on the Fields & Functions button.

Send: Allows you to setup the basic options used when replicating documents in the database.

- *Do not replicate deletions to replicas of this database.* Allows you to delete documents from your local database, but doesn't replicate these deletions to other databases – useful if you have to save space on your local server, but want to preserve the data elsewhere.

Other: Allows you to temporarily disable replication, setup replication only for documents that are younger than a certain date and to set the priority of the replication.

- *Disable replication of this database.* As you can imagine, this prevents this database from being replicated – useful for confidential information or if a database has been corrupted.

- *Priority.* The priority setting of a database works together with the priority setting in the connections database. For example, if you want to replicate certain databases every hour, and others every three hours, configure the hourly databases as high priority and the three-hourly databases as low priority. Now, create two connections documents – one that defines how to replicate high-priority databases, the second limited to low-priority databases.

Advanced allows you to setup basic rules that define which databases or subsets are replicated when your server is called from another server.

Monitoring replication

Replication can, unless carefully configured, cause all sorts of headaches. If schedules clash, one server might never be replicated. If you forget the priority settings of a database, it can cause havoc. If a database designer doesn't tell the system manager how he's added selective replication, user's will never get a straight answer. To allow a system manager to monitor replication, Notes provides a replication history report. These histories list when replications occurred, the name of the database and whether data was sent or received. To access the replication history, select *File ▸ Replication ▸ History* menu option.

Note   If you clear the history for one server, the next time a replication occurs, Notes will have to carry out a full search of all the documents to check their times and dates. This increases traffic and takes a lot longer to complete.

Setting up mail routing

Tied in with the process of replicating databases is another function – routing mail messages between servers. If you address a message to a user on another server, mail routing ensures that it gets there. There are a number of rules relating to mail routing that you must watch out for; if you miss one, you might find that mail is never delivered between two particular servers.

Between servers on the same network and in the same domain Mail routing is carried out automatically at the same time as a scheduled replication.

Between servers connected via a modem link or in different domains Mail routing has to be specified or messages will not be transferred.

To ensure that mail messages are correctly transferred you should set up connection documents on each server and for each other server. These documents specify when and how to transfer mail messages. Normally, messages are routed if there are more than the threshold specified in the connection document (this limit is normally five). If there are more than five messages waiting to be routed to another server, the connection is made according to the connection document and the messages transferred.

You should make sure that mail routing works in both ways. As you will see, it can be the case that replication is only initiated by one server. Mail routing, on the other hand, has to work both ways or one server might never be called.

Configuring mail routing between servers

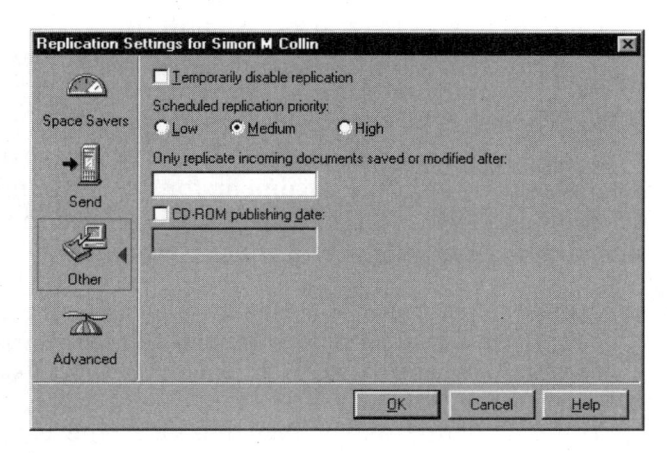

When routing mail, you should consider how to handle the different priority mail messages. Normally the following happens:

- **High-priority mail** – the connection is made immediately and the message transferred.
- **Medium priority** – the connection is made on schedule or if the threshold for waiting messages is reached.
- **Low priority** – will only use a connection at off-peak hours as specified in NOTES.INI (normally midnight–six a.m.).

Configuring mail routing

Mail routing is carried out according to the instructions in the Connection document. These Connection documents are stored within the Public Name & Address Book database. To minimize problems, you should limit the number of users that can set up Connection documents to one or two managers.

To create a mail routing Connection document

1. First, open the public Name & Address Book database on the server.
2. Choose *Server ▸ Connections*.
3. Click on the Add Connection button to create a new Connection document (or edit an existing one).

Fill in the information fields with the database to be called, the port to call through (normally LAN0 or COM1 for a remote server). Next, set-up the schedule to call the server. Typically, you need only call for mail routing every hour or two.

Under the tasks field, select Mail Routing. The options for this are Replicating or Mail Routing or both. It is more flexible to set up Connection documents for the different types of data transfer, but awkward to manage. Most supervisors will set up combined replication and mail routing within one Connection document. You could, however, set up one connection document for Mail Routing that specifies a scheduled call every three hours, while a replication Connection document might need a connection once per hour.

Tip — To give your installation flexibility, use a different Connection document for mail routing and replication. You can also use different Connection documents to specify different weekend call schedules.

You can define which mail messages the connection document refers to using the Replicate Databases of Priority field. Use the [Space Bar] to cycle through the choices. You could create a Connection document for high-priority mail that routed it immediately, and another that routes low- and medium-priority mail at the scheduled time.

Tip If you have a large network of servers, you could find splitting the tasks of the servers to manage mail or databases separately helps overall system management. In this case, your Connection documents need only specify mail routing or database replication according to the server's task.

How to decide a schedule?

This problem can keep you awake for nights as you mentally try to work out which server should call another and in which order. What happens if schedules overrun? Have you remembered all the mail routes as well as the replication paths?

To save a lot of this frustration, some companies have a full-time supervisor who's sole job is to worry about scheduling replication of different databases across the company. As the numbers of servers, databases and users grow, the problems of scheduling while still maintaining a reasonable response time can become all-consuming!

Database replication

- Try to set schedule times when there's less network or server activity – after work or at lunch time.
- Use the priority settings of different databases to help stagger replication – high priority immediately, low priority at night.
- Don't forget about time zones when setting multiple schedules – don't overlap push–pull schedules or one replication will be missed.
- You can schedule several replications at the same time – useful for hub-based systems or to access multiple servers that are all on the local LAN.

Mail routing

- Don't over-schedule – remember that mail is normally transferred at the same time as a replication.
- It's often easier to get one server to call another regularly, but remember to create at least one Connection document in the opposite direction.
- In a busy network, you will spread the load evenly if you can try to use low-priority mail delivered overnight.

- Notes can cope with routing mail through several COM ports at the same time.

7

How Notes sees the world

About this chapter

Central to any Notes server is its public Name & Address database (stored in a file called NAMES.NSF). This is really a directory of all the recognized users, servers and connections between servers (for example, for replication). A Notes domain is any group of servers that share the same public Name & Address database. In practice, this means that one administrator can manage the single public Name & Address database – and so manages the domain.

A domain – the collection of servers – is not limited by physical constraints. You could have a domain of the servers in your building, or you could set up a domain to cover a company's widespread servers dotted around the world.

This chapter looks at how Notes uses and shares its Name and Address files, how to create, edit and manage both the Public and your Personal Name and Address files and, lastly, how to manage the problem when multiple Notes servers are connected.

The public Name & Address database

Before we can go much further, it's worth looking at this important database. It was used when setting up replication and mail routing connections (see the previous chapter), but it deserves a little more attention – especially on the subject of domains.

The workspace shows the server-based and personal address books

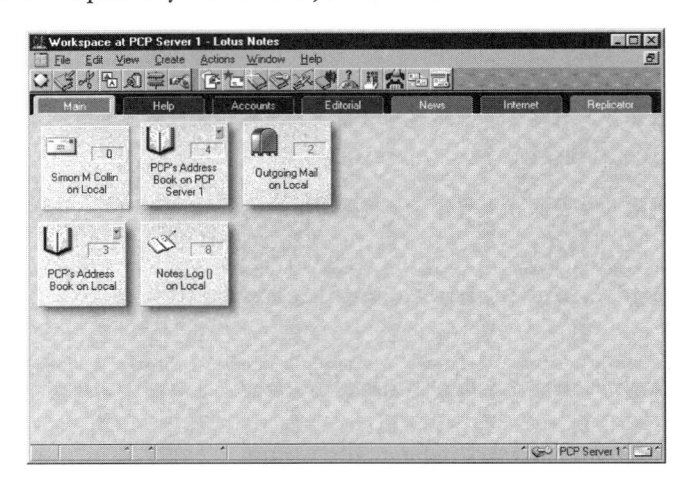

The public Name & Address database has two functions: it's primarily a directory of every user, group and server in a domain; it also contains all the instructions that define when and how servers should communicate. Its primary use, as a directory of users and servers, it is mostly used by Notes electronic mail. Type in a name in the To: field and Notes will check this against the entries in its Name & Address book. However, if you have another e-mail system installed and are not using Notes mail, you will still need the Name & Address book for its second task – storing the instructions for used for server communications (replication and mail routing) and server management (statistics and automatic program execution).

When you install your first Notes server, it will create a new public Name & Address book. Once this has been set up, any new servers within the domain will have a replica of this Name & Address book listing the current users and servers that make up the domain.

It's worth noting that there are two types of Name & Address database: the server-based public N&A book, called NAMES.NSF and, for each user, a personal Name & Address database stored on the workstation's hard disk and also called NAMES.NSF. This personal Address book is used to store a user's personal address lists – its contents are not in the public book, nor can they be read by any other user. Only if you have author access, can you add or edit the documents in the public Name & Address database.

Notes directory services

The primary function of the public Name & Address book is to operate as a directory service – listing all the user and server names and addresses that are within the domain. The Name & Address book contains a directory of the following: users, servers, certifiers & cross-certifiers, and groups. Each new user or server added to a domain is automatically added as a new document to the Name & Address database.

Document structure used to configure a server

- Server
  - Certificates
  - Clusters
  - Configurations
  - Connections
  - Deny Access Groups
  - Domains
  - Licenses
  - Mail-In Databases
  - Mail Users
  - Networks
  - Programs
  - Servers
  - Setup Profiles
  - V3 Stats and Events

The Name & Address database has eight types of document that can be added (some automatically, some created manually by managers):

1. When a new user is created, Notes adds a Person document. This contains the user's home domain, personal and security details and is mainly used for mail routing.
2. A new server adds a new Server document. This document is used mainly to establish the domain of the server and so the path to be used for mail routing.
3. Connection documents (discussed in the previous chapter) are used to hold information and schedules that define how and when the server should communicate with other servers to

route mail or replicate. There are Network Connection documents (used for local servers) or Remote Connection documents (used to call servers using a modem).
4. Program documents allow a manager to set up automatic execution of an application at a pre-defined time.
5. Certifier documents contain details of certifiers and cross-certifiers within the domain.
6. Group documents are used to define groups of users for mailing lists or database access lists.
7. Mail-in documents specify a database to which users can send mail.
8. Domain documents specify foreign domains and how to communicate with them.

As you can see, the Name & Address database contains all the basic information that defines the connection data for users and the servers in a Notes setup. How this connection information is configured and what Notes uses it for are decisions that you have to make when configuring the domains in your Notes system.

Multiple Name & Address books

If you decide to separate your multiple Notes servers into several domains you will find that you have to manage multiple Name & Address databases – one for each domain. There are two options when storing the Name & Address books: to store only the local domain Name & Address book on each server or to store copies of all the Name & Address books for all the domains on each server. There are advantages to both methods, which are covered later in this chapter. However, if you are investigating the databases on your Notes server and discover several Name & Address databases, you will know how it's been set up! In either case, the local Name & Address databases is called NAMES.NSF while the books from the other domains stored locally are called different names.

Mapping the world with domains

As stated at the beginning of this chapter, a domain is a group of Notes servers that share the same public Name & Address database. Over the last few pages, I have described what this database is and why it's important. The Name & Address database is a real entity – it's the NAMES.NSF file on your server. A domain, in contrast, is nothing more than a convenient name to call the collection of servers.

If you have one single Notes server within your company, you automatically have only one Name & Address database and your server is the sole member of the single domain. If you have multiple servers then you have a choice – should you set up your system within one big domain encompassing all the Notes servers in your company that might be spread across a city or even the world? Or should you divide the company up into separate domains – perhaps one for each country, or one for each city? The arguments for and against these two choices can are summarized in the table below:

Pros and cons of domain types

Domain type	Pros	Cons
One single domain	It's easier to manage one domain	Uses more server RAM for larger N&A book
Addressing mail is simpler	Address lookup time is worse	Mail routing is efficient
Multiple smaller domains	Each domain has more control – local manager looks after his N&A book	Addressing mail is more complex (must specify domain)
Address lookup time faster	Central management is very difficult	Uses less server RAM for smaller N&A book. Mail routing is slower

Setting up domains

When you install a new Notes server and first start the Notes program, a dialog box pops up to ask you if this server is the first in the organization or if there are others. 'Organization' is Notes-speak for domain therefore, if you want to set up a new domain, select the option 'The first Notes server in the organization.' If you are adding a new server to an existing domain, select the second option 'An additional Notes server in the organization.'

Setting up a new server

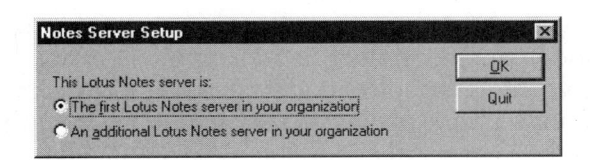

Setting up a new domain

If you are setting up a new domain (the first option in the previous dialog box), you'll be prompted to enter more details about the new domain including the server name, organization name (the domain name) and the administrator's name.

Managing multiple domains

If you have just set up a second (or other multiple) domain in your Notes system, you will have to decide how to manage the multiple Name & Address (N&A) databases. There are two choices: for the servers in each separate domain to hold only their own domain's local N&A database. Second, for each server in each domain to hold copies of all the N&A databases for all the other domains. There are advantages to each method.

One address book per server

This is the simplest setup, in which each server in a particular domain holds a single Name & Address database for that domain. It's actually a replica of the original N&A database created by the first server in that domain.

This setup uses less disk space, gives each domain autonomy but requires mail sent between domains to include the correct domain name (for example: `Simon_Collin@LONDON-HQ`).

Multiple address books per server

This setup is a little more complex than the previous single database, but has a number of advantages. In this scheme, each server in each domain holds copies of all the N&A databases from every domain. The server's local domain Name & Address database is always called NAMES.NSF, the copies of the other address books for the other domains are given different names (with the NSF extension).

The great advantage of this system is for the user: they do not have to include domain names when sending mail to other domains – Notes will search through all Name & Address books stored on its drive and so can identify users on other domains. The disadvantage of this method is that it's slower to address mail – since Notes has to search multiple Address books – and it takes up more disk space. In fact, unless you want separate managers for each domain, you are effectively providing the same service as one single large domain, and getting the same disadvantages and advantages, but also can cause more work managing each domain.

If you are using this configuration with multiple address books on each server, you will have to tell Notes that these other Name & Address databases exist, but are called different names. To do this, you will need to enter a line at the Notes console:

```
SET CONFIGURATION "NAMES=NAMES, USANAME, UKNAME"
```

This command tells Notes to search NAMES.NSF and two new Name & Address databases called UKNAME.NSF and USANAME.NSF. Once you've entered this command you will have to shut down, then restart the server for the changes to take effect.

Editing the Name & Address Book

To open the public Name & Address book, double-click on its icon in your workspace. This displays a Navigator bar to the left, showing the major views by types of documents on the server. For example, at the top of the Navigator are folder icons for people and groups, below this are folder icons for the documents that configure the server itself.

To view any document, click on the folder icon in the Navigator bar. For example, to view the registered users on the Notes server, click on the People folder icon and the right-hand side of the window displays a list of all users. To edit any user's document, highlight the user name and click on the Edit button on the Action bar at the top of the screen. To add a new user, click on the Add button and fill in the details as described in Chapter 8.

Network names

One configuration parameter that is sometimes confused with the domain name is the server's Network name. In some Notes setup screens, the domain name is referred to as the Organization name. However, the Network name defines the local network to which the server is connected (although it doesn't have to be the same as the name specified in the LAN's network operating system). For example, the default Network name for servers is Network1. Sticking with this default is fine until you start to define multiple servers and multiple domains. Any servers that have the same Network name are assumed, by Notes, to be connected directly by a LAN and so can communicate directly without using a Connections document. If you have a server that can only be connected via a modem link, you should give it a different network name to indicate that it is not directly connected. The Network name for your server is set up under the Advanced Server Settings box that follows the First Server Setup dialog box.

Defining the settings for the first server

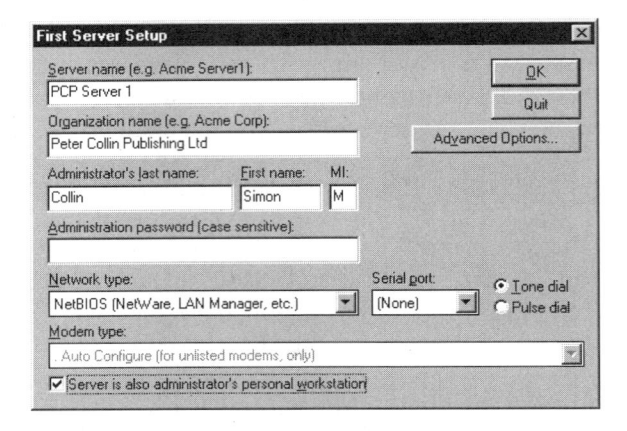

Setting the initial domain name

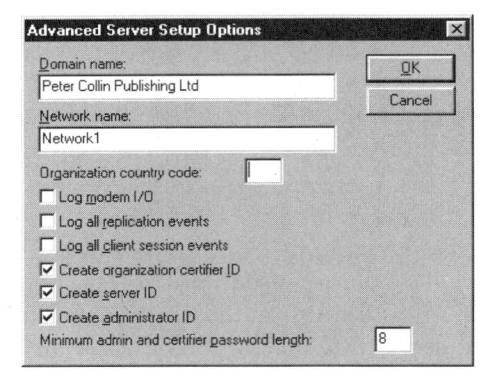

Personal Name & Address database

So far in this chapter, I've covered the public Name & Address database. This is replicated to all other servers in the domain and is used by Notes to deliver mail and set up connections between servers. If your user name does not appear in this public address book, then you will not be able to receive mail. The public Name & Address database is normally large and can be removed from a user's workspace with only a little loss of functionality.

If you do not have the public N&A database on your workspace, you cannot use the Address button when sending mail. Nor will Notes be able to automatically check and correct addresses in your mail as you type them.

Personal Name & Address database

There are other address books – the personal N&A database that's private for each user. These databases are stored locally on the user's workstation (or on the server, if you're using diskless workstations). A personal N&A database can have duplicates of the entries in the public address book, together with nicknames or group lists created by the user. This database is not replicated to other servers and its entries are private from other users.

Setting the basic preferences for a user's workspace

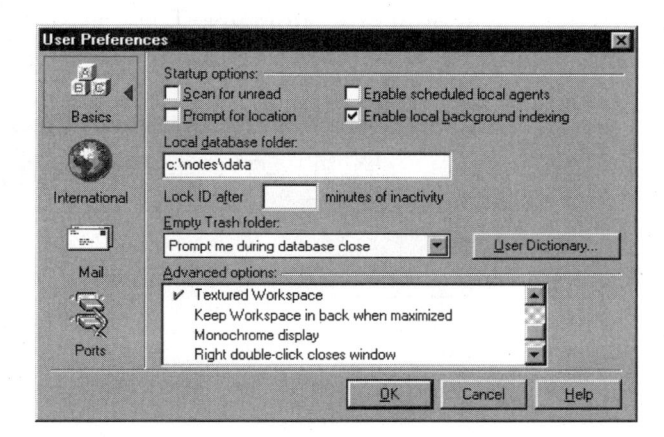

A personal Name & Address database can be used to store: names and addresses of other users on other electronic mail systems that communicate with Notes via a gateway; private mailing lists; nicknames of other users in your domain.

Using nicknames

One time-saving feature of a personal Name & Address database is that it lets you use nicknames to address other users in your domain. You can type in a short nickname for a user instead of their full name. For example, if you have a user called Edward Spode-Smith, you might find this rather tedious to type in – especially if you send him lots of mail. Instead, it's easier to set up a nickname of 'Ted' or 'Ed.' To do this, access your personal N&A database and choose View/People to show your existing users. Now, edit the entry for Edward Spode-Smith and type in the nicknames under the field for his Full Name (separated by a coma). Make sure that his full name is entered under the Full Name field. For example, if you want to add the nicknames Ted and Ed to our user Edward Spode-Smith who is resident on the Marketing server, you could enter:

```
Edward Spode-Smith/Marketing, Ted, Ed
```

User groups

As a side issue within this chapter on Name & Address databases and domains, it is worth mentioning user groups. These are groups of users, under one name, that are usually created by users in their personal Name & Address database. The list of users can contains users in the current domain or in other domains. These lists are useful when sending mail to a large group of users – just specify the group name.

Defining a new group and its members

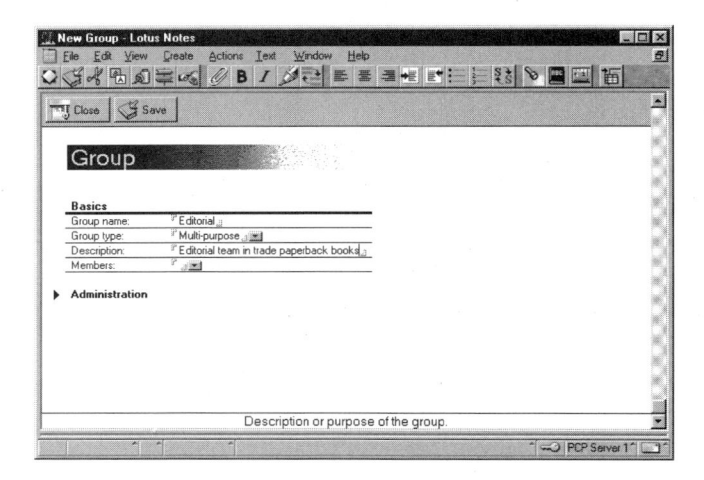

It is also possible to create user groups within the public Name & Address database – however, only someone with Author rights to the database (normally the administrator) can do this. The user groups within the public Name & Address database are available to any users in the domain.

To create a group, open the personal Name & Address database (or the public N&A database, if you want to create global user groups). Choose the Groups item from the Navigator bar – you'll now see a list of existing groups. Click on the Add button in the Action bar and you will see a new Group document: you can now add a list of users that are part of this group, enter the group's name and set its use (either as an ACL, mail list or general purpose group).

8

Managing Notes

About this chapter

As a Notes administrator, there are three main areas that require administrative time to ensure that Notes and your network are running efficiently and correctly. You won't need to tackle these administrative jobs every day, but you will have to look at them on a regular basis.

The three areas that you have to look after are:

- Database administration
- User administration
- Server administration

In this chapter, we look at all three areas and show you the main tasks you'll have to carry out and how to get the best from Notes.

Database administration

Databases are the core of Notes and so to ensure that Notes is working efficiently, you must look after the databases stored on the server. Some database tasks, such as designing a new database, editing or modifying databases and arranging database replication are often divided between the administrator and the database managers. In this book, these tasks are covered in other chapters (see Chapter 6 on database replication and Chapter 11 on designing a new database). In this chapter, we cover the basic administrative tasks which are split into defensive tasks, such as monitoring database activity to spot problems early on, and proactive tasks, such as aging documents in a database and compacting and tidying the contents of a database.

Managing data directories

When you store a database file on the server you can give a number of users or groups of users access to its information. All these database files are stored in the Data folder on the computer. However, if you want to sort databases into other folders, organize them by groups or if the file gets too big for the server or if you want to free up disk space on the server, it is useful to be able to relocate the database file to another server or onto another disk.

Notes 4.5 provides a way of fooling the Notes software into using database files that are not stored where they appear to be! The feature is called *directory pointers* and lets you create a text file on the local computer that Notes workstation thinks is a local directory. In actual fact, the text file will point Notes to another directory where you can access any of the files.

To create a directory pointer that will point away from the Notes Data folder and tell the workstation software to look in the [Project] folder do the following steps:

1. Create a plain text file called Project.DIR in the Notes Data folder.
2. In the first line of the Project.DIR file, enter the name of the new directory that Notes should look in. For example, D:\PROJECT\DATA.
3. In the following lines of the text file, enter the names of users and groups that you want to allow to access the new directory.

Database administration 133

> Note   There are a couple of points to bear in mind with directory pointers. The first is that anyone not listed in the DIR file will still be able to see the directory, but will not be able to access it. The second is that the new directory must be a subdirectory – it cannot point to a root directory.

Managing database files

In exactly the same way as mentioned above for directories, you can also create database pointers. These point Notes to a new location for the particular file. The only differences with directory pointers is that the text file should be given the .NSF extension and the first line of the text file should contain the directory and name of the database. For example, if you want to create a database pointer to a SalesLeads file that is stored in the D:\SALES\DATA subdirectory rather than in the Notes Data directory, you would create a text file called SalesLeads.NSF in the Data directory and in the first line include the text:

```
D:\SALES\DATA\SalesLeads.NSF
```

The users will be automatically redirected to the new database whenever they try and access it. The normal security and ACL controls are still active.

Cataloging database files

If you begin to loose track with the number of database files you have stored across your system, it's useful to maintain a catalogue of all the databases and where they are stored. You can do this automatically with a Notes database: create a Database Catalog file called CATALOG.NSF on the server. The Notes Server runs a Catalog application at one a.m. each morning and this stores its results in the CATALOG.NSF file.

Library of database files

A nice feature that you should offer your users is a library of all the available databases – each entry has a short description beside it and allows users to view databases that are of interest to them.

Any manager or user with Create rights to the Library template can create a central or local library. To do this, select *File ▸ Database ▸ New*, enter a server, title and filename for the library. Select the Database Library – DBLIB4.NTF – file as a template and click OK.

Chapter 8

Creating a new library for a collection of databases

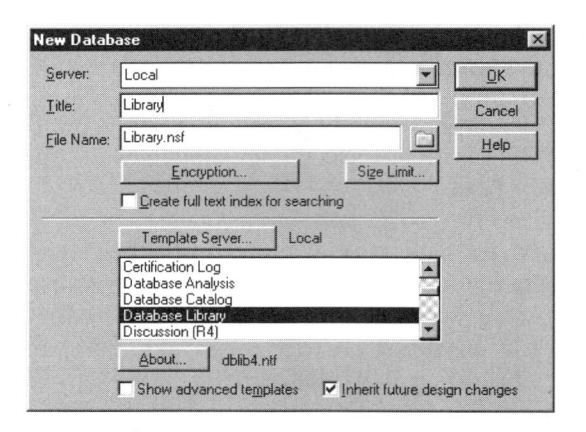

Removing old documents from a database

As your databases grow in size, they take up more disk space. Unfortunately, the multitasking operating system that's running on the server (be it OS/2, NetWare or Windows) needs disk space to store temporary files, to use as virtual memory and for the network management files. In short, unless you can afford to fit new disk drives as your databases grow, you will have to start to prune out old documents.

In some cases, you won't want to cut down the database – especially not if it's a library or client records. However, in some cases, such as the server log file and, if it's used heavily, the mail file.

Defining which documents to delete during a replication

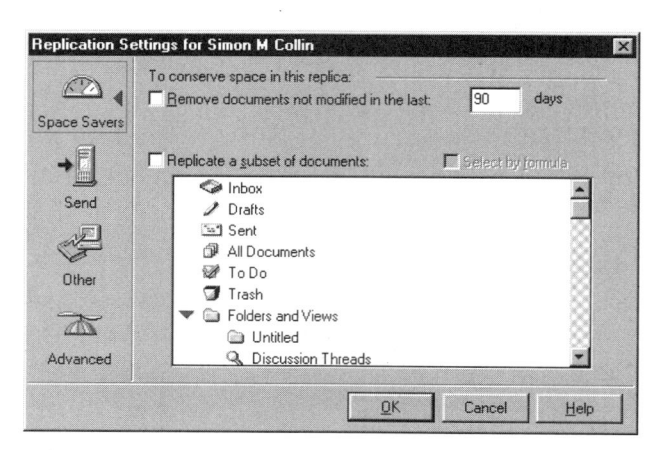

The process of removing old documents is called *aging*. This means any document that was created or last edited before a certain cutoff date is deleted from the database. In order to carry out aging, you'll need to change the replication settings for the database, and for this you will need manager status for the database. Aging is carried out automatically when a database is replicated, according to the replication settings (see also Chapter 6 for more on replication). To specify the cutoff date for documents, select the database icon from your workspace, choose *File ▸ Replication ▸ Settings* and select the Space Saver icon.

The first option lets you define the oldest documents that will be kept, enter the number of days – typically around 90 or 120 days is sufficient for many logs and mail files. Select the third check box Remove documents not modified in the last *xx* days. Click on OK to accept these changes. When this database next replicates, all the old documents in each replica of the database will be deleted. This might not be what you want! In some cases, it could just be your local server that's running out of disk space, in which case you should read the following section on deleting versus purging documents.

To delete or purge documents?

The way in which documents are removed from a database could have unexpected repercussions in light of database replication. If you delete a document from a database, Notes removes the document, but leaves an identifier in its place. This identifier continues the deletion during replication: it's transferred to the replicas of the database and deletes the corresponding documents from these files. If you purge a document, you remove the document identifier from the file. This frees the space taken up by the identifier and also means that the document is not deleted from the replica databases (since Notes no longer has a reference to do so). To automatically purge aged documents from your local database, but not make any changes to the replica databases, you should use the *Remove documents saved more than ☐days ago* option together with a number of days setting in the Replication Information screen for the database.

Monitoring database use

Under normal circumstances, Notes maintains an activity log for each database. This log is part of the server activity log recording details of replication, mail routing and database use. The most useful spin-off of this information is that a manager can view the activity of a particular database – to see who's using which database or to monitor which databases are being used. From this, you can base decisions to archive unused databases, compact large files or check that users are still accessing a database.

User activity

To view user activity for a particular database, highlight the database icon and select the *File ▸ Database ▸ Properties* menu option. From the options, choose the '❶' page tag and click on the User Activity button. Notes displays a scrolling list of user read and write operations to the database, together with a summary of use at the bottom of the screen. (The summary information lists 'Use' when the database was opened and at least one read operation occurred, 'Reads' when a document has been opened and 'Writes' when a user has created, edited or deleted a document.)

One drawback of the user-level activity log is that no trail will be recorded for a user that just opens the database and looks at views without actually opening a document. If you want to monitor all user activity, including all access to views, you should read the following section on database use. This log records each time a user accesses the database rather than the document-level trails stored in the user activity log.

If you want to keep track of user activity over several months – or years – you will need to cut and paste the user activity data to a wordprocessor or Windows WordPad. To do this, select the Copy to clipboard button, then switch to the wordprocessor and select *Edit ▸ Paste* to insert the data.

Note   When you start to record user activity for a database, you increase the size of the database by 64Kb. Notes adds on this overhead to store the tracking information of each user as the open, read and delete documents.

User transactions

Switching your view of the log file to Usage by User displays a summary of how often each user has accessed each database and how much disk space they are using.

From this screen, it's easy to spot over-active users, users that perhaps don't use the Notes resource enough (perhaps a tutorial would help them) and those users that hog too much disk space.

Database use

The main activity log allows you to view the data in various ways. You have seen how to view the activity by user, but another useful view is activity by database. Select *File ▸ Tools ▸ Server Administration* and then choose the Databases icon – from the pop-up menu select the Statistics option and Notes displays a list of the databases together with every access by either a user or server.

Database administration 137

To set statistics, click on the Databases button

This general overview of all database activity can be more useful than the user-level activity trail mentioned previously. Not only does it show similar information, but it does not require the 64Kb overhead on each database that you incur when recording all user activity. A second advantage is that you can check which users access the database in any way, which would include users who only look at views of the data rather than individual documents: this activity would not be recorded by the user-activity log because no document is opened. It is recorded by the database usage log as a session.

Database size and statistics

The third view on to the database and user log gives you a summary screen showing the size of each database (in kilobytes) together with the number of times the database has been used in the last week. This screen gives you an immediate impression of the popularity of each database.

For example, if the Notes Help database is top of the list in user access you might consider giving your users a Notes tutorial or a brief summary of the functions of Notes. If, on the other hand, a database has had zero access during the previous week, you might consider archiving the file off the main server to help save disk space.

Starting the activity log

By default, the activity log that records the user information described above is active for each database. If you find that you cannot view user activity, it could be that the log has been disabled in the NOTES.INI file. To check this, open the INI file in a text editor – such as Windows Note-Pad – and see if the following line is present:

```
NoForceActivityLogging = 1
```

If this line is present, you will not be able to record any user activity. To override this setting (for which you need to have designer or manager status) do the following:

Chapter 8

1. Highlight the Databases icon, choose *File ▸ Database ▸ Properties* and select the '❶' page. From this page, click on the User Activity button.

View user activity from the pop-up dialog box

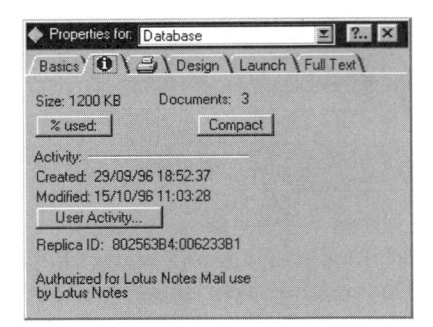

2. You will now see the history file for user activity on this database. If you want to record user activity, check the Record Activity check-box.

From now on, as users access the database, their activity will be recorded to the log. If you want to analyze the log file outside of the Notes environment, you can cut and paste it via the Windows Clipboard to any Windows wordprocessor or spreadsheet using the Copy to Clipboard button at the bottom of the reporting window. (See later in this chapter for more information on what is recorded in the Notes log file.)

Monitoring database replication

All replication activity is logged by Notes so that you can keep track of which database has replicated and when it last successfully replicated. To view the replication history of a particular database, select the database icon and choose the *File ▸ Database ▸ Properties* menu option.

A dialog box pops up giving you a choice of options. Select the Basics page tag and click on the Replication History button to view the replication history of the database. A second dialog box is displayed. Two radio buttons at the top of the screen give you the choice of ordering the replication activity By Date or By Server.

The contents of replication history

Any database that has successfully replicated at least once will have a history file. This history file plays an important part in the actual replication process. During replication, Notes will check the history file to determine the date of the last replication and so select the documents that should be included in the current, incremental history.

A copy of the replication history file is included in the local database and in all the replicated files. As a new replication occurs, the new replication times are recorded in each database's history file as the replication ripples across the servers.

Clearing the replication history

Be very careful of the implications if you choose the Clear history button (you need at least manager status to clear the history). This will clear the replication log on the current database and on all the replicas. Not only this, but at the next replication, Notes will no longer have a log of previous replications, so it will perform a full replication rather than an incremental replication of just the documents that have changed. A full replication will take longer to carry out and create more network traffic than an incremental update.

Compacting a database

As you delete documents from a database, space is freed in the file (called white space). If you create a new document, Notes will try to store it in the white space to make efficient use of the space. However, if you delete a range of documents, or a document with a large attachment, your database will effectively remain the same size, but will have a higher percentage of white space. Compacting removes the white space by copying the documents in the database to a new copy of the database, in the process eliminating the white space. Unlike a database copy operation, compacting preserves the document read/unread markers for all users.

To make the most efficient use of your disk space, try to compact all the databases once a month. If, on checking the status of the database, you find that there's more than 10% of white space, try to compact this database every week. To see how much white space is present in your database, either use the database log described earlier in this chapter, or select *File ▸ Database ▸ Properties* and choose the '🛈' page tag. This displays the size of the database and the size of the content in the top right-hand corner of the window.

Note Before you compact a database, make sure that you have at least as much free disk space as the size of the database, since compacting makes a temporary copy of the original database.

To compact a single database, highlight the database icon on your workspace, select the *File ▸ Database ▸ Properties* menu option, select the '❶' page tag and click on the Compact button.

To compact a set of databases, you'll find it simpler to enter the server administrator screen. Select *File ▸ Tools ▸ Server Administrator* and click on the Database icon in the bottom-left corner. You'll see a list of available databases. Highlight the database you want to compact and click on the Compact button.

If you want to compact a database that has a full text index, you will find it quicker to delete the index, compact the database then re-create the index. (To delete a full text index, use the *File ▸ Tools ▸ Server Administration* menu option, select the server that stores the database, select the Database icon and choose Database Full Text. Select the database from the list and click Delete option.)

To compact all the databases on the server, it's more convenient to use the console operation:

```
LOAD COMPACT
```

This will run and compact all databases on the current server. You can limit the compact operation to only those databases that have more than a certain amount of white space. For example, to only compact those databases that have more than 10% white space, enter the following:

```
LOAD COMPACT -S 10
```

Tip   Users will see a database in use message during compacting: try to schedule compacting for off-peak hours or use a program form to schedule the compacting to run automatically. (See Chapter 11 for more information).

User administration

Within your company, the users cannot be relied upon as a constant: people leave, new employees join or change their name. All these user-related tasks have to be managed by the Notes or network administrator. (For details on how to add new users, see Chapter 11, Setting up Notes.)

When Users move jobs

If a user moves job or leaves the company completely, you will need to do some basic security and administrative tasks.

A user leaves the company

If an employee leaves the company, you should quickly make sure that there's no way that the now ex-employee can gain access to your Notes system. To remove a user from Notes, do the following:

1. You should delete the user's Person document from the public Name & Address book.
2. Delete their mail file from the server.
3. Deny the user access to all servers by changing the access control lists to deny access to any server or database.

Setting a forwarding address if a user moves

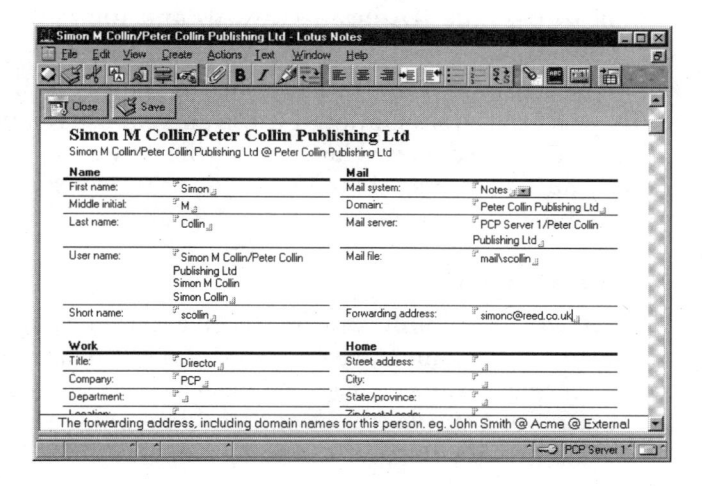

Lastly, if you have multiple servers, issue a Replicate command at the server console to immediately update the changes across the other servers.

When deleting a user from the system, you want to remove all their rights to access any database. The easiest way to do this is to create a group called DENY ACCESS in the public Name & Address book. Make sure that this group is included in the Not Access Server field of each server document in the Name & Address book. Now, to remove the rights from any user, add them to this group.

A user moves job within the company

In this case, there's no need to delete the user, you need to reset any rights and make sure that mail is correctly forwarded. If in moving job, the user moves server, you will need to re-direct mail. To do this, edit the old user's Person document and add the new mail address within the Forward Address field. This should only be a temporary measure and you should then make sure that their document reflects their new home server.

Change a user's name with Notes Mail

Changing a user's name within Notes is not quite as simple as it is within network operating systems, such as Novell NetWare. In Notes you must not only change the user's name, but also certify the new name and ID. The most convenient way of doing this is to use Notes Mail to pass the ID files backwards and forwards between user and administrator.

The user who wants to change his name selects the *File ▸ Tools ▸ User ID*; select the More Options button and choose Request New Name. In the field marked 'New Name' enter the new name you want to use and send the mail message in the To field to the person that certified your ID file – the server administrator. Click Send to send the request.

Certifying the ID

When you, as administrator, receive this message for a request to change a user's name, you must first certify the ID file that is attached to the message. Choose the *Actions ▸ Certify Attached ID File* menu option; Notes displays a list of files, highlight the name of the attached ID file (normally the user's existing name).

Then enter the certifier password after which Notes will display a dialog box with the ID's information. This dialog box also gives you the chance to change options for the user. Click on Re-certify button.

Finally, you can change the user's name by using the Change User Name menu option. This gives you the opportunity to enter the first and last name together with an initial.

You can now mail the certified ID file back to the user – Notes creates a message for you with a preset message regarding the name change. The user opens the received mail message from the adminstrator (that contains the new ID) and selects *Actions ▸ Accept Certificate*. This will automatically merge the new ID into the user's file and change the user name accordingly.

User administration | 143

Note You must also remember to change the user's name in the Name & Address book and in any database in which the old user had an entry in the ACL (this also includes the user's mail file).

Changing the user's name without Notes Mail

The previous section described how to change a user's name using Notes Mail to carry the certified ID file as an attachment. If, for some reason, Mail isn't working, you will have to resort to a rather more lengthy method of changing the name and re-certifying the ID file. First, the user must make a backup copy of his or her ID file. Exit Notes and use the Windows or DOS COPY command to copy the file with an .ID extension, normally stored in the \NOTES subdirectory. Name the new file with the user's new name.

Creating a new key for a user

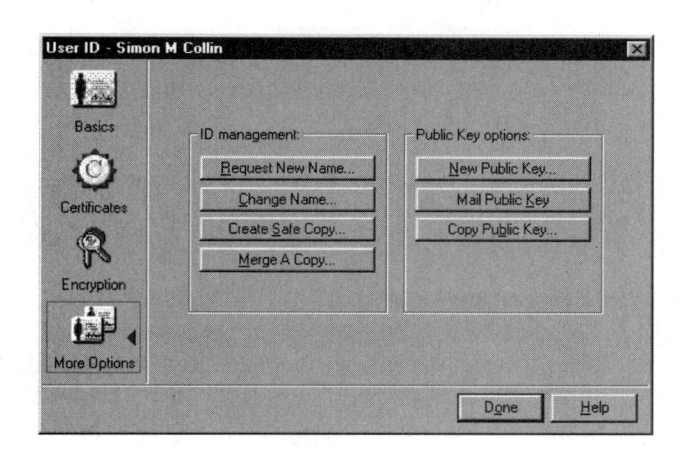

The user now inserts a blank floppy disk into their PC and selects *File ▸ Tools ▸ User ID*. Select the More Options button and click on Change Name. The user can now enter the new user name he or she wants to adopt and click on the Create Safe Copy – this prompts the user to enter the path for the new ID file – which should point to the floppy disk. The user then gives the floppy disk to you, as administrator.

When the user gets the floppy disk back from the administrator with the new ID, they select the *File ▸ Tools ▸ User ID* click on More Options and select Merge A Copy; from the file list box that's displayed he or she should select the filename on the floppy disk and click Done.

The job for the administrator is to re-certify the ID file: insert the floppy disk with the safe copy of the user's ID file and choose *File ▸ Tools ▸ Server Administration*. From the choice of icon options, select

Chapter 8

the Certificates button and enter the path to the user ID file supplied on disk. Notes prompts you for the certifier password – enter this and it will now stamp the ID file with the new certification. As in the previous section using Notes Mail, the last job for the administrator is to change the name settings in the Name & Address book.

Selecting the correct ID from a disk

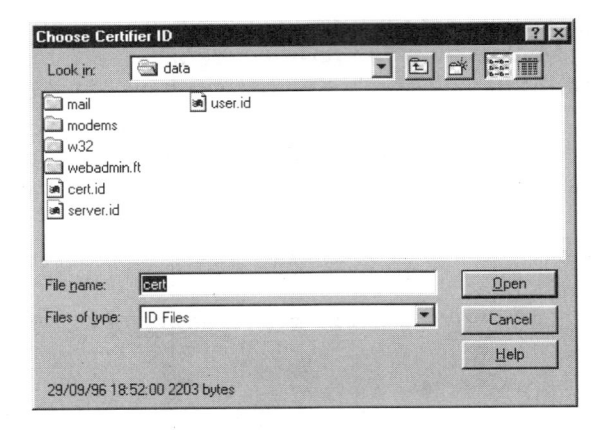

Tip If you want to make sure that mail addressed to the user's old name still reaches them under their new name, insert their new name before the old name in the Full Name field within the Name & Address book.

Editing a user's Person document

Each registered Notes user has their own Person document created in the public Name & Address book by Notes when the user was created. There are a number of common changes that you might be asked to carry out on a user's Person document. To access a user's Person document, open the public Name & Address book and choose the View People menu option to show the documents by user.

Move the highlight bar down to the user that you want to edit. To make any changes, you'll need to switch to edit mode: either hit [Ctrl]+[E] or select the Edit button option.

A user might want to add a nickname which is recognized like their full name by Notes. To do this, add the nicknames, separated by semicolons, within the First Name field. Do the same under the Full Name field.

Another change might be that a user moves location or office. In this case, you would want to change their Electronic Mail Information setup so that mail is redirected to their new home server.

If a user is visiting another office or wants to be kept up to date with Notes proceedings, you could add a routing address in the Forwarding Address field. This would normally be used if the user can only be contacted by another mail system – perhaps a commercial service or by fax or by the company's own brand of e-mail software – all of which would require a Notes gateway.

Recovering a user's ID or password

If a user forgets their password or deletes their ID file by mistake there's, unfortunately, almost nothing you can do to help – unless you have a backup ID file. There is no way to work around a forgotten password.

The only solution is to create a new ID for the user. This means that the user cannot access any signed or encrypted mail received with their old ID. To create a new ID file, but still keep the user's original mail file do the following:

1. First, delete the old user ID from the public Name & Address book.
2. Next, create a new user ID by selecting the *File ▸ Tools ▸ Server Administration* menu option and click on the People icon.
3. From the drop-down menu, select Register User. It's important that you specify that Notes creates a TEMPORARY mail file (it will be called TEMP.NSF). This avoids Notes overwriting the user's existing mail file.
4. Switch out of Notes and delete the file TEMP.NSF that it automatically created.
5. Switch back into Notes and open the new user's Person document (choose the View People menu option to see a list of users and move to the new user's entry, press [Ctrl]+[E] to edit the Person document).
6. Within the Person document, change the reference from TEMP.NSF to the user's original mail file.

If there's any chance that someone else got hold of the user's password or ID file, it's worth adopting a slightly different strategy: create the new ID file with a slightly different name (for example, EDJONES instead of EJONES). This means that anyone who's in possession of the file cannot use it. To make sure that the user's new ID will still receive mail, open the old Person document in Edit mode (see above) and add their new ID in the Forwarding Address field as a temporary measure.

Registering a new user

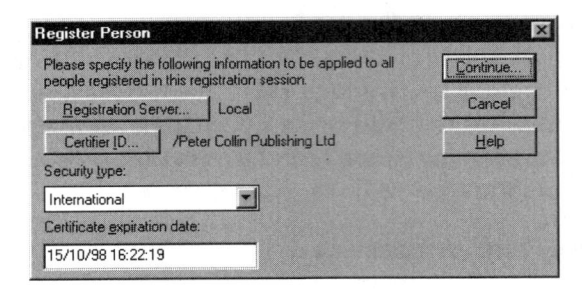

Groups and users

One of the most convenient ways of dealing with your users is to set up groups. Your network operating system probably already uses groups, perhaps by department or office. Groups under Notes can contain users, servers or other groups and it makes the management of mailing lists, access control lists and server access lists much easier. When you create a group, you are creating a Group document within the public Name & Address book. You can see existing groups using the Group View menu option in the Name & Address book database.

Notes starts life with two groups:

- LocalDomainServers
- OtherDomainServers

These contain the existing server and if you add a new server to the Notes network, you should add it to one of these groups.

Creating a new group

To create a new group you must create a new Groups document within the public Name & Address database. Open the public Name & Address book and select the Groups line on the Navigator bar. You can now click on the Add button on the Action bar at the top of the window.

Action bar for groups

Now enter the name of the group together with a brief description of the document and, lastly, a list of the members. If you have multiple Notes servers and want to use this group on other servers, you should replicate the Name & Address book so that changes are made across the network. If you have database managers, mail them a message so that they know this new group exists and can add it to any database access control lists.

Editing a group

To edit a group document, normally to add new users, open the public Name & Address book and click on the Groups entry in the Navigator bar; move the highlight bar to the group you want to edit and click on the Edit button in the Action bar.

Configuring a new group

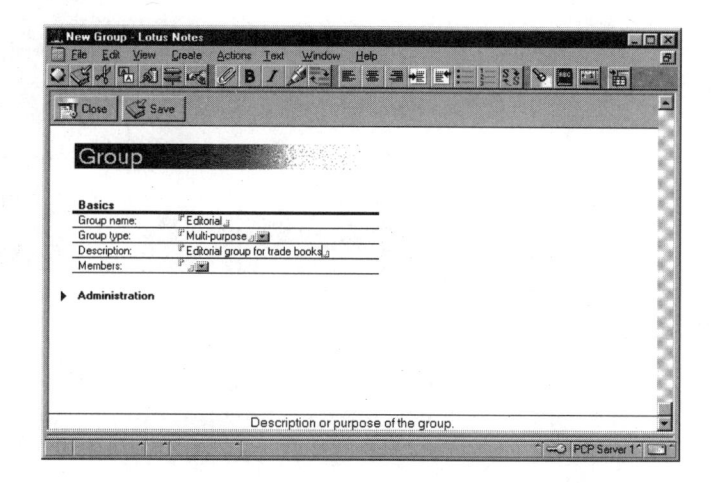

Server administration

Notes 4.5 now includes a single page that brings together all the main administrator's jobs. This gives you access to all the basic server definitions which are stored within the Server document in the public Name & Address book. You can either go directly to the N&A book and edit this 'raw' or you can use the interface provided by the Server Administration page – reach it via *File ▸ Tools ▸ Server Administration*. Important tasks that are carried from within the Server document are changing the Notes server administrator and setting up an Access Control List. Both are generally concerned with security of the server, either against ex-employees or to prevent users being able to access the server. For more details on Notes security, see Chapter 11.

*Main adminis-
tration screen
for the servers*

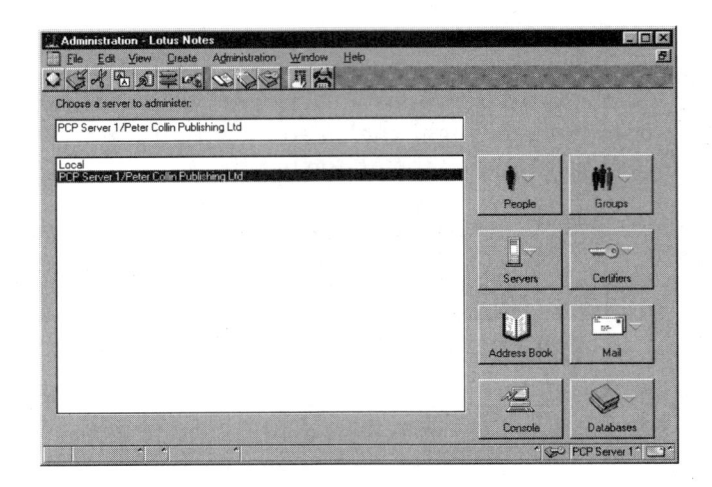

Daily server administration jobs

In order to keep your Notes server running smoothly and keep your users happy, you will have carry out a number of administrative jobs daily. The following section describes the jobs that you should try and carry out each day.

Check for dead mail

If your company is using Notes for its electronic mail capability, you should try to ensure that the e-mail works smoothly and efficiently. If there's one thing that is sure to bother your users, it's the chance that their mail won't get delivered. This is just as likely to be their fault as a hardware or router problem: the user might have wrongly addressed the message.

Dead mail is a message that Notes could not deliver; these messages are stored in the server's mail box and you should try to check for dead mail each day. If there's any dead mail present, you can then run the supplied macro that will return the mail message back to the sender, with a note explaining that it couldn't be delivered.

To check for dead mail, enter the SHOW TASKS server console command (see later in this chapter for more details on console commands). You can either enter this command at the server keyboard or use the remote server console utility, run from the *File ▸ Tools ▸ Server Administration* menu option and click on the Console button. In response to the Show Tasks command, Notes displays a list of current tasks including a report on the status of tasks, mail and transactions processed.

Server administration

Remote Server Console lets you issue server commands from your workstation

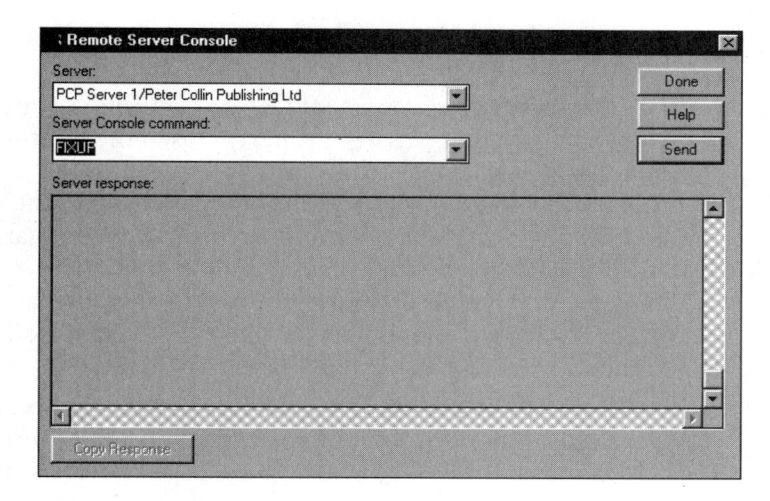

The line that's important for this task reads:

```
Pending mail: 0 Dead mail: 0
```

Normally, unless there's a configuration fault, there should be no dead mail. If there are dead mail messages indicated, you should open up the server mail box so that you can return the messages to their senders.

At your Notes workstation, choose the *File ▸ Database ▸ Open* menu option and select your local server. In the Filename field, type in the name MAIL.BOX (the name of the server's mail box) and select the Open button.

You can carry out a similar task from the workstation. The Server's MAIL.BOX database icon will be added to your workspace. In order to access the database, you need ideally to be administrator or at least Editor status in the database's ACL. In order to return the dead mail messages to their sender, open the MAIL.BOX database and choose the *Actions ▸ Release Mail* menu option. This will automatically try and release any dead mail or resend undelivered mail.

Running database FIXUP

One of the main cause of server problems and crashes is corrupted databases or documents. Preventative action will help ensure that Notes stays running smoothly and for as long as possible. To try to prevent corrupt documents, you should use the Notes server utility, FIXUP (see the end of this chapter for more details on server commands). The

FIXUP utility automatically checks the integrity of databases and documents and does its best to fix any problems it finds.

One other very important feature of the FIXUP utility is to check for any database that was not properly closed the last time it was accessed. If it finds any database that wasn't properly closed, it re-opens the database and carries out a full integrity check on all the documents in the database. If any damaged or corrupt documents are discovered, the utility will delete the document. It's important to note that these deleted documents are not replicated to any other server; in fact, at the next replication these Notes will try to pull valid versions of these documents from any replica database to fill in the gaps in the local file.

If there's no replica of the database – perhaps because you have only one Notes server – then Notes will not be able to replace the deleted documents. If this is the case, you should retrieve your last backup and manually copy the documents from this into the database on which you ran FIXUP.

FIXUP runs, by default, each time you start up the Notes server. Its actions are controlled by the Fixup = variable in the NOTES.INI file; by default, the value is 0.

FIXUP values within NOTES.INI

0   Scan all databases and delete corrupt documents.
2   Scan all databases even if properly closed, and delete corrupt documents.
4   Scan all documents carefully (and slowly) and delete corrupt documents.

When FIXUP deletes a document, it leaves a report trail of the document number in the Notes Log file (see under the Miscellaneous Events view). Once FIXUP has deleted a corrupt document, you should try to replace it from a replica as soon as possible; use the PULL or REPLICA server commands to override the scheduled replication times.

If you are concerned that a database might have been corrupted or damaged (perhaps, by a short server power or network failure), you can run FIXUP manually. Since FIXUP is a normal Notes server utility, you should run it in the same way as any other server utility, using the LOAD command. At the server console command prompt, or using the *File ▸ Tools ▸ Server Administration* menu option click on the Console button. In the command field, enter the following:

```
LOAD FIXUP
```

Server administration

FIXUP will run on all databases and carry out a full document scan, reporting on screen as it progresses. It will not be able to work on open databases, such as NAMES.NSF and MAIL.BOX.

If you don't want to wait for FIXUP to process all the databases, you can run it on just one named database using the command:

```
LOAD FIXUP <database> options
```

where the options are:

-L logs each database as FIXUP processes it

-Q skips the long, thorough scan and performs just a quick scan.

> **Tip** If you want to run FIXUP regularly, at the same time each day, you could set up a program document, or set the NOTES.INI variable to carry out the task at the same time each day or create an Agent that will do the job automatically according to a fixed schedule.

Backing up the server

However you use Notes, one thing remains the same: the data you build up in the databases is the most important part of the system. Therefore it's worth taking considerable care of your data. Like every other book, this one is no different in stressing the importance of making regular backups. If you lose your data, you will have to start again, from scratch.

What to back up?

You should make secure copies of the server ID file, any design templates or custom workstation shells that you would want in order to re-create your Notes setup in case of a complete failure. If you've edited it, you should also back up your NOTES.INI file. In case your users have problems or one of their workstations crash, it's safest to make secure copies of the User ID files.

Finally, we come to the database files themselves. In addition to your custom-designed databases, you will also need to back up the standard Notes databases: NAMES.NSF, MAIL.NSF and the Notes Log file (LOG.NSF). These last three files cause more problems than your own databases, since Notes requires that they are always open, and you cannot back up an open file. The only solution is to shut down the Notes server, back up the files then re-start Notes.

Note   Do not rely on replicas stored on other servers as secure backups. You should always make separate backups of your data and, ideally, store one copy off-site in case of fire or theft.

How to restore a database

If you do have the misfortune to lose a database, you will need to turn to your backup copies in order to restore the server to its previously saved condition. If you have been carrying out full backups, the simplest method of restoring a database is to copy the file from the backup media (e.g. tape) to the server's hard disk. If your server is one of a number of linked Notes servers, you could restore the database from a replica stored on another machine. To do this, delete the database's replication history via the *File ▸ Replication ▸ History* command (see Chapter 6 for more details). The next time a replication occurs, Notes will rebuild the entire database from the replica.

Devising a backup strategy

There is also a question mark with backup strategy. System managers can get concerned that they are not backing up often enough but there's no fixed set of rules that state when you must back up your system. You should know what your users are doing on the network, and be able to judge the importance of the information. If you already have a network server backup process in place, your mail backup is likely to be part of this. When installing new backup media, remember to first try a complete backup and restore of sample data to make sure that the software and hardware works and that you know how to use it.

Full backup

Full backups are a complete backup of every file and directory structure. This makes restoring a complete system very easy. If your hard disk crashes with no signs of life, then plug in a new disk and restore the whole structure. All applications, files and system information will be restored to its previous condition.

Full backups are easy to administer but expensive in tapes; tapes are filled quickly and if you exceed the capacity of a tape, the software will just sit and wait until someone replaces it with a new, empty tape. Calculate your total data requirements before setting a full backup running – you might have to wait around to swap tapes. You should carry out a full backup at regular intervals, typically once or twice a month for a small office network; more often for a larger installation.

Incremental backups

For everyday backups a more efficient system is to use an incremental backup. In this, only the files that have changed since the last backup are saved. Under Notes this could be the most active databases, but not the Name & Address book or the configuration files.

Whenever the contents of a file are changed, the operating system automatically turns on the file's Archive flag. Backup software then scans through all the files on your system, backing up files with the Archive flag set. All Archive flags are reset after the file has been backed up.

Because only a few of your data files are likely to change (application files should not), an incremental backup will take less time to execute and take less backup media than a full backup of every file. They are preferable as a more time efficient and less costly daily backup solution.

The disadvantage of incremental backups becomes apparent when you have to restore a system. Take an example in which you do a full backup once per week, on Mondays, then an incremental backup every day. If your disk fails on Thursday you will have to restore Monday's full backup, then feed in tapes for Tuesday and Wednesday to restore the system. If a user asks you to restore a single file, you might need to search through a stack of tapes, but good backup software will keep a catalogue of the contents of each tape.

When to carry out backups?

Look at your database usage patterns before you fix a time to backup. If you are running a small installation doing a full back up once a week, do not start this backup as you leave on Friday night. If you do, the tape will sit in the drive all weekend – if there's a fire, it will all have been for nothing.

It's obvious, but if your network is busy during normal office hours, schedule your backups when there are likely to be fewest users on the system. Backups will hold open any mail files and can take up server processor time and network bandwidth which will slow down mail delivery for users.

Media rotation

For an efficient and safe method of backing up you must organize a rotation of your backup media. You should at any one time have at least three copies of the mail data. One copy is up to date and stored on your server's hard disk. The second is slightly out of date on tape in a fire-proof safe in the office.

The third is stored off-site. This way, you can respond quickly to user demand with the backup data on-site, but protect against fire or theft with secondary data off-site.

Any tape rotation method will be expensive in tapes or other backup media. For a large site you might carry out a full backup every morning, with incremental backups on to separate tapes during the day. This could take up five tapes per day, with different sets for each day, and duplicates rotated off-site.

This rapidly becomes expensive, but you have to choose between the initial cost of the tapes and the price of the mail data.

Checking for problems in the server log

One of the most useful aids to the administrator is the Notes log file. This is a server-based database in which Notes records events, actions and problems. By looking in the Notes Log file on a regular, daily basis, you can spot symptoms early or before they become a problem. It's also very useful to find out why something isn't working correctly.

To access the Notes Log file, add the icon to your workspace: use the *File ▸ Open Database* and select the LOG.NSF file from the list of available databases.

Recording activities

In addition to recording a mass of information and activities about users, disk space and replication, the Notes log also gives you the option to record activities for a particular database or communications port. These can be very helpful when trying to establish how popular a database is or why a modem isn't working correctly.

Starting to record user activity for a database

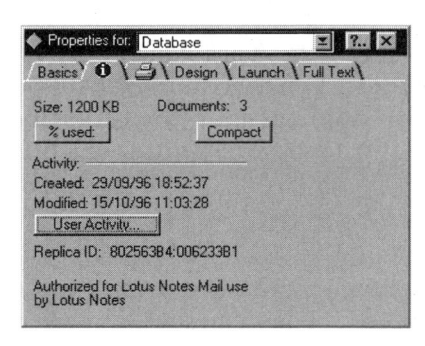

To start recording the database activities, open the database and select the *File ▸ Database ▸ Properties* menu option and select the '**ℹ**'

page tag; from here, click on the User Activity menu option and select the Record Activity check box. (Watch out, when you activate this option, the database immediately grows by 64Kb to accommodate the activity records.)

To start recording the activities of a serial port, select the *File ▸ Tools ▸ User Setup* menu option and choose the Ports icon in the navigator bar. Select the COM port you are interested in and select the Log Modem I/O check-box. This will then record all the modem activity; you can view the results within the Miscellaneous Events view of the Notes Log database. If you use the modem regularly, you should cancel this activity recorder once you've sorted out any problems, because the disk space taken up can be considerable.

View the Notes log file

All the records for the Notes log file are stored within the LOG.NSF file. This comes with a number of pre-designed views indicated in the navigator bar on the left of the screen – these cover most eventualities – but since this is Notes, you could always add your own design of view if you are interested in monitoring some particularly group of activities.

Server log file

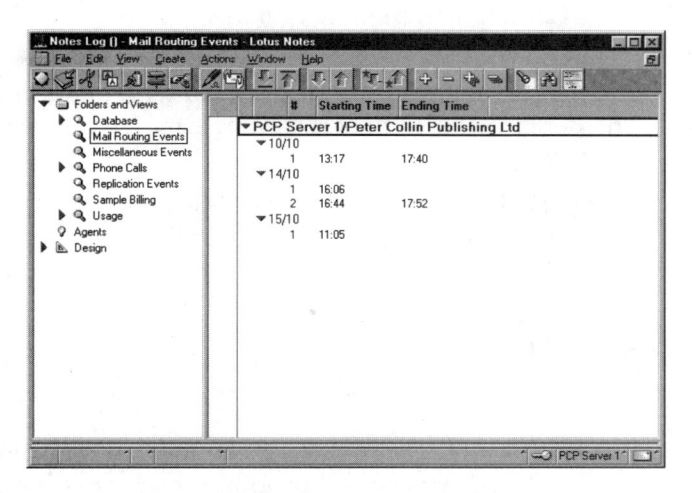

Database Sizes View Displays the size and activity of all databases, sorted by size. This is useful when calculating disk space requirements or pruning out unused databases.

Database Usage View Displays the amount of data transferred to and from a database by users, number of documents read and written and the replication history. Most useful in sorting out replication problems.

Mail Routing View Displays the movement of mail messages, together with the time the transfer started and finished.

Miscellaneous Events View Displays a mixed bag of activities, including modem I/O, mail routing activities and the number of corrupted documents encountered. Very useful to check on corrupted databases, why a server crashed and mail routing problems (for both software routing and modem hardware).

Phone Calls View Displays the calls made by and received by the server together with the amount of data transferred to and from the server. Useful when billing users or when sorting out the correct scheduling of replication calls.

Replication Events View Displays the history of replication events between servers together with details of the documents transferred and the time taken for the replication. This log only records the new documents sent from the local server to the remote server. For changes to the local server during a replication you have to, paradoxically, look at the remote server's log.

Sample Billing View A sample view that gives you an example of a view design to help when billing users.

Usage by Date View Displays the number of sessions between users and the server and between the local server and other remote servers. The detail includes the amount of data transferred, number of documents and the duration of sessions.

Usage by User View displays the same information as the previous, Usage by Date view, but sorted according to user.

Administrator administration

You will, at some point, have to change the name of your Notes administrator. Either your existing administrator has left the company, or is replaced by another person. Whatever the reason, you need to change the setup for the administrator name that is registered on the server. This process is similar to that described above which you would need to carry out if a user leaves the company.

Replacing the administrator

Your administrator leaves the company

This is simple: you need to make sure that the now ex-employee cannot gain access to your Notes system. You should delete the administrator's Person document from the public Name & Address book, delete their mail file from the server and, finally, change the Access Control Lists (ACLs) to deny access to any server or database. (This last stage is more easily done if you set up a 'Quit' group which has no access, and copy the administrator's name to this group).

Once you've made quite sure that the old administrator cannot gain access to your network, you will need to set up the new administrator – which is described below.

Your administrator moves to a job within the company

In this case, there's no need to delete the administrator, you need to simply reset their rights and make sure that mail is correctly forwarded. To change the name of the administrator, see the next section that tells you how to edit the Server document so that it contains the new administrator's name. If in moving jobs, the old administrator moves servers, you will need to re-direct mail. To do this, edit the old administrator's Person document and add the new mail address within the Forward Address field. This should only be a temporary measure and you should then make sure that their document reflects their new home server.

Adding a new administrator

When your administrator moves jobs in or out of the company, you will need to carry out some basic security measures, as described in the previous two sections. Once you've made sure that any ex-employee can no longer access the system, you need to inform Notes of the new administrator's name. This information is stored in the Server document.

The basic setup of the Notes server is defined in a Server document that is stored within the public Name & Address database. To add a new administrator, open the Server document in Edit mode: view the Server document and press [Ctrl]+[E] or select the Edit button. You can now delete the old administrator's name and type in the new name. If the old administrator had Manager access listed in the Name & Address book's ACL, you will need to delete the old name and enter the new administrator.

Adding a new administrator to the Server Document

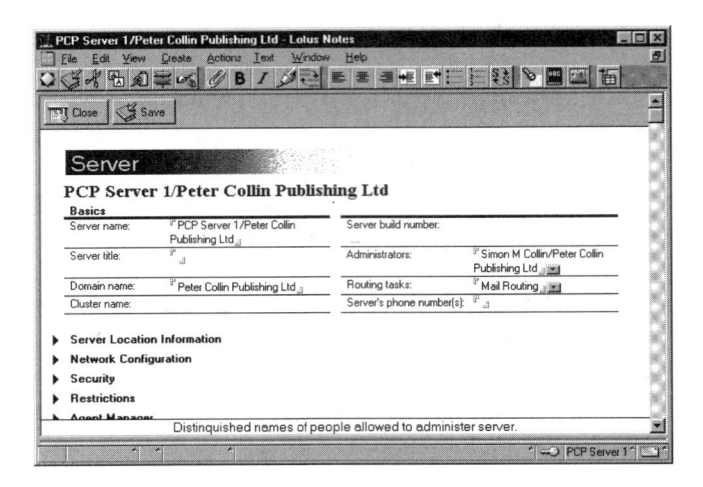

Once you have made the changes to the public Name & Address book, it's a good idea to replicate this database immediately to all other servers – type the REPLICATE command at the Notes console to force Notes to replicate now rather than waiting for the next scheduled replication.

Server access lists

One of the best ways to protect your Notes server from unauthorized use is to set up a server access list. A server access list offers another level of protection above the usual user access control; it offers control over the entire server and its hardware component.

Defining the access list for the server

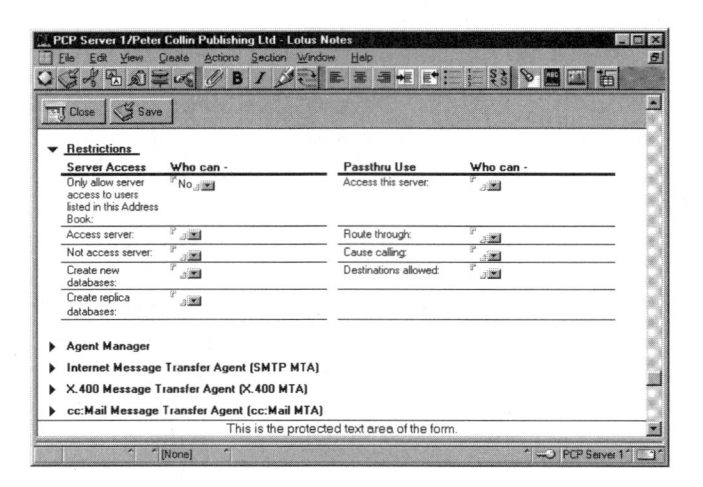

A server access list is stored in the Server document within the public Name & Address book. The access list is normally set to administrators only, but you can change this to include particular users or groups that are defined in the Name & Address book. To edit this document, open the Name & Address list and view the Server document, press [Ctrl]+[E] or select the Edit button to edit this document.

The most important field in the Server document is labeled Can access Server. If you don't include a server access list in this field, any certified Notes user can legitimately access the server – not a very secure setup. Include in this field the names of the users or groups of users that you want to grant access to the server. Working in an opposite way to this field is the second, Cannot access server. This contains a list of groups or users that are denied the right to access the server. If a user is in both fields, Notes takes the deny-right as the dominant right, overruling the inclusion in the grant access field. A convenient method of adding a range of users to any of the access control lists is to use views. For example, if you want to grant the right to access the server to all the users, they are all listed in the People view of the Name & Address book. To enter this view, precede it with an asterisk: *People in the Can Access Server field. (If you do use views, this will slightly slow down log in to the Notes server since it has to calculate the view and check the user against the results.)

Controlling the server

When Notes is running on its server PC, you can control many of its basic functions from the server console. There are two ways of entering commands: either from the command-line prompt, '>', at the server PC itself or, if you're at your workstation you can issue server commands remotely.

Remote server console

The remote server console screen allows the administrator to enter server commands and control the Notes server as if he were at the console. To be able to run this utility, you must be listed as an administrator in the target server's Server Document.

To start the remote server console, select the *File ▸ Tools ▸ Server Administration* and click on the Console icon and highlight the server's name from the displayed list.

Commands are entered in the single-line window. Once you have composed your command, click on the Send button. Any server response is sent back and displayed in full in the scrolling display window. If you want to keep a record of the server status, you can copy the server's response from the display window to the Windows Clipboard by clicking on the Copy Response button (then, paste it into your word-processor or Windows text editor).

Server commands

The Notes server responds to a range of commands that let you configure the server and display its status. In addition, you can protect the server from intruders with a password or force replication to update the databases on the server.

BROADCAST or B "message" <users>

Sends a message to all users of this server

For example: B "Server shutting down in 35 minutes."

DROP or D "username"

Closes one or more sessions. To close two or more at a time, separate each name with a space.

EXIT or E

Shuts down the Notes server.

For example: E

HELP or H

Displays a list of the server commands available.

For example: H

LOAD <program> or L <program>

Loads and runs a Notes server program (see later in this chapter for a list of applications). This command is normally used for occasional use. If you want to always load an application, add it into NOTES.INI or use a program form to run it automatically at a scheduled time.

For example: L REPLICA

PULL "<server>" or PU "<server>"

Forces replication from the named server to your local server; this command overrides any scheduled replication documents in the Name & Address book. Note that this command only carries out replication in one direction, updating your local server from the distant server. For a two-way replication, use the REPLICATE command.

As with any form of replication, this command will only work if the remote server has a server document in the Name & Address book or a remote document (for remote servers). If the server is already in the middle of a replication when you issue this command, the PULL command will be queued. You can check on the status of the queue by using the SHOW TASKS command.

Note Use quotation marks around the server name if it is more than one word. For example: PU "LONDON OFFICE"

PUSH or PUS "<servername>"

Forces replication from your local server to the destination server; this command overrides any scheduled replication documents in the Name & Address book. Note that this command only carries out replication in one direction, updating your local server from the distant server. For a two-way replication, use the REPLICATE command.

As with any form of replication, this command will only work if the remote server has a server document in the Name & Address book or a remote document (for remote servers). If the server is already in the middle of a replication when you issue this command, the PUSH command will be queued. You can check on the status of the queue by using the SHOW TASKS command.

Note Use quotation marks around the server name if it is more than one word. For example: PUS "LONDON OFFICE"

QUIT or Q

Exits the Notes server program – this has the same effect as the EXIT command.

REPLICATE "<server>" or REP "<server>"

This command forces an unscheduled replication between the named server and the local server. Unlike the PULL command, this command starts a full, two-way replication process. (The sequence first starts with the local server pulling data from the remote server; control then passes to the remote server which pulls data from the local server.)

If the remote server has a replication document that specifies a scheduled replication at the current time, the two-way replication will occur; if this forced replication is outside the time boundaries (the time or repeat interval) specified within the replication document of the remote server, only the local server will pull data – equivalent to the PULL command.

It's also worth noting that the two-way replication will only occur if it's necessary. If a database has been recently updated on one server, then only a one-way replication would happen if that's all that's necessary to bring both into line. If the Notes server is already in the middle of a replication process, your command is placed in a queue. You can check on the status of the queue by using the SHOW TASKS command.

For example: REP "LONDON OFFICE"

ROUTE "<server>" or RO "<server>"

This command immediately routes mail to another server, overriding any scheduled mail routing document in the Name & Address book. If there are no mail messages waiting to be routed, Notes ignores this command. This command is only really useful for sending mail to a server linked by a dial-up connection, since servers linked by a network have mail routed between each server almost immediately.

For example: RO "LONDON OFFICE"

SET CONFIGURATION <variable> = <value>

This command is used to set variables used in the NOTES.INI file (for a list of NOTES.INI variables, see the Appendix). If you add or change any variables using this command, you need to shut down the server (using the EXIT command) and then restart it in order for them to take effect.

You should use the SHOW CONFIG command to see the setting of a variable before you change it using this SET CONFIG command and ideally, again once you have set the variable to check that it's been correctly set.

SET SECURE <password> or SE SE <password>

This command sets up a password on the server console to prevent casual users using the console without authorization. Once the server has been protected using this command, you cannot run the LOAD, TELL or SET CONFIG commands, nor can the server run any other Notes application (including the workstation program on a Windows-based server). If you want to change the password, add it after the existing password.

For example: SET SECURE password

To change the password:

SET SECURE old_password new_password

Note   If you forget the password, you can bypass it by accessing the NOTES.INI file and deleting the line:

Server_Console_Password=

SET STATISTICS or SE ST <variablename>

Resets the counters used for additive statistics to zero.

For example: SE ST Server.*

will reset all the Server statistics back to zero

SHOW CONFIGURATION <variable> or SH C <variable>

This displays the settings of variables used within the NOTES.INI file. This command is normally used before or after the SET CONFIG command to check that the variable has been correctly set. (See the Appendix for a list of the variables used in the NOTES.INI file.)

SHOW DIRECTORY or SH DIR

Lists all the Notes databases (including all NSF and NTF files and replicas) stored in the Notes Data folder or directory on the server. You cannot specify any other directory.

SHOW DISKSPACE <drive> or SH DIS <drive>

Displays the amount of free disk space available on the named drive. (The drive letter should be entered without a colon.)

For example: SH D C

SHOW MEMORY or SH ME

Displays the amount of available RAM on the server. On an OS/2 server this displays the amount of available RAM plus the swapping memory for the boot drive. On a NetWare server, the command displays the configured memory (you should use the Monitor command for a more useful result). This command does not work on Unix servers.

SHOW PORT <port> or SH P <port>

This command displays statistics for the named port (which can be a serial port or network adapter card). The statistics include the level of traffic and the number of errors processed by the port. This information is also available from the Notes Workstation under the *File ▸ Tools ▸ User Preferences ▸ Ports ▸ Show Status* menu option. The ports available are normally: LAN0, LAN1, COM1 or COM2.

For example: SH PO COM1

SHOW SCHEDULE or SH SC <servername>/<programname>/<location>

Displays the time at which the next program is due to run on the server or the schedule for a particular program.

For example: SH SC Fixup

will display the schedule for the Fixup program.

SHOW SESSIONS or SH SE <servercommand>

Displays information on the current sessions to the Notes server including the port, buffer size and other useful debugging information.

SHOW STATISTICS or SH ST <statisticname>

Displays the statistics for the server. For a complete list of all the available statistics, type the command with no arguments.

SHOW TASKS or SH TA

Displays information about the current server including its name and the path to the Notes program directory, together with details of the tasks it is currently executing.

SHOW TRANSACTIONS or SH TR

Displays the transaction statistics for the server including tasks running, router details and basic statistics.

SHOW USERS or SH U

Displays a list of the users that currently have sessions established at the server. The display lists the name of the user, any databases that the user has open and the number of minutes since the user last used the database.

TELL or TE <serverprogram>

Allows you to send an instruction to a separate Notes server application, such as the indexer or router. It is normally used to shut down an application without having to shut down the entire server.

To shut down the Router application, enter: TELL ROUTER QUIT

Controlling the server

Server utility applications

To carry out some tasks, it's necessary to run separate applications. These run on the Notes server and are loaded and executed using the LOAD command (see above). The main utility applications that run on the server carry out replication, database management, index management and updates. These separate utilities are listed below:

    CATALOG, CHRONOS, COMPACT, DESIGN, FIXUP, INDEXER, LOGIN,
    REPLICA, ROUTER, STATLOG, UPDALL

Running server commands automatically

All the server commands and applications discussed in this chapter can be set up to run automatically according to a pre-defined schedule. In fact, this also applies to any third-party Notes application or any Notes application that does not require user input. To run any Notes server command automatically you need to create a Program Document within the public Name & Address book. This document will execute any server command at a particular time or day or repeat a command regularly – such as a backup command in the middle of the night when there are no users logged in.

To create a Program Document, open the public Name & Address book and select the *Server ▸ Program* entry in the navigator bar. Click on the Add button to add a new Program document to the server.

In the first line of the form, enter the name of the program that you want to execute. In the second line, enter the command (as you would type it at the command line) that would start the program, together with any arguments. In the third line, identify the name of the server on which you want the application to run.

The Schedule fields let you define when the program should be run, and any repeat interval (for example, if you want the program to run every night).

9

Electronic mail and communications

About this chapter

Within Notes 4.5, Lotus has provided a full featured electronic mail system that uses the same front-end as the popular cc:Mail product. This addresses what had been one of the weaker points of Notes and makes it just as capable as any other commercial e-mail system. Notes is often mistaken for an e-mail system – it's not – Notes is a distributed database system that lets you create custom front-end applications. The e-mail system supplied with Notes is actually a custom form and navigator that's been designed to look and work like Lotus cc:Mail. Electronic mail is one of the best ways to boost productivity in your company: if you want to get in touch with someone you don't have to wait in a phone queue or rely on the postal service. With e-mail, delivery is almost instant and guaranteed – you can see exactly when your mail was read, thus resolving plenty of office politics.

Within Notes 4.5, Lotus has dramatically improved its e-mail feature to make it one of the best around. Easily as good as many standalone e-mail software packages: you can write memos, customize templates, create rules, send files and start applications from within Notes' e-mail. Notes' e-mail includes functions to generate a receipt message back to let the sender know his mail has been received, a function to encrypt sensitive messages and a method of signing your messages to guarantee authenticity. Best of all, if you don't like the standard e-mail application, as supplied, you can rewrite it using Notes programming language.

In this chapter, you'll see how to use the extended features of Notes' e-mail and how to integrate it with other software systems, such as Lotus cc:Mail and Microsoft Mail.

Using Notes mail

Notes mail works in a similar way to any other Notes database in that the documents are stored on the central server and can be transferred between servers either as part of a replication cycle or as a specific transfer (see Chapter 6 for more information).

Mail messages are created within your local mail box (another name for the mail database). When you save the message, it's sent to the central server which checks the name of the intended recipient and passes the message on to their mail box. When you receive a new message, your workstation alerts you (normally with a little tune) and by displaying a small envelope icon on the Status bar at the bottom of the Notes workspace screen; the count of unread messages in your local mail database increases by one.

The user's e-mail front-end

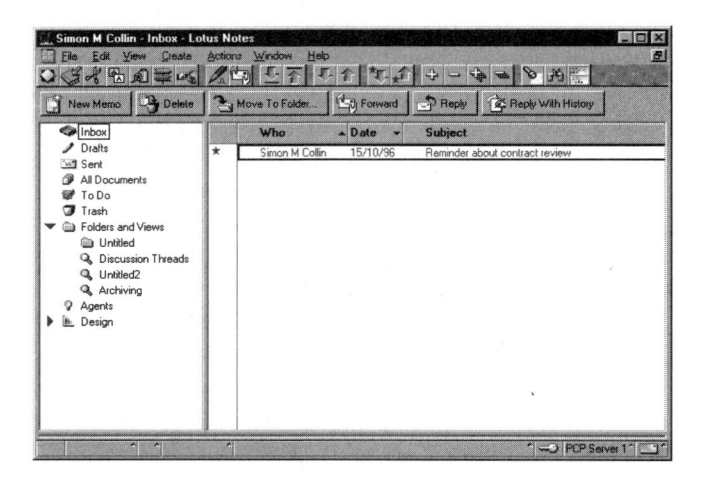

If you think of Notes mail as if it were any other Notes database, then the mail box is the local database; when you read a message it's the same as reading a document in a database and when you send a message it's the same as creating a new document. The Notes mail icon is normally on the first page of your workspace. Its label gives your full Notes name.

When you double-click on the icon, you open up your mail box and see a navigator screen with the various mail folders listed on the left and their contents listed in a pane on the right.

The Mail Folder Structure

Within Notes 4.5, the e-mail application now supports a full set of folders for each mailbox. These let you and your users bring some order to their mail messages. The most important folder is right at the top of the structure – the InBox. This receives any new mail messages as they are delivered by the server.

Basic folder structure used by the e-mail database

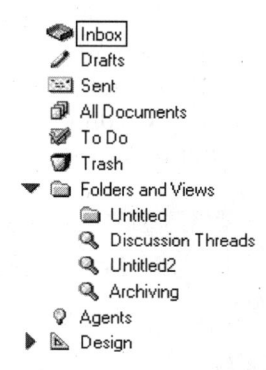

- Inbox
- Drafts
- Sent
- All Documents
- To Do
- Trash
- Folders and Views
    - Untitled
    - Discussion Threads
    - Untitled2
    - Archiving
- Agents
- Design

Beneath this are a series of folders that contain the following:

Drafts – holds unfinished mail messages that have not yet been posted.

Sent – holds messages that have been posted.

All Documents – holds copies of all your messages.

To Do – the organizer that displays the set of tasks left within a workflow selection or lets you organize meetings by mailing a group of users a custom message (use *Create ▸ Task* menu option).

Trash – the recycling bin which holds messages that are to be deleted.

Folders & Views – your user-defined folders and user-defined views that can display particular details of messages.

Agents – lists the current agents (automated tasks) that are available.

Design – gives you access to the designs for views, forms and navigators used in the mail system.

Writing a mail message

Sending a mail message is just the same procedure as creating a new document in any other Notes database. Select the *Create ▸ Memo* menu option and you will see a blank message form displayed. Alternatively, click on the Memo button in the Smart bar.

The message layout is pretty spartan (in version 4.5 there are just as many options, but they've been hidden). You must fill in the fields of the name of the person (or multiple users) to whom you want to send this message, the subject field and the rich text field that contains the message itself. The delivery options are hidden within a menu and these are covered below.

Addressing the message

If you type part of a user's name in the To: address field, Notes will try to match this with entries in its Address Book. If it finds a match, it fills in the user's full name and their server. If you want to send the message to several users at once, separate their names with a comma.

Adding a name from the list of registered users

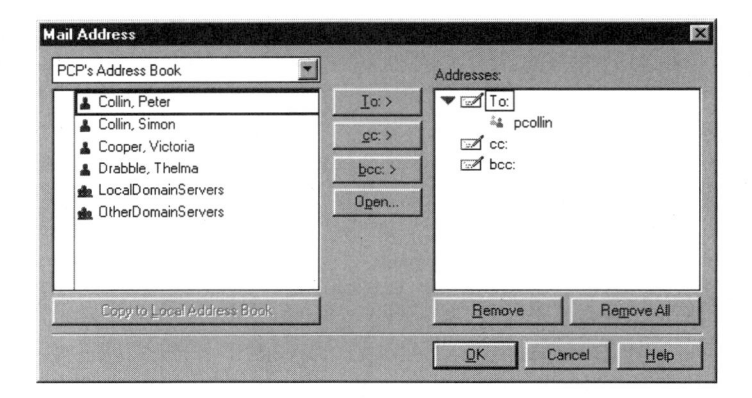

If you cannot remember the user's full name, click on the Address button in the top right of the Smart bar. This displays a list of possible Address Books; below this are the domains, groups and user names stored in the Address Book. Highlight one of the names, groups or domains and click on the To: button in the center of the dialog box. Similarly, if you want to fill in the cc: and bcc: fields, highlight a name and click on the button in the center of the dialog box. You must fill in a name in the first field To:, but you can leave the rest blank.

The second field cc: sends a copy of the message to another user or list of users. There's often some confusion about the various send options, especially when you want to send a message to several people.

To: send the message to each user listed, none of the users know about the others in the list.

cc: send the message to a user, the original person in the To: field sees entries in the cc field.

bcc: the user listed gets a copy of the message, but other users don't know he or she has a copy.

For example, if you want to send a message to fire an employee, James, you must also send a copy of the letter to the personnel manager, Fiona, but you want to send a secret copy to your friend, Pete, so that he knows there's a job opportunity:

To:James
cc:Fiona
bcc:Pete

The message

The main body of the message is stored in the rich text field in the center of the mail form. Normally, this would be just type, but because this is a rich text field, you can change the fonts and look of the type and insert graphics. One example is to add your signature at the bottom of the screen – draw it in Windows Paintbrush, then cut and paste it into the message. Notes supports OLE 2 and can import a range of text and graphics files and will store them in the message field – you can then move them or resize them.

There are a few extra features that let you create more complex messages, for example, you can add buttons or hotspots into your message. Then, when the recipient opens the message and clicks on the button it will carry out the commands you have described. (This is a good way of upgrading drivers or software.)

Adding Features to your Message

Notes 4.5 lets you add features to the message or body of your e-mail. For example, you can insert a table of data or a hotspot that, when the user clicks on it, will jump the user to another point in the message or execute any other Notes command. Lastly, you can insert a button that can execute a series of commands when clicked by the recipient.

Table

To add a simple table to format data that you type into the message, click on *Create ▸ Table* and you will be prompted for the size of the table in rows and columns.

Link Hotspot

This creates a section of text (the hotspot) that provides a link to another view, a doclink or another article. To create a Link Hotspot, first copy your link (move to the document you want to link to, select *Edit ▸ Copy* as Link). Now back in the mail message, highlight the text that you want to act as a hotspot and select the *Create ▸ Hotspot ▸ Link Hotspot*.

Setting up a hotspot

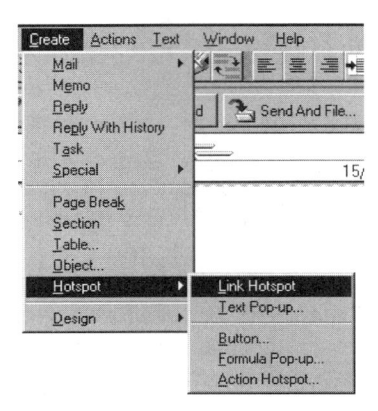

Text Popup

These are useful for explaining complex terms within a message. When the user clicks on the hotspot, a panel will popup displaying more text about the object. Hightlight the text that you want to act as a hotspot, select *Create ▸ Hotspot ▸ TextPopup*. A dialog box appears. Type the explanatory text into the text field and select OK.

Defining the pop-up text for a hotspot

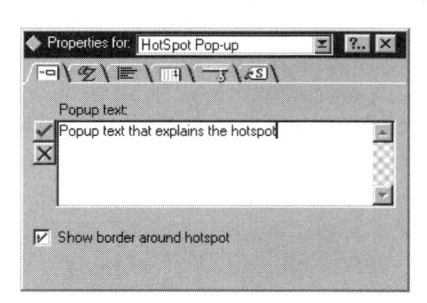

Button

You can insert a button into a message and attach a set of commands to the button that will be executed when the user clicks on the button. Select *Create ▸ Hotspot ▸ Button*. A properties dialog box appears – enter the text for the button caption in the Caption field. A new pane

Using Notes mail   173

appears beneath the main mail message. You can select to add a simple action or a complex set of formulas. In either case, Notes makes life a little easier by listing the available commands and the fields that you can use as arguments – click on the Add Action button to see these commands.

Adding a button to the message

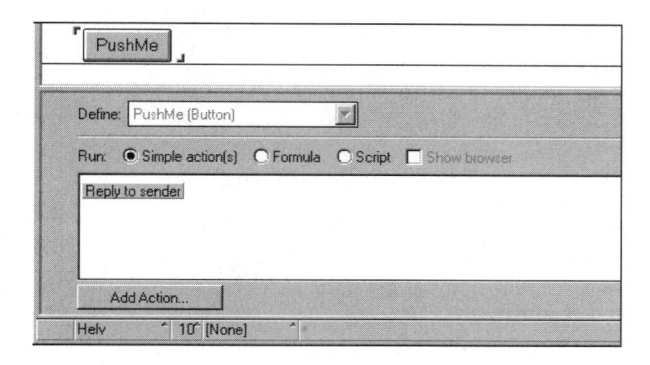

Delivery options

When you send a message, Notes can be instructed to deliver it at one of three different priority levels: Normal, High or Low delivery priority. To define the priority (and so the speed at which the mail is delivered) click on the Delivery Options SmartButton. If you are connected to the recipient on a single LAN, then the priority setting makes little difference to the time it takes Notes to deliver the message. If you are sending a message to a user that's on a different server or is accessed via a remote link, then the priority becomes more important: high priority sends the message as fast as possible, regardless of the cost of the transfer media; low priority sends the message as cheaply as possible, regardless of speed (normally at night to take advantage of low-cost phone calls).

Setting Delivery Options for a message

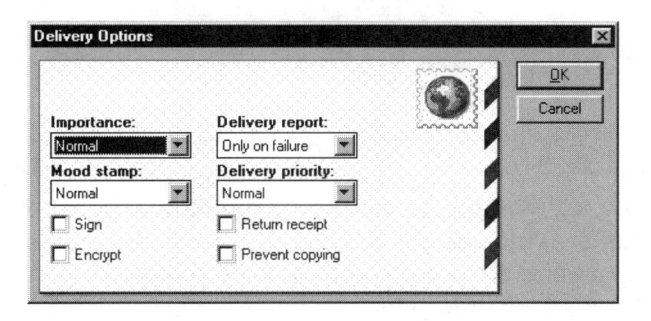

Chapter 9

The Delivery report option produces a report that tells you that the message was successfully delivered. Normally, Notes only tells you if there was a problem delivering the message.

Mood stamp attaches a banner graphic to the mail message, beneath the address panel that is supposed to indicate the tone of your message. This is something of a gimmick, especially since you can modify the mail header graphic.

Return receipt option generates a return message that tells you exactly when the recipient read the message.

Sign lets you authenticate a message.

Encrypt automatically encrypts the message – normally messages are sent as plain text.

Adding a file attachment

You can attach any type of file to any mail message – you can send spreadsheet files, documents or programs. When you attach a file to a message, Notes inserts a file icon into the message and you can attach several files to a single message.

Adding an OLE object to a message

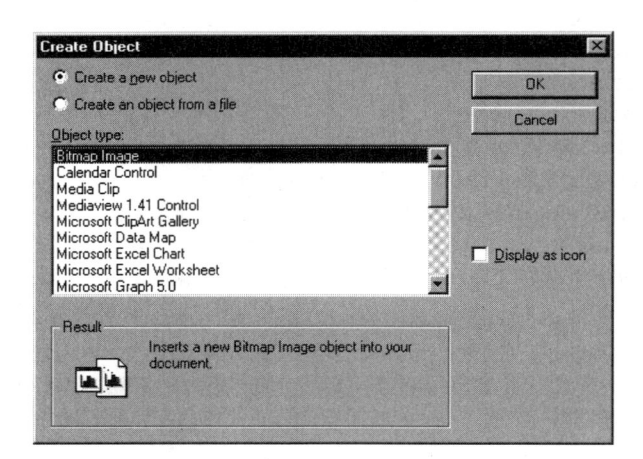

To attach a file, either click on the paperclip icon in the button bar at the top of the Notes screen or choose the *File ▸ Attach* menu option. If you use Windows for most of your applications, you'll probably find it easier to include a file as an OLE object – select the *Create ▸ Object* file menu and choose the type of data object that you want to include: an Excel file or video clip.

Compress

You'll notice a compress check-box on the right of the file attachment dialog box. This gives you the option to compress the attached file. If you are sending a document or graphics file, these can be substantially reduced in size (and so cut down on transmission time) if you compress them. Program and many data files don't compress well. The recipient doesn't need to worry whether an attached file has been compressed since Notes de-compresses files automatically.

> **Note:** When you view the list of messages, those with attached files have a paperclip icon beside them.

Receiving an attached file

If you receive a message with attachments, there are several ways in which you can access the files. The simplest is to double-click on the file icon in the message. A File Attachment Information dialog box pops up and gives you the option of saving the file on to your disk (it doesn't detach the file, but it does make a copy) or to launch the application that was used to create the file and load the attached file. Obviously, this will only work if the recipient has the same applications installed as the sender.

Deleting an attached file

Sometimes you might need to delete an attached file – perhaps you attached the wrong file. To do this, you have to get back into the message that contains the file and switch to Edit mode (press [Ctrl]+[E]). Now, highlight the file icon and press [Delete].

Importing versus attaching

There is another way of sending documents, graphics or data to another user: import the information into the body of the message. This has the advantage that the recipient doesn't need the same application software to read the information. For example, if you have Microsoft Word, but you're not sure of the type of software the recipient uses, it might be safer to import it into the message. To import a file, select the *File ▸ Import* menu option when you're in Edit mode within the message field.

Secure messages

One of the problems of electronic mail is that it is possible, in theory, for a dastardly intruder to read your mail or intercept your mail messages. Most of the time, this isn't a worry. But if you want to send a particularly sensitive memo or you are sending a memo to a remote user – and so the message passes over a phone link or bulletin board – then you could encrypt the message.

Notes gives you the option to encrypt a message from the Delivery Options dialog box. If you select the check-box at the bottom left of the Save dialog box, Notes will scramble the contents of the message. The recipient doesn't need to do anything, since Notes will automatically decrypt an encrypted message. This feature prevents Notes from sending plain text messages, and so reduces the risk when using telephone links. However, it's not so useful if you're trying to protect against an internal attack by another nosy user – if they can gain access to your workstation there is a chance they could read your mail. If you work with particularly sensitive mail messages, always try to log out before leaving your desk, or use a screen-saver with a password built in (you can do this from MS Windows through the Control Panel).

Signing a message

Sometimes you will need to provide a guarantee that it was actually you who sent a message. For example, a joke message telling someone they're fired can backfire! In these cases, where you need to assure the recipient that you are the real sender, you should sign the message.

Like the encryption option, the sign option is available from the Delivery Options dialog box. It adds authentication data to the message that proves you sent it.

Accessing your mailbox from another PC

There will be times when you need to check your mail, but you are not at your normal PC. Perhaps you're at another office in your company, or your PC has broken down. To access your mail box from another PC (even if it's running Notes under another operating system), all you need is one file: your Notes ID file. You can also access Notes from your laptop or over a dial-up telephone link – see Chapter 5 for more information.

You should always keep a spare copy of your Notes ID file, just in case your PC breaks down. Notes stores all the vital details about you in

Using Notes mail   177

a local file with the extension .ID. The file name is your user name: for example, Simon Collin could have an ID file called SCOLLIN.ID. This is normally stored in the C:\NOTES\DATA directory on your local hard disk.

To create a spare, backup key disk which contains a copy of your ID file, insert a blank floppy into your PC's drive and type:

```
COPY *.ID A:
```

Setting the Location Document to access a mail database

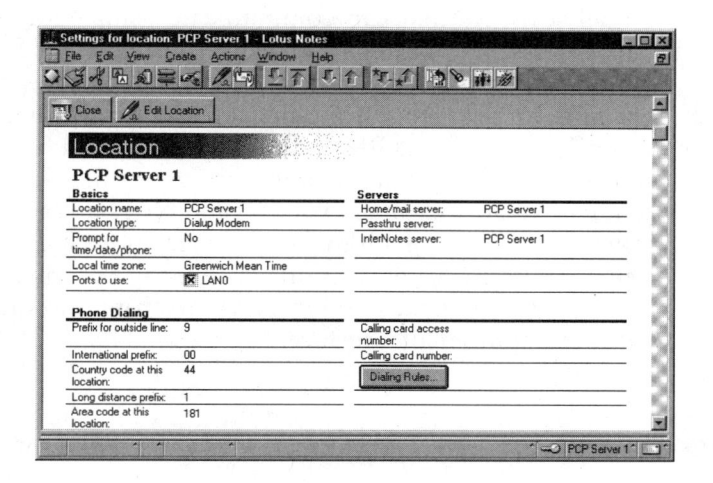

You will also need to know the name of your home server (unless Notes is only running on one server). To find out your home server, select the *File ▸ Mobile ▸ Locations* menu option which opens the Location section of the personal Address Book.

You should keep your ID disk carefully – even with this disk, another user cannot access your mail box unless they also know your password.

Logging on to Notes with an ID disk

To log in from another workstation, first start Notes. When it asks for your password, press Cancel. Insert your key ID disk into drive A: and select the *File ▸ Tools ▸ Switch ID* menu option. Enter the drive and name where your ID file is stored.

Notes will load your ID file and ask for your password; type your password. Notes finally displays an information box with your ID number and name. Select OK and you are logged into Notes and can access your mail box. To open your mail box, select *File ▸ Database ▸ Open* menu option. This lists available databases – choose your home server then scroll down the list of databases and select the MAIL directory:

Chapter 9

select this and you will see a list of user names from which you can open your own mail box.

Alternative e-mail front-ends

Notes Mail is a VIM-compliant application. This means that any other e-mail software that can communicate using VIM codes can act as a front-end to the Notes Mail delivery engine. In fact, there are two front-ends that are commonly used with Notes to provide more functionality for users that want more from their e-mail system than Notes can offer. The first is BeyondMail from Beyond Inc. The main benefit of this program is that it offers intelligent rules that allow you to program it to read your mail messages and file them according to their contents. If you receive a lot of new messages each day, BeyondMail can help you keep the messages tidy. The second product is Lotus cc:Mail – although there's little point in using this front-end since it's near identical to the Notes mail interface

Gateways to other mail systems from Notes

Lotus is well aware of the wide number of standards used by different electronic mail systems. In order to link Notes to any other mail system (including the Internet or SMTP systems) you'll need a specific Notes MTA (message transfer agent). If you've already got a company-wide e-mail system that works well and your users can rely on, then there's got to be a very good reason to change away form it. To allow Notes to work with other mail systems, Lotus and other third-party software companies have developed a number of gateways that sit between Notes and another e-mail delivery system. Since the capabilities of the MTAs are always evolving, it's best to check the Lotus WWW page (www.lotus.com) for details of the new MTAs that are available.

Electronic mail standards

If you have a single Notes installation, you will have no problems exchanging mail messages because it's all handled by Notes. If you want to connect to another Notes server, Notes looks after the connection and delivery of mail messages. However, if you need to send mail to another type of e-mail system – perhaps a user on a commercial on-line service (such as CompuServe) or a user of a mainframe, you'll need to install a special piece of software to connect Notes to the foreign system and translate the message format. This software is called a gateway; the next section describes the major gateways that are available.

When sending mail to another mail system there are two major considerations. First the e-mail system must be able to identify the intended recipient of a message. Next it must be able to locate the receiver and find a route along which the message can be transported and delivered intact. There are some 400 different 'standard' methods of addressing, routing and commanding a system to perform enhanced message handling functions. Among the contenders for survival, one of the favorites is the group of companies that have opted to pool their resources and applications program interface specifications to produce a standard they have dubbed VIM for Vendor Independent Messaging interface.

The VIM consortium includes Apple, Borland, Lotus and Novell. Other favorites include Microsoft with its Messaging Application Programming Interface (MAPI) e-mail interface. In the meantime, though, the neutral mail exchange system is from Novell whose Message Handling System (MHS) standard is claimed, by Novell at least, to have emerged as the most widely used e-mail standard and API over local area networks.

Novell MHS

One e-mail standard, developed in part by Novell, is MHS (Message Handling Service). This is unusual in that it's not tied to any particular product or vendor – unlike MAPI and VIM. Because of this, it's the only neutral gateway and often the only way of connecting dissimilar mail systems to allow them to swap messages.

The beauty of MHS is that it is supported by almost all e-mail vendors. This includes Notes which supports an MHS gateway. Other e-mail packages can concentrate their efforts on the front-end, safe in the knowledge that the delivery is being taken care of by MHS. If you need to connect Notes to another mail system or other sites without Notes, you will probably find that MHS proves to be the simplest and most efficient solution.

MAPI

Microsoft's MAPI is a set of standard functions and calls within compatible e-mail software that a developer can use to provide mail functions within another application. MAPI was developed by Microsoft and is supported by a number of e-mail applications – but not by any Lotus products (which use the rival VIM standard). Therefore, if you want to connect a MAPI product with Notes or any other VIM product, you will need a third neutral gateway such as MHS to connect the two.

VIM

A group of software companies including Lotus, Apple, Borland, IBM, Novell Inc. and WordPerfect formed the VIM Consortium to define a new independent API that could be used for front and back-end mail applications as well as mail-enabled applications. VIM is used in all Lotus products, including Notes, to send and deliver mail.

X.400 and X.500

If you want to send a message from your PC to a user on mainframe in another country, you are going to come up against a number of problems. The first is that two different computer systems, each running a different e-mail program, want to talk. To solve the problem of data exchange there are a number of proprietary solutions. To bring standards to the issue, the International Consultative Committee for Telegraphs and Telecommunications (CCITT) published a set of recommendations (called X.400) intended to define how dissimilar computer messaging systems can exchange information. There are gateways available for Notes to connect to other e-mail systems but beware, not all implementations of X.400 are necessarily the same. Nevertheless, X.400-based e-mail products offer one of the most reliable standard available for meeting the integrated electronic messaging needs of the corporate environment.

PROFS

PROFS has the largest installed base of any mail system: it runs as a mini and mainframe mail software either as IBM PROFS System, OfficeVision/VM or CMS Notes. PROFS will really only find its way into a PC environment if it is being used as a mail backbone within a company or if a small PC workgroup wants a friendlier Windows-based front-end to PROFS. Notes has an optional PROFS gateway that lets you send mail messages to and from a central mainframe.

When running a PROFS gateway, your local users will appear as another PROFS node to existing mainframe users of PROFS. The gateway utilities should allow you to download the PROFS nickname file to include within your local mailing list so that local users have immediate access to any user name and nickname.

SMTP

Simple Mail Transport Protocol (SMTP) is widely used in the Internet and in Unix sites – it's sometimes known by its less obvious name of RFC-821 – and specifies the protocols required when transferring mail messages between two computers. Of minor historical interest only, SMTP replaced MTP (Mail Transport Protocol) which was generally considered to be too complex for most installations.

Unlike some of the high-level mail interfaces mentioned earlier, such as MAPI and VIM, SMTP is very simple. It defines the protocols required by a sender to deliver a message on to the disk of the recipient's computer; the sender contacts the recipient's computer directly so there's no need to use intermediate mail routers (which could delay or misroute a mail message).

What makes SMTP so simple to use and understand is that not only does it do all the message delivery itself, all its messages are readable as text and all start with an identifying number to make processing even easier. SMTP is the most prevalent mail system on the Internet and is commonly used with TCP/IP and in Unix systems. If you want to connect Notes Mail to the Internet or to a Unix network or host, you will likely to need an SMTP gateway, which is available for Notes.

Facsimile

Fax machines are pretty much everywhere and can provide an alternative means of transport for mail messages to a recipient who doesn't have a workstation able to receive mail. Notes supports a fax gateway that lets you send mail messages (or any document) as a fax message to a normal fax machine. This gives the user the benefit of being able to deal with distant users who aren't on the main mail system easily and within the same environment as all other mail messages.

In order to integrate faxing seamlessly with all your other Notes operations, you'll need to add the Lotus Fax Server product. This sits on a nominated Notes server and accepts mail directed to it. The mail messages include the user's fax number in their To: line. The Fax Server will render the mail text and any images into a fax graphic format and send it from one or more fax cards installed on the fax server.

In addition to sending outward-bound faxes, the Fax Server software can route inward-bound faxes, although the method it uses depends on the phone system you have in your company.

Telephony

Notes 4.5, like many products, can integrate with the new set of Telephony standards. This allows Notes to provide a full voice service to customers calling in – which has the benefit of tying in Notes database material with the voice output.

There are several Telephony software packages that run on dedicated servers within your company network and create a link between the Notes server and the PBX. One popular product is by Remark! and supports a range of Telephony boards and scripting commands.

Internet

The links between Notes and the WWW are covered in detail in Chapter 10, however this won't help much if you want to link Notes e-mail to the Internet. In order to create an e-mail link, you will need an Internet mail MTA which is available as an optional extra from Lotus. This will provide the transport via the TCP/IP protocol stack that actually connects your LAN's traffic to the Internet server. An Internet server is normally a Unix machine; Unix comes with mail and networking built in, so it was a natural evolution to produce the Internet. Within the Internet there is no directory synchronization – you need to know who you want to mail and their mail address.

To add Internet access to a LAN, you can use a TCP/IP or Internet gateway for Notes – which is available. Internet providers will furnish you with accounts for your company and generally charge you by connect time. As an alternative, there's no need to connect your LAN to the Internet, nor to have a LAN-based e-mail system running. You could, instead, use a special package (that many of the TCP/IP or Unix vendors sell) that runs under Windows and gives users direct access to the Internet. In this way, the Internet is doing the work of the back-end messaging engine that would otherwise have been Notes. The alternative is to subscribe to CompuServe that offers a Notes gateway and limited Internet access.

Commercial services

An alternative method of linking remote sites, or keeping in touch with colleagues from your industry, is to use a commercial on-line service. Originally, bulletin boards offered crude mail services, but current on-line services provide a mass of information and gateways to other services. For example, the main USA-based services (which all have local dial-in numbers in most countries) such as America Online, Compu-

Serve, Delphi, Genie and Prodigy, all provide business reference, electronic mail to other subscribers and, in many cases, a gateway to Internet. For an electronic mail only service, MCI offers a global network of dial-in points, but very few on-line databases.

Some on-line services, notably CompuServe, have added mail backbone support that could provide the links to remote offices. In this setup, CompuServe can work as a central hub for Notes or any MHS-compatible e-mail software system. A modem on your local mail server and software gateway transfers messages to remote users to CompuServe. CompuServe then re-directs these to either the local CompuServe user, an Internet user or a fax machine, depending on the delivery and addressing instructions.

There's no point in using a commercial service if all you need is a simple method of sending memos around your dozen workers in one office. However, if you need to access business data, such as share information, or you want to provide a central number for remote users to send mail via a hub, then a commercial service has a number of advantages over doing it yourself. Primarily, although the hardware costs won't be much less, since you still need to equip the remote users with modems, you won't have to install, manage or worry about the day-to-day service required to keep it working efficiently.

10

Notes and the Internet

About this chapter

Lotus Notes 4.5 provides an excellent set of applications that let you connect to the Internet and browse Web pages from the comfort of your Notes workspace. By default, Notes 4.5 includes an application that provides the functionality to browse Web pages via a central InterNotes server. In addition, later releases of the software will have a suite of applications that let you connect Notes to the Internet or create your own intranet within the company. These can be downloaded from the Lotus WWW site for free. These applications include a Web Publisher application allows you to convert a Notes database and publish it in HTML form that can be displayed by any WWW browser. Users can browse WWW pages using the Web Navigator and can read newsgroups using the InterNotes News utility.

These four Internet applications let you fully integrate Notes with the Internet. If you want to make databases accessible to other users via the Internet, the Web Publisher simplifies this task tremendously. If all you want is to allow your users to have access to other Web pages on the Internet this is easy to setup using the Web Navigator software.

This chapter covers all these applications showing how to integrate Notes with the Internet or an intranet. It does not cover in any detail the physical links between your Notes server and the Internet, since this will vary according to your setup and operating system.

The InterNotes suite

The series of applications that lets you integrate Notes with the Internet is called InterNotes and is comprised of three main products: Web Publisher, News and Web Navigator. Respectively, these three applications let you convert a Notes database and publish it in HTML format, view newsgroups and browse WWW pages.

The main Notes Web Navigator front-end

How to get InterNotes

Currently-shipping versions of Notes 4.5 do not come with the full InterNotes suite. As a basic, you get just the Web Navigator software, but the rest – including Web Publisher and a Web server application – are available for free download from the Lotus WWW site. Currently, you can download Web Publisher for Notes 3 or Notes 4 for a free evaluation from Lotus' Web site at:

```
www.lotus.com/inotes
```

In addition, you can download an evaluation copy of the Lotus Domino application that turns a Notes server into a full-function Web server application platform. Again, as this book was being written, both these impressive applications are available for download to any supervisor.

InterNotes Web Navigator

The main application that lets your users browse Web pages on the Internet is Web Navigator. This ships with Notes 4.5 and provides most of the functions you would expect of a standard WWW browser – similar to those of popular software such as Netscape Navigator or Microsoft Internet Explorer.

Web Navigator lets you view Web pages that have been designed using the standard HTML markup language. It displays GIF images and links to other pages. Web Navigator also provides FTP (File Transfer Protocol) functions to transfer files to and from the main Web server (probably located at the Internet Service Provider) and a Gopher function that will find items on the Internet.

Setting up Web Navigator

It takes just a couple of steps to setup Notes Server to provide all the functions that support Web Navigator. To provide this support, you need to create a Web database and define your local Web server name so that users can access its correct home page. This sounds complex but is very simple:

1. Make sure that your link to the Internet has been setup – this depends upon the server operating system you are using, but will require the TCP/IP protocol and a modem, ISDN or router link to your local ISP.
2. At the Notes Server prompt, enter the command LOAD WEB.
3. Back at the Notes workstation, open the public address book.
4. Open the Location document for the server and enter the home server name in the InterNotes server field.
5. Your users can now access the Internet by clicking on the Open URL button in any view of Notes.

Action bar button to the Internet

The InterNotes server name you setup will be used by the Notes workstation software to check whether a user is allowed access to the Internet.

Note If you want to provide direct routing of Notes mail messages to foreign Internet addresses, you'll need the SMTP gateway add-on (either from Lotus or other third-party suppliers).

Defining how to access the Internet

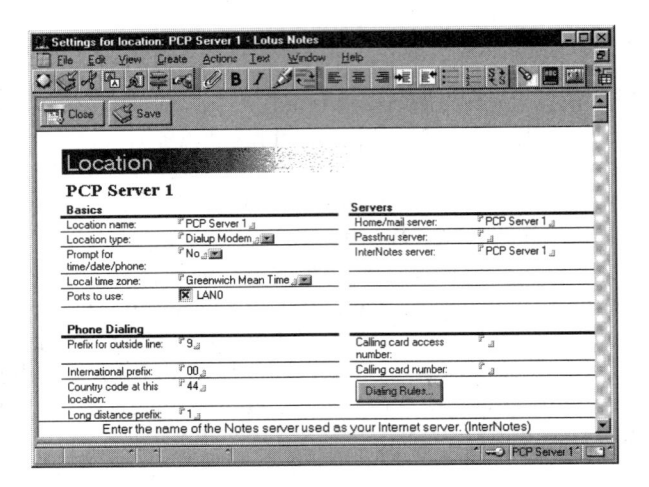

Configuring InterNotes

Many of the InterNotes options are simple to configure and will depend entirely upon the way in which you configure your access to the Internet. For example, the Web pages that you visit are stored in a database – the Web.NSF file. This means that any mobile user can still access Web pages by opening a copy of the Web.NSF file – admittedly, these will be saved pages rather than live data. You can limit the size of this Web database, and the way in which older documents are purged – but the process for doing this is no different to any other Notes database. In this section, are two extra functions that you should setup to get the best from InterNotes – and make InterNotes different from other Notes databases.

Keeping pages up to date

Since Web pages are always changing, it's a good idea to setup an agent that will periodically refresh the contents of the database from the original page on the Internet. InterNotes is supplied with a Refresh agent that will go off onto the Internet and retrieve new content for pages that have been accessed. It does not, however, refresh FTP or Gopher pages, nor those pages that are in a user's private folder.

To setup the Refresh agent, you must first make sure that the agent has the security clearance to run on the InterNotes server. To do this:

1. Open the Personal address book for the InterNotes server and edit the server document.

2. In the Agent Restrictions section, enter your user name in both the 'run restricted LotusScript agents' and 'run unrestricted LotusScript agents' fields. This will let you run the Refresh agent from your workstation on the InterNotes server.
3. From your workspace, open the Web Navigator database.
4. Select *Views ▸ Agents*.
5. You will a list of three pre-defined agents in the right-hand pane. Select the Refresh agent tick box.
6. You are prompted to enter the name of the server on which this agent will run – select the InterNotes server.

Agents help manage your Web pages

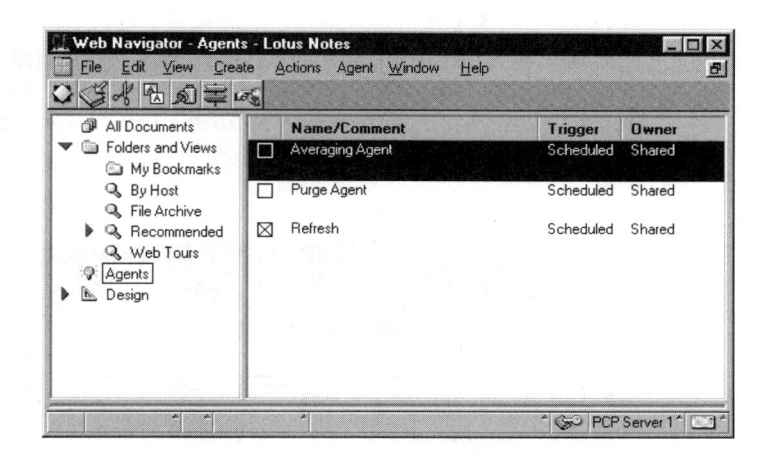

You can setup the agent to run at certain times, or to run periodically using the Personal address book entry on the InterNotes server or select the Agent from the list and right-click on its Schedule option. Alternatively, if you want to force an immediate refresh, select the Refresh Now button.

Accessing the Internet

When a user wants to connect to the Internet and view the first Web page, he or she needs to enter the URL (uniform resource locator) address for the WWW page. A good start is the Lotus site itself which tells you about current Lotus products and Notes itself – for this a user would click on the Open URL button and enter the address www.lotus.com. You don't need to enter the usual prefix of 'http://' since Notes adds this itself. A new icon is automatically added to the user's workspace: Notes Web Navigator. From now on you can access the Internet directly by double-clicking on the Web Navigator icon.

Controlling Access to the Internet

One useful feature that you should setup as soon as possible is the Allow access field of the Administration document. This lets you control access to various Web pages, FTP and Gopher sites on the Internet. It's a simple way to prevent your users accessing unsavory material from your company's server.

To deny access to a particular Web site, open the Administration document for the Web Navigator and move to the Access control section. You'll see two fields: one provides the option to define the sites that can be accessed, the other lets you define the sites that cannot be accessed.

If you want to limit access to prevent users visiting just a couple of sites, enter a '*' in the Allow Access field and list the sites in the Deny Access fields. For example, if you don't want users to visit a site called rude-things you would enter www.rude-things.com in the Deny Access field.

Setting up access control to the Internet

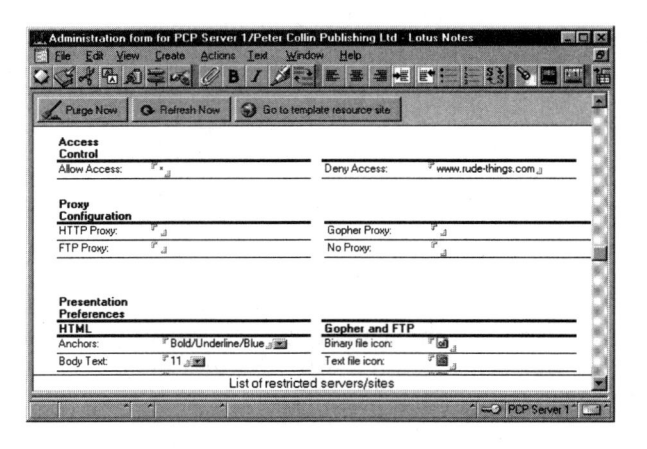

Web Navigator

The main opening screen of Web Navigator shows a graphical workspace with icons representing areas you might be interested in. Each icon links to a particular URL, for example to the Yahoo search engine at www.yahoo.com. You can, of course, change the URLs for this graphical welcome screen or choose to view the data through the usual folder and pane structure. The Web Navigator software lets you display any Web

Web Navigator

page that's been created using the standard HTML page tags. It pulls up pages from the Web.NSF database or accesses a URL on the Internet to retrieve a page directly from a remote server on the Internet.

Editing the graphical home navigator

When you start the Web Navigator, the first thing you will see is a graphic image with icons that provide links to areas on the Internet. These are actually hotspots defined over a simple bitmap and point to different sections of the Yahoo search engine at www.yahoo.com. You can easily modify either the URLs to which the hotspots point, or you can even change the entire Navigator background graphic image.

Setting URL links to hotspots on the Navigator front-end

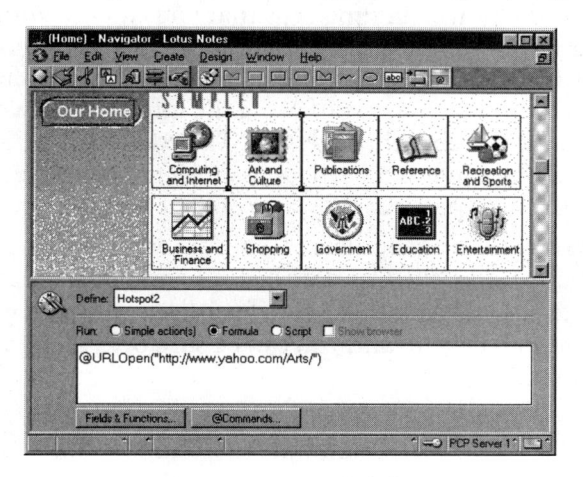

To change one of the icons so that it points to another URL, open the Web Navigator database and carry out the following steps:

1. Choose *View ▸ Show ▸ Folders.*
2. Select the Design-Navigators option and double-click on the <home> from the list of Navigators on the right.
3. You'll see the Navigator window displayed. This shows the background graphic file together with the hotspot areas defined and the URLs to which they point.
4. Highlight any of the hotspot areas and you'll see the command this hotspot executes listed in the window below the graphic image.
5. To change the URL, edit the command in the window beneath the graphic image.

Chapter 10

There are three @-commands that are specific to the WebNavigator and that can be used with any of the hotspots in the home Navigator graphic:

- **@URLGetHeader** – returns information about a particular URL (or site).
- **@URLHistory** – allows you to move through the entries on the history list of sites that have been visited.
- **@URLOpen** – lets you open a specific URL address.

Searching the Web database

One of the powerful functions that you can use with the Web database is the usual Notes search engine. This works in just the same way as usual and lets you search the database for any documents referring to particular text. One way of using the information would be to create an agent that searches through your Web database periodically to find any articles referring to a particular subject. This is a good way of looking through news pages as they are refreshed by the main Refresh Agent.

To create an agent that searches through the articles in the local Web database, select the *Create ▸ Agent* menu option and enter the text you want to search for. Set the article options so that it will only search new or modified articles and you can be sure of keeping your run time down to a minimum.

InterNotes Web Publisher

One of the most powerful features of the Notes 4.5 package is Web Publisher. Originally, this was sold by Lotus at a high, premium price. You can download the software from the Lotus WWW site and it will soon be integrated into the package and provides an excellent way of publishing information onto the Web. If you have not got the Web Publisher (or News) programs on your distribution CD, you can download these applications from the Lotus Web site at:

    www.lotus.com/inews/

Web Publisher will automatically convert any Notes database into a format that can be viewed by WWW browsers. This means that the information will be saved into an HTML format (HTML is a system of codes that represent fonts, links and so on and is used to describe WWW pages). What's wonderful is that Web Publisher does almost everything for you! It will convert a database to an almost exact HTML replica. It converts not only the data and the formatting, but also any images (which are automatically converted to GIF format) and any documents (which are automatically converted to URL links). It even provides a way for WWW browsers to access the database index to search for documents.

To give you an idea of how simple life becomes with Web Publisher, here are two scenarios for ways of publishing data onto the Internet:

- Publishing via a traditional method:
    1. Import data into an HTML editor.
    2. Format data, headings and text.
    3. Add jumps to other pages and links to documents as HTML commands.
    4. Save individual files.
    5. Upload files using FTP to your Web server.

- Publishing with Web Publisher
    1. Allow any user to edit the Notes database that contains your data.
    2. Run Web Publisher to convert all data, graphics and doclinks to HTML.
    3. The pages are now on the Notes server and can be accessed by any user. That's it!

To load the Web Publisher application and setup the server, enter the command Load Webpub at the Notes Server command line – and that's about it. The bulk of Web Publisher works automatically and there's very little for you to configure or setup! You can add any of the standard @commands to enhance a form, and Web Publisher will do its best to translate these into the correct HTML form commands. However, for ease of use, Web Publisher is hard to beat. It does what you want, automatically.

InterNotes News

One of the best ways of keeping up to date with the information that's available on a particular topic is to subscribe to one of the Internet's news groups. These have gained a certain notoriety over the past years, but the majority are informative and provide an excellent resource. InterNotes News lets you subscribe to any of the 20,000-odd news groups that are active at any one time. You can view the articles in a news group and the article itself. If you ever used a commercial news reader or the News window of products such as Netscape Navigator, you will be familiar with the way these groups work.

To startup the News function, enter the command 'Load InNews' on the Notes server. Before you can start to use the News feature you will need to ensure you have an Internet connection for the server. You must also get specific information from your ISP (Internet Service Provider) – the address of its news service server and a password or filter that might also be required. The News database needs to be configured with this information, and is then ready to run.

Domino Web Server

The latest addition to Notes is the release of the Domino software application that turns any Notes server into a full Web application server. The best way of getting hold of the Domino application is to download the latest version from the Lotus WWW site. Since the application is still evolving, it's best to check the Lotus Web site for current details, but it provides a simple way of creating a powerful Web application server that integrates well with the Web Publisher software to provide a total Web solution.

Security and the Internet

One of the important points that must not be forgotten is that when you connect to the Internet you are opening a potential doorway for hackers to gain access to your server. There are all sorts of tricks to prevent this from happening, but there are in practice three main options. All these require you to configure and setup third-party Internet software that will work with your TCP/IP protocol and connection to the ISP.

Firewall security

This system is as good as the firewall software that it is running. An InterNotes server is connected to your company network and can only gain access to the Internet via another server running a firewall software protection program. This firewall software will try to prevent unauthorized users from gaining access to your network.

Isolated LAN security

You can setup a similar security feature to the firewall configuration by adding a passthru server between your main Notes server and the InterNotes server. In this setup, the InterNotes server connects directly to the Internet but is located by itself on an isolated network. It can only be contacted via a passthru connection (see Chapter 5) between it and the main Notes server.

Protocol security

Lastly, you setup a secure system using two separate network adapter cards within the InterNotes server. In this setup, the InterNotes server is connected to the Internet via a network adapter running TCP/IP and is connected to the main company network by a network adapter running the SPX (or any other – but not TCP/IP) protocol.

When you connect your Notes server to the Internet, in any way, you must bear in mind that this can provide all sorts of potential security implications. You should make quite sure that the ACLs are configured to prevent any unauthorized users or guests gaining access. You should make sure that your Public Name and Address books are protected and you should be extra careful with virus scanning.

If you are using Web browser software other than the Web Navigator software, for example either Netscape Navigator or Microsoft Internet Explorer, you should also watch out for applets. These are tiny programs that boost the functionality of a browser during the session. There are two main types supported by newer browsers: Java and ActiveX. Both add great functions to the Web pages but can also be used to plant timebombs or a virus in your system – beware.

11

Agents and automation

About this chapter

Notes 4.5 provides a new feature for users and administrators – Agents. These are actually very similar to the old macro function of Notes 3 and allow you to automate tasks. With an Agent you can carry out a housekeeping chore, such as moving incoming mail from one folder to another, or you can carry out a simple data archival at a particular time. One Agent is triggered by an action (the arrival of a mail message) the other by a timer (to happen at a particular time).

Agents can be written to use any Notes command and to be triggered from a variety of events, user actions or timers. They are an excellent way to tailor your user environment and to save time with administrative tasks. This chapter shows you how to create and program Agents and how to configure them to run from a certain event.

Automating tasks with Agents

Agents carry out tasks at a particular time or when triggered by an action. They can help speed up tedious tasks, such as filing or sorting documents and archiving old material, or can be used by users to add a degree of rules-based intelligence to the Notes e-mail system. There are two types of Agent: personal Agents that are created by and used solely by you, and shared Agents that are created by an administrator (called the designer, in this case) which can be used by a group of users. You should decide its type when you create your Agent, since the personal or shared flag cannot be changed once it's been designed.

Creating a new Agent

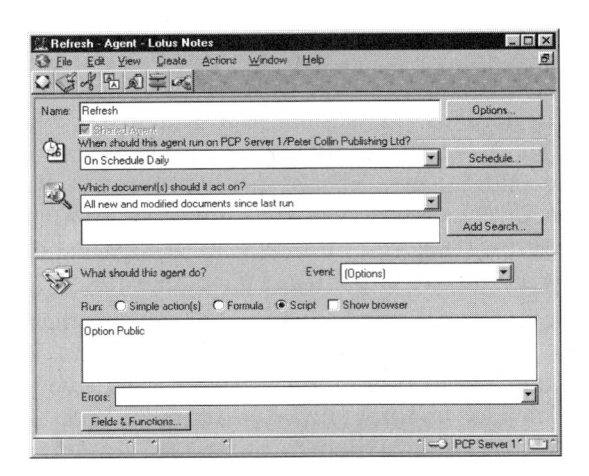

Agents are simple in concept and consist of just three basic elements:

1. A selection formula that selects a particular document or range of documents.
2. A trigger that activates the Agent – either a timer or a selection procedure. The triggers can be a time or event (such as new mail, a document changes or user selection).
3. A series of commands that is carried out when the Agent runs. This can be by a Notes-supplied action, an @function or a LotusScript program, however the commands will only work on the documents selected by the selection formula in (1.).

Automating tasks with Agents   199

Creating an Agent

If you want to create a personal Agent, you will need to have your Create Personal Agents option selected in the ACL. If you want to create a shared Agent, you'll need the Designer or equivalent permission set in the ACL. Once you have the correct rights setup, you can get down to the business of writing Agents. There are two ways of creating Agents: copying an existing Agent (and then making changes) or creating an Agent from scratch. Agents are associated with a database, but you can copy an Agent between two databases.

- Viewing Agents

To view the Agents associated with a particular database, select the database and choose the *View ▸ Agents* menu option.

Viewing the Agents you have created

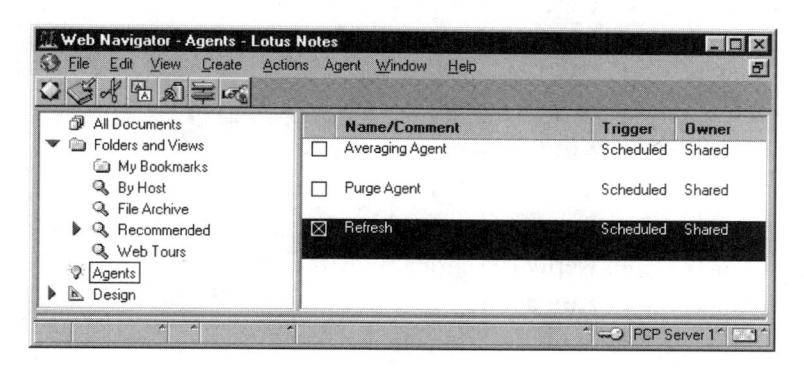

- Copying Agents

To copy an Agent, highlight the Agent from the list and select *Edit ▸ Copy* and then either move to the new database or stay in the existing database and select *Edit ▸ Paste* to create a new copy of the Agent.

- Creating New Agents

To create a new Agent, open the database and select *Create ▸ Agent* menu option and enter a name for the Agent.

Configuring an Agent

Once you have copied an existing Agent or if you create a new Agent, you can then start to configure the way in which it works and responds to actions. When you use the *Create ▸ Agent* menu option, the dialog boxes step you through the elements that make up the Agent and ask you to define the selection formula, the actions and the trigger. To edit

Chapter 11

the actions of an Agent, view the list of Agents for the database using the *View ▸ Agent* menu option and double-click on the Agent that you want to edit.

Actions for an Agent

An Agent can carry out simple actions – or multiple simple actions – that you pick from a list. The actions you define will carried out in the order in which you insert the actions (except for the Delete from database command which is always performed as the final action).

Agent Actions:

- Copy to database
- Copy to folder
- Delete from database
- Mark document read
- Mark document unread
- Modify field
- Modify fields by form
- Move to folder
- Remove from folder
- Reply to sender
- Run agent
- Send document
- Send mail message
- Send newsletter summary
- @function formula
- LotusScript program

Agent Triggers

There are several ways in which an Agent can be triggered to run:
- User chooses the Agent from the Actions menu.
- User highlights Agent in Agents View pane using the *Actions ▸ Run* menu.
- Document is mailed to the database.
- Document is changed in the database.
- Document is pasted in the database.
- At a particular time according to a schedule.

Automating tasks with Agents

Actions that trigger an Agent

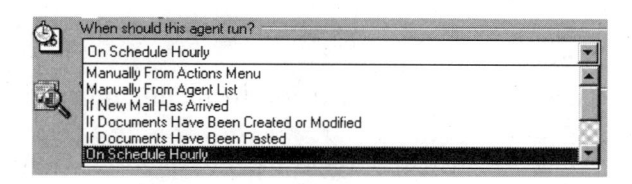

Agent document selection formula

Unlike other formulas, Agents will only work on a range of selected documents. These documents can be chosen in a number of ways according to a set of criteria:

- All documents in the database.
- New and modified documents (since Agent was last run).
- Unread documents.
- All documents visible in the current open view.
- User selected documents.
- Current document.

Example: Vacation Agent

As you can see, Agents are straightforward and simple to create. The range of basic actions is wide enough to cover most situations and, if not, you can always turn to @formula.

Creating an e-mail reply Agent

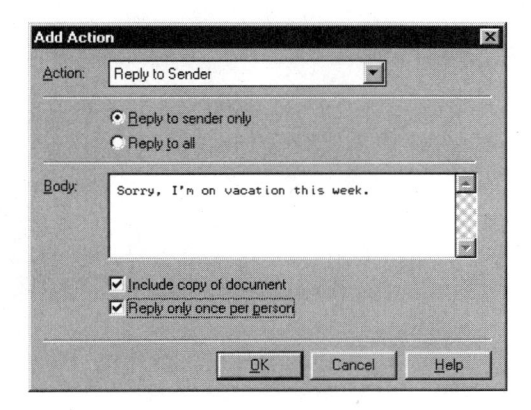

To give you an idea of how simple it is to create an Agent, the following example will look after your e-mail when you're on vacation. If any mail messages are received, it will reply with a simple message telling them that you are currently on vacation, but will look at their message on your return.

Chapter 11

1. Open the mail database and choose the *View ▸ Agents* menu option.
2. Select *Create ▸ Agent* from the menu and call it 'Vacation reply agent'.
3. Select the way the Agent will be triggered – in this case, a scheduled run, select On Schedule Hourly.
4. Select Run once every 4 hours.
5. Select Don't start until this date and enter your vacation start date, do similar for Stop running on this date.
6. Click Simple Actions and click on the Add Action button.
7. Select Action: Reply to Sender.
8. Of the options listed, click on Reply to Sender Only
9. Type in the reply message 'Sorry, I'm on vacation this week.'
10. Click on the Reply only once per person option to prevent one person getting more than one automatic reply.
11. Click OK and close and save the agent.

12

Creating Notes applications

About this chapter

One of the greatest benefits of Notes is that it contains a fully-featured programming language. This lets you create any application that can look at a new or existing Notes database. In this chapter, you will see how to create a new database and a visual interface to go with it – this is the simplest way of creating a basic Notes application and involves almost no programming: just point, click and drag to create the database. Notes 4.5 now lets you design panes, windows and folders for applications – these are covered in detail – together with the ways of creating a full-text search index. Lastly, this chapter shows you how to setup the final parts of a database: defining the ACL for security, designing an icon and writing an About… and Using… documents.

Designing a database

Notes applications center around a database. This contains documents that hold the data; within each document are pre-defined fields into which data can be inserted. Some applications use just one database, some extract information from several databases. The information is shown to a user through a form; most applications have several forms that show the data in the database in different ways. For example, in a diary one form will show your day's appointments, another your week's appointments and a third a to-do list. All three display some of the information that's stored in one database. In addition, views arrange the documents according to the data in a particular field – for example, an invoice-tracking system could list invoices by number, customer or date.

Types of database

Before you start creating a new database application, it's worth outlining the different types of application that can be created and the individual elements that make up an application. This will give you a broad overview and help you understand the terms in the rest of the chapter. There are five main types of application that are normally created with Notes.

Broadcast

An application that has (normally) fixed data that is displayed to users. Good examples are a news-service that displays news stories; a company newsletter; financial share information. In each example, the user sees an updated version of the information which can be real-time perhaps for the share-price information – and does not normally allow a user to edit, change or enter new data.

Reference

Applications similar to the broadcast type, but that are not real-time and form part of a library resource that can be searched by users. Examples include back issues of articles from a newspaper, market research information for the previous few years or a company policy and mission statement.

Tracking

This type of application relies on users updating information to provide an accurate, up-to-date source of data. A good example is a client-tracking system in which users enter when they last contacted the client or what was done for the client.

Discussion

These applications can be very structured or completely free-form, but all rely on users reading the display and entering their own remarks or comments that are then seen by the other users in the discussion. This could be good for meetings connecting remote users, to argue through policies or to produce user-feedback on something over a period of time.

Approvals

Workflow applications are the most sophisticated from a programmer's point of view. These carry out jobs automatically, for example sending orders via a particular chain of users, each requiring an authorization, or a diary that sends out reminders for meetings.

In each of these types of application, the designer can now use the Notes 4.5 NotesFlow feature. This lets you route forms or data between users, between databases or to and from other applications or to run batch programs on a process.

Extending Notes Applications

To make the most of any Notes application you can use the range of built-in commands and functions, together with its support for the platform's native range of features. For example, under Windows you can use OLE 2 and DDE; on a Macintosh you can use the Subscribe feature; database access is now considerably easier with support for ODBC drivers and standard commands. In Notes 3 you might have had to turn to C programming to reach the Notes API, but in release 4.5 you can use the LotusScript tool to program just about any function you might want to implement.

What makes a database?

Any Notes database is made up of four main elements: forms, fields, documents and views.

Form

A form defines what a document looks like. How the fields are arranged, layout of headings, logos or text. Applications normally have several types of form: for example, a diary has one form to enter a new appointment and another which displays your day's appointments.

Field

A field is a named element in a form that can contain a particular type of data. For example, in a Name and Address book, the person's telephone number could be stored in a field called 'HOME_TEL' that can contain up to 10 numbers. The field can then be referenced by commands.

Document

A document is equivalent to a record in a database. It contains all the information that a user entered using a form. For example, in an invoice system, each separate invoice would be stored as a separate document – which was created by entering data into the fields displayed on a form.

View

A view is a particular way of looking at data stored in the documents within a database. For example, an invoice system might have a view to show invoice documents by invoice number, another by customer name and a third by data.

Folders

Folders allow users to collect and organize information and documents. They are often linked to Views, in that they can display particular sets of documents, however the user must manually transfer the documents to the folder – folders cannot have selection formulas. Folders are usually used within Navigators.

Navigators

Navigators are a new feature of Notes 4.5 that allow users to see, graphically, how documents are organized and allows users to move around a database structure without having to select a new View or menu command. Notes includes standard Navigators that include folder icons that are nested like a directory tree to show how elements of a database are organized. Navigators are also an excellent way of transforming any existing Notes 3 database. You can keep the same forms and data and create a stunning graphical Navigator that uses icons to lead users to common views.

Formulas and scripts

Formulas are built-in commands that allow a programmer to process data in fields or do something to a document. For example, an invoice system might use a formula command to check that there's no other invoice with the same invoice number or might retrieve the price of each item as it's name is entered.

Scripts are based on the LotusScript language that makes it easier to program complex rules that would otherwise take a long @formula. LotusScript also provides access to ODBC drivers and other external routines. As mentioned at the start of this chapter, LotusScript is Lotus' common tool that will work across almost all its Windows applications including Approach, 1-2-3 and WordPro.

Agents and actions

Agents – which were previously called *macros* – let you add automation to any application. You could create an Agent that checks automatically through a database of expense claim forms and, if they have not got signature approval, will remind the accounts department – by e-mail – of the list of outstanding claims. Agents are covered in greater detail in Chapter 10.

How to create a database

There are three paths that can be taken when designing a new database. The first is the most straightforward where you create the new database from scratch, defining the forms, views and fields that make up the database. You will normally store the fledgling database on your local hard disk until it's finished.

The second method is faster; you use one of the existing example template databases supplied with Notes as a basis for your application. You can then easily edit and tailor the database to your requirements.

It's also possible to use a design template as a foundation that links to your application. If you want, you can arrange it so that any changes made to the design template you used are reflected in your application. If linking to the template, you must be sure to save your application on the same server as the template.

The last method is used for large, complex applications. In this case, there will be a team of programmers each working on one section of the application. The application file should be stored on the server during development and each programmer given Designer rights within the file's ACL rights list.

Creating a new, blank database

To create a Notes application from scratch, you must first create an empty, blank database. To do this, select the *File ▸ Database ▸ New* menu option and select the '-Blank-' design template from the list on the left of the dialog box.

Creating a new, blank database

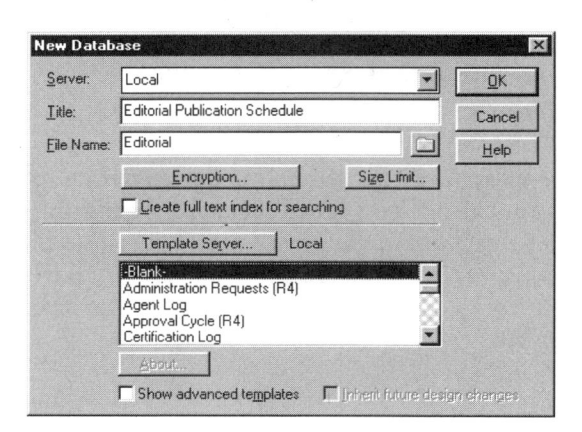

Give the application a title. The title is displayed under the icon in a user's workspace (it can be up to 256 bytes long – which might not be 256 characters long if you use multi-byte accented characters). Notes will generate a filename for the new database. Lastly, normally you will not want you new application to inherit any changes made in the template – so make sure that the check box is not selected.

To create the new database, select the New button. Notes creates the new file and opens the applications ready for you to start modifying it.

Creating a database using a template

By far the simplest method – and the best way to start experimenting with Notes – is to use one of the templates supplied with Notes. These have a defined form, view and associated formula but don't have any data stored in documents. There are templates for a range of applications including: customer tracking, things to do, general discussion and news.

If you are taking over as manager of a Notes site, or are particularly pleased with an existing application you use, you can turn it into a template by copying the database without any documents (a check-box option) and giving it the NTF extension.

Creating a new database from a template

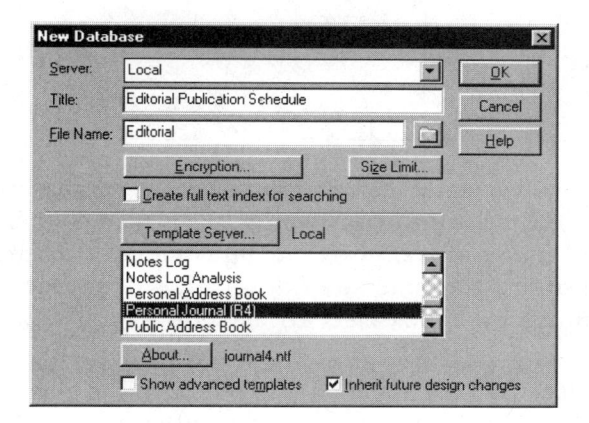

To create a new database that's based on an existing template, select the *File ▸ Database ▸ New* menu option. To the left of the dialog box is a list of the available templates (you might need to select the server with templates if you didn't install templates on your server).

Enter a new title for the application. The title is displayed under the icon in a user's workspace (it can be up to 256 bytes long – which might not be 256 characters long if you use multi-byte accented characters). Lastly, normally you will not want you new application to inherit any changes made in the template – so make sure that the check-box is not selected.

To create the new database, select the New button. Notes creates the new file and opens the applications ready for you to start modifying it.

Creating a database by copying

If you have already created a database that you think is similar to the design of your new application, you could just copy the existing database. In some cases, you might want to copy the entire database, with all its documents and data (such as for a new stock list or a price list), but normally you will only want to copy the design of the database.

Copying a database and its data

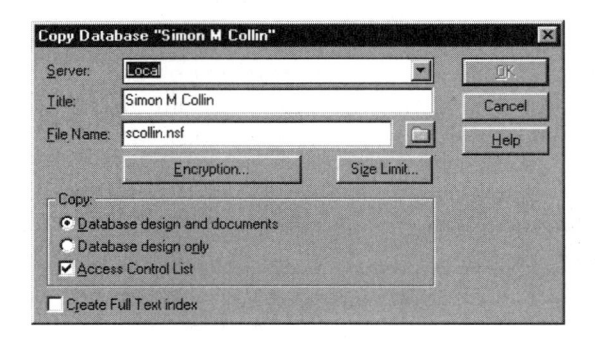

To copy a database's design, select the database icon on your workspace (install it into your workspace if it's not there), and choose the *File ▸ Database ▸ New Copy* menu command. The dialog box lets you enter a new filename and title for the copy, together with the server location for the file (select Local if you want it copied to your workstation).

Select the Design Only radio button at the bottom of the dialog box and de-select the Access Control List check-box before you click on the New Copy button to create the copy. If you select the ACL check-box, the rights list will also be copied and, unless you have at least Designer rights, you won't be able to change the design of the newly copied database.

How to create a form

Once you have created a new database, the next job is to design the panes and forms that a user will use to enter or view data stored in the documents. A form defines the layout and structure of data stored in a document. A form normally contains fields that are placed on the form (a field is a named element that can hold a particular type of data) and static text, logos or pictures that help a user understand how to enter information or just make the form look good.

A form is used to add data to a database. If a user wants to add a new document, the user normally selects the Create menu which gives a list of possible forms. Choose a form and fill in the fields to create a new document. An example of this is the electronic memo database supplied with Notes – select the Create menu option and you see the option to create a new memo – this is a form that lets you enter the address of the recipient and the text of the message. The fields are the white boxes into which you enter the name of recipient, the subject and the memo. Any other descriptive text in the form is static text that's just there to clarify the form.

If you created a new database by using a template or copying the design of an existing database, then you will already have the forms that are associated with the database. If you created an empty, blank database, then you must create new forms and add fields, text and other elements to it. Just like the previous section, regarding creating a database, there are three possible ways of creating a form. You can use an existing form that was part of a design template. Secondly, you can copy a form from any database or template – and, if you want, you can link the new form to inherit any changes made to the original form. Lastly, you can create a form from scratch.

Viewing the forms in a database

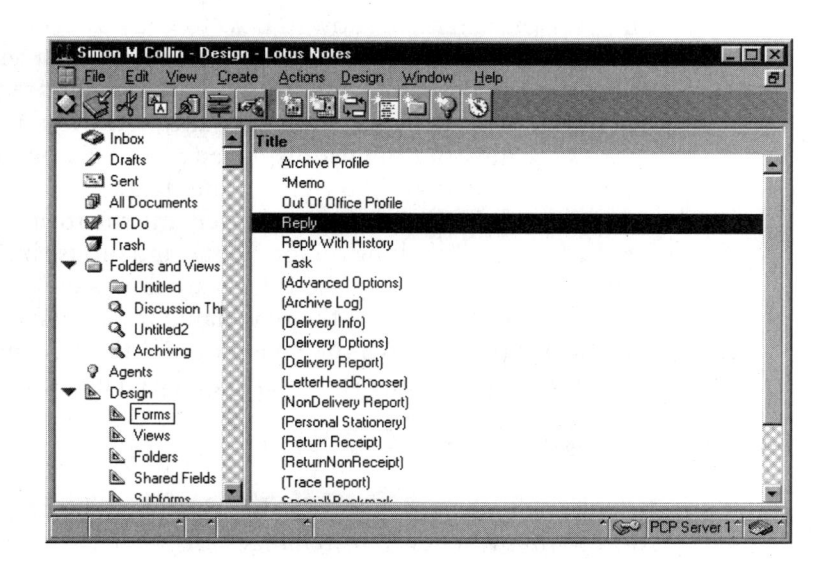

Copying a form from a different database

Copying a form cuts the time it takes to create an application, but if you plan on making a lot of changes, you might find it quicker to create a new form. To widen your scope, Notes lets you copy a form from one database and it use it in another, or copy a form and use it in the same database. To copy a form, select the database that contains the form that you want to copy. Select the *View ▸ Design* menu option and double-click on the Forms item in the pane displayed on the left of the screen (the other elements that can be designed are also displayed in this pane). A list of available forms is displayed: highlight the form you want to copy.

Select the Copy button at the bottom of the dialog box (in the Clipboard section). As you might guess, this copies the form design to the clipboard. Now select the database into which you want to insert the form. Choose the *View ▸ Design* menu option and select the Forms item from the pane on the left of the screen which will list the existing forms – if any. Choose the Paste button at the bottom of the dialog box. This pastes the previously copied form into the new database. Choose Done to finish and save your new form.

Copying a form from the same database

The previous example showed how to copy a form from one database to another. It's even easier to copy a form within the same database. Select the database you want to work in and choose the *View ▸ Design* and select the Forms item from the pane on the left of the screen. Highlight the form from the list displayed in the dialog box and select the New Copy button on the right of the dialog box. A copy of the form opens on screen. You now have to rename the form – do this by selecting the form and clicking on the right-hand mouse button and selecting Properties. This pops up the form's attributes dialog box listing background colors, etc. Enter the new name in the Name field and choose the OK button. To save the changes, and the new name, select *File ▸ Close Window* and choose Yes to save the changes.

Inheriting changes to a form

Just like a database design, it's also possible to link a form to a template form so that whenever any changes are made to the design of the original form, these are reflected in the new form. To do this, select the database that contains the new form. Choose the *Design ▸ View* menu option and highlight the Forms item in the pane on the left; choose the form you want to work with from the list shown in the dialog box. Choose the Info button which displays the date the form was created and any links to inherit changes.

At the bottom of the dialog box is a field that holds the name of the design template which holds the original form design. If the name is present, any changes made to the original form will be reflected in this new form.

Removing form design inheritance

If you do not want the new form to inherit changes, delete the form name from this field. When you do this, the check box below is activated – select it to prevent the new form inheriting any changes.

Create a new, blank form

If you want to create a new, empty form or you created an empty database not based on any template complete the following steps.

1. Select the database that you want to work in.
2. Choose the *Design ▶ View* menu option and select the Form item from the pane on the left of the screen which pops up a dialog box listing any existing forms for this database.
3. To create a new, empty form choose the New button; Notes creates a new blank form, opens it and places you in Design mode within the form.

Creating a new form from the database

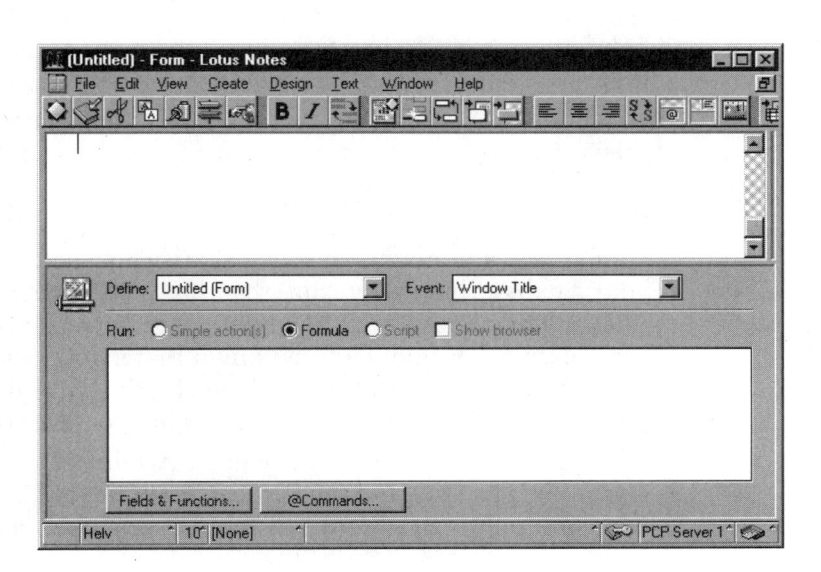

The form still has no attributes – no name, title or colors let alone any fields, or static text.

Setting a form's attributes

When you create a form, you should, before you start placing fields, define the form's attributes. This sets the form's name, together with its form type and a number of other important attributes. To set any attributes for a form, open the form (if you have just created a form, you will already be in the form) and select the *Design ▸ Form Attribute* menu option.

Naming a form

If you have just created a new, blank form or if you have copied a form and need to give it a new name, you will have to use the Form's attributes dialog box. To give a form a name choose the *Design ▸ Form Properties* menu option which pops up a dialog box listing the form's background colors and an empty field at the top into which you can enter its name. When entering the name, remember that Notes orders forms alphabetically within the Compose menu, so try to name the forms logically and, if possible, so that they will appear in order. Notes will use the first letter of the Form's name as an accelerator key (so you choose the form by pressing the key from within the Compose menu). If you want to choose a different letter within the name as the form's accelerator key, place an underscore character ('_') before the letter. For example: a form named 'New Entry' will have 'N' as its accelerator key. To force Notes to use 'E' enter the name as: 'New _Entry'. Note that a Macintosh doesn't use accelerator keys.

Choose OK when you have finished entering the form's name and then use the *File ▸ Save* to save the form under its new name.

Using pseudonyms in forms

Sometimes, you might want use a particular name for a form within your database, but then realize that this doesn't mean much to the users (they might complain or you might create a foreign edition of the database). Notes lets you add a synonym that's displayed in the Compose menu instead of the form's real name. Nothing else changes: all the formulas for the form work as before and old documents can still be read.

To give a form a new display name, while keeping its original name within the program, use the vertical bar symbol ('|') when entering the name in the *Design ▸ Form Attributes* dialog box. For example, to display the word 'Lettre' instead of 'Mail' in an e-mail database you want to convert to French, type 'Lettre | Mail' in the name field.

Types of form

Notes organizes forms within a database in three categories. These are defined in the *Design ▸ Form Attribute* box, below the form's name. Click on the down-arrow to the left of the Type field and select from the three types of form available:

Document for forms that create new main documents within the database.

Response to document for forms that will create a document that's a response to a main document entry; in the hierarchy view, response to document entries appear under the corresponding document, indented to the right.

Response to response for forms that will create a document that's a response to a main document, or a response to a response; in the hierarchy view, these documents are arranged below their related document and indented to the right.

Setting a default form

Each database should have one default form (only one is allowed); this is normally the main document type of form specified above. If you want to set your current form as the default, make sure that the Default Database Form check-box is selected in the Form Attribute dialog box. An asterisk (*) will appear beside the form's name when the database's existing forms are viewed.

One useful feature is the next check-box option in the Form Attribute screen, Inherit Default Field Values. This will copy the data from the form displayed when the user selects the Compose menu option and inserts the data into the new document that's been created – which is particularly useful for response forms.

Designing a form

The design of a form affects the way a user sees the data in a database and how easy the application is to use. The form contains not only the fields that hold the data, but also static text that describes field names together with graphics, color and design that help make the form user-friendly. If you have just created a new, empty form Notes automatically opens the form and places you in Design mode. If you want to open and start designing a form, select the *Design ▸ Forms* menu item, from the dialog box, highlight the form name you want to edit, and select the Edit button to open the form in Design mode.

General design guidelines

When designing a form, try to follow some simple basic guidelines; your forms will have to be used by tens or hundreds of users – so try to make them simple and straightforward to use. One point that's often forgotten by the designer is that not every user will have the same setup as he or she does. The size of screen, resolution and color capabilities can vary greatly in any company. The basic Windows $3.1x$ resolution is 640×480 pixels, but many users will have graphics that are compatible with SVGA or higher (up to 1024×768). This talk of graphics resolution and color means that you cannot be certain of how your form will look on a user's screen. If it takes up the entire screen on your SVGA system, only part of the screen will be displayed on a normal VGA system. If you use a dark background color, it will be difficult to read anything on the LCD screen of a laptop computer. In short, try to stick to plain, pale (preferably white) backgrounds, limit the use of colors and make sure that the form's still usable even if the user has to around due to a low-resolution screen. These limits might make you give up hope of creating a good-looking form design. However, there are plenty of tips that will help you design a form that looks good and is usable:

- The most legible font on any screen is a sans-serif, such as Arial or Helvetica. Don't mix more than two or three different fonts in a form, or it will look like a mess.
- Use static text to make fields easily identified. Try to align the text vertically and align fields to give a cleaner, less cluttered feel
- Group related buttons or options into an area to make it easier for a user to navigate the form. Often, designers put a box around the options, with a caption.
- Arrange fields and buttons in a logical order so that, for example in an e-mail application, the user enters the recipient's name before the users to receive a carbon copy.
- Use small graphics or icons to break up a block of options or fields. Also make sure that there's plenty of vertical space between fields or lines of text.

- When adding captions to buttons, give some thought to accelerator hot-letters. If a user's on a laptop, they might find it easier to use [Alt]+[hot-key] combinations to navigate than to use a mouse.

Adding text to a form

Adding static, descriptive text to a form is simple, if not very flexible. When you have opened the form in Edit mode (*Design ▸ Forms ▸ Edit*) you will see a flashing vertical cursor indicate your position on the form. A form accepts text just like a basic text editor – all text is left-aligned unless otherwise formatted.

To place text at a particular location, press the [Enter] key to add new lines and move down (you can use the arrow keys once you have entered lines) and then either use tabs or spaces to move the text in from the left.

To center a line of text, position the cursor in the line (you don't have to highlight the line) and select the *Text ▸ Alignment* menu option.

You can change the font, attribute, size or color of any word, character or line by highlighting the text, then selecting the Text menu option.

Tip　To create a horizontal line separating related fields, highlight the entire line and set it to underline using the *Text ▸ Underline* menu option.

Defining all the attributes of a paragraph is easy: move the cursor to the paragraph, then select the *Text ▸ Paragraph* menu option. This displays a dialog box that lets you set the inter-line space, tabs, alignment and so on.

If you want to organize yourself in large, complex forms, you will find a time-saver is using paragraph styles. These, just like any word-processor, let you store all the definitions of a paragraph of text under a name. Set the paragraph with the attributes you want, then choose *Text ▸ Paragraph Styles* menu option. You can save the style of the current paragraph by entering a name. To recall the style and apply it to another paragraph, move to the new paragraph, pop up the same dialog box and highlight the previously saved style.

Tip　If you have already roughed out a template in your wordprocessor, you can import most common WP formats directly into the form – use *File ▸ Import*.

Adding graphics to a form

There are two ways of adding graphics to a Notes form: first, you can use the Windows Clipboard, second you can use Notes' import filter. Whichever method you use, remember that adding graphics makes the forms bigger, which slows down the speed of display and, if you get carried away, could bog down your network with traffic.

The simplest method ideal for small logos or even a signature is to use Windows' Paintbrush. Start Paintbrush (in the Applications group) and create your image. Now copy it to the Clipboard (via *Edit ▸ Copy*) and move back to Notes.

Move to the line in the form where you want to place the graphic and choose *Create ▸ Layout ▸ Graphic* menu option.

Including a graphic on a form

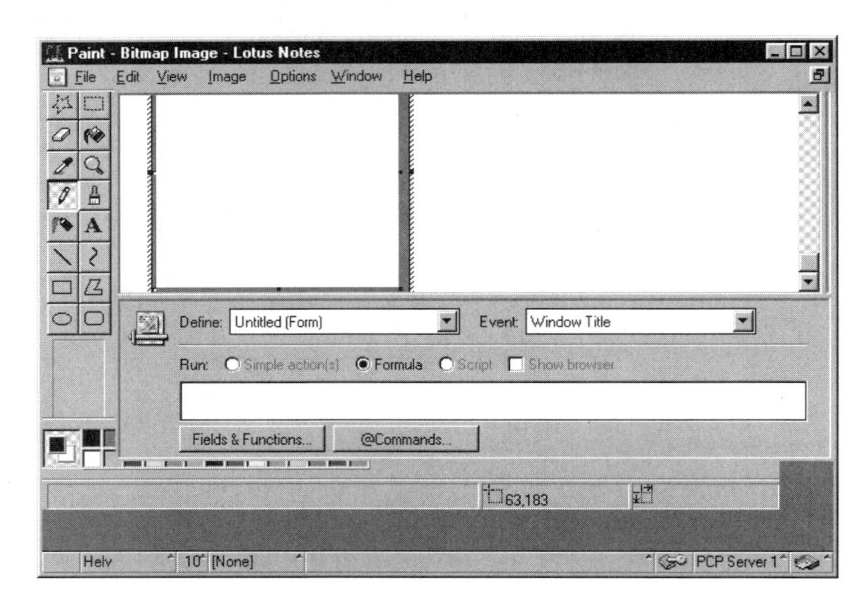

Note: If you want to add a graphic that will carry out an action when clicked – a hotspot graphic on the form – you should choose the 'Graphic Button' option rather than a simple 'Graphic' option when placing your graphic on the form. (To place a graphic, choose *Create ▸ Layout* menu option.)

Defining fields

Now that you have created a new form and added static text and graphics to it, it's time to add the fields. Fields are named elements that can contain text, numbers, dates or pictures. If you have copied an existing form, you will see that it's already got fields in place – you can edit or move these around or add new fields. Fields carry the information that makes up a particular document in a database: they can carry just a date or a report several pages long. When you are in form Edit mode (use *Design ▸ Forms ▸ Edit* option) the form is presented rather like a simple text editor. If you are starting with a blank form, you will need to press the [Enter] key to create blank lines. Any text or fields you create will be left-aligned by default. You can then position them using the *Text ▸ Alignment* menu options. If you are going to copy, edit or create new fields you will need to have at least Designer rights in the database's ACL. If you are editing a database that's on your local hard disk, you will automatically have Manager rights.

Adding a new field to a form

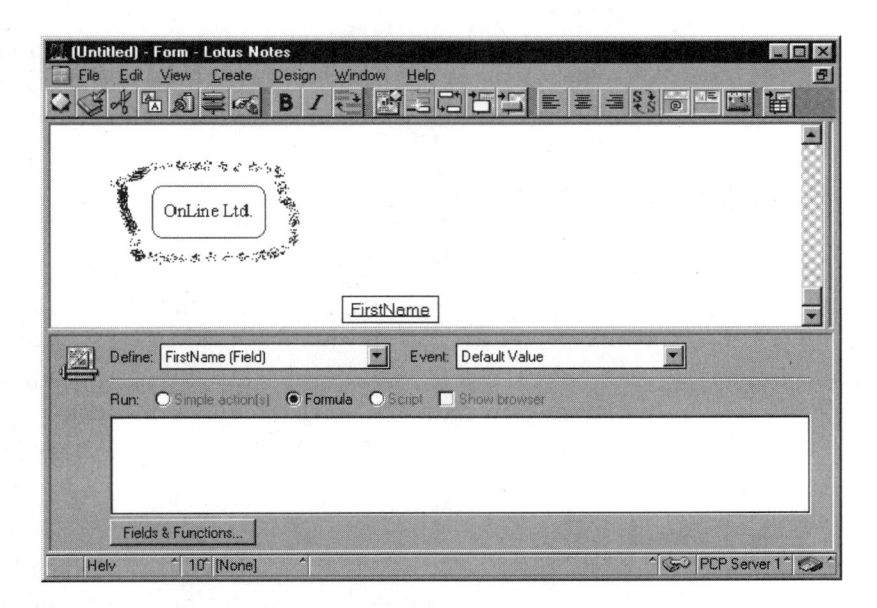

Notes displays fields on a form as boxes. Inside each box is the field name; the size and depth of the box are defined within the field definition dialog box, discussed on the next page.

Chapter 12

Create a field

To create a new field on a form, move to the point where you want the field to be placed (you can always move it later) and select the *Design ▸ New Field* menu option. A dialog box appears asking whether the field should be accessible to other forms. Some fields you will want to access from other forms, but the default is the first option – to create a new field that's only used within the current form. Click on OK and the field definition dialog box pops up. See below for details on how to complete the Field Definition box.

Single-use fields

Single-use fields are the most common field type: they can only be used within the current form. The data they contain cannot be accessed from another form in the same document. Even if you use the same field name in another form, the two fields are in no way related. To create one of these fields, choose the first option.

Shared fields

A shared field can be used in any form within a database. Each time you change a shared field from one form, its new value is reflected in all the other forms. If you create a shared field, it is shown with a heavy, bold border to the field box.

Delete a field

To delete a field, first highlight the field by moving the pointer on to it and clicking as you drag across the field. The field inverts (black on white), you can delete it by choosing the *Edit ▸ Clear* menu option.

If you do delete a field from a form, you don't change the data in the database – any data that was previously entered through this field is still in the database. You can view this data again by pasting the field into a form.

Copy a field

To copy a field, highlight the particular field by moving the pointer on to it and clicking as you drag across the field. The field inverts to show it's selected. You can now use normal Windows copy and paste tools that are accessed from the Edit menu. To copy a field, select *Edit ▸ Copy*, move the pointer to the position where you want to place the new field and select *Edit ▸ Paste*.

You will see that Notes appends '_1', '_2' and so on after the field name of any copies. You can change these field names within the field definition box described later.

Move a field

To move a field, use a combination of the previous two commands – Delete and Copy. First, highlight the field you want to move, select the *Edit ▸ Cut* menu option, move the pointer to where you would like to place the field and choose *Edit ▸ Paste*.

Setting a field definition

The position and alignment of a field are all set using normal text editing commands – in the Edit and Text menu options. To set up the definition of the field itself (it's name, what it contains and how it operates) you need to access the field definition dialog box.

Setting the text alignment properties

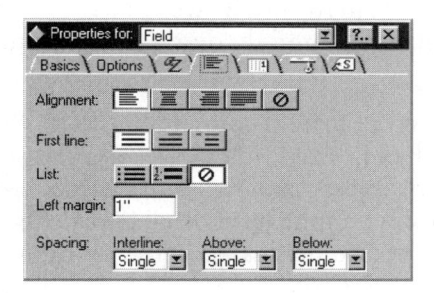

To change any of a field's attributes, highlight the field and select the *Design ▸ Field Definition* menu option (you can also highlight the field and press Enter or double-click on the field to pop up the field definition window).

Name:

The first attribute is the field's name. This can be up to 32 characters long but cannot contain spaces. You can use the underscore character, however, and the name is case sensitive.

Help description:

The second attribute is a line of help text that appears in the status bar at the bottom of the window when a user selects the field. On most monitors, you will have room to display around 65–70 characters.

Data type:

Data type defines the type of information that the field will contain. There are nine types of data that you can choose from the pull-down list box:

Text The field can contain plain text, with no attributes or styles (see Rich Text). Normally used for the name, address and title of forms.

Number The field can contain any standard mathematical number (0..9, +, -, E, e, .). Notes can operate with up to 14-digit numbers.

Time The field contains letters and numbers that describe a time or date. Once you have selected this data type, choose the format for the display of the time and date by clicking on the Format button. (Some @formula in the Notes programming language are useful in these fields, such as @Modified which displays the date the entry was last modified.)

Keyword A keyword field has a pre-defined set of possible entries and a user picks from the list. You define the keywords, which could be colors of a product or flight destination, to ensure that the entries are consistent.

Rich Text A rich text field can contain text which is formatted in different typefaces, sizes or colors. Graphic images can also be inserted as can objects such as OLE objects, sound or embedded items from another application. Rich text fields cannot be shown in a view and cannot be processed with any other field when using a Notes @command.

Author Names This data type contains a list of users that can edit a document after it's been created. The list does not override any ACL list, but it can be useful to limit editing rights of users.

Reader Names Similar to the Author Names list of users, but it controls the read-access attribute rather than the edit attribute. If the document already has a read access list (created with the *Edit ▸ Security ▸ Read Access* command) the names in this field are added to the access list. Users included in the Author Names list have automatic read access to documents.

Names Contains a list of user or server names, for example in an e-mail form, this could list the available users that can receive mail.

Section An area of the form that can be programmed to carry out particular tasks.

Allow Multi-Values

If you select this option, users can enter multiple values into the field. Select the Separators button to choose the separator that's to be recognized (normally a comma or space).

Field type

This option defines the type of operation that can be carried out with the field; bear in mind that not all field types are applicable to all data types. There are five main types of field:

Editable Used with most fields and available for all data types. The user enters data and formula can check, or supply default data.

Computed A formula calculates a value and stores it in this field. The user cannot edit the value; you can use this with any data type except rich text.

Non-editable Similar to computed (above), but only available for rich text data types. A formula calculates a rich text value which is stored in the field, but cannot be edited by a user.

Computed for display A formula calculates a value, users cannot edit the value. This value is not stored in the document, but instead is re-calculated each time the document is opened. The value cannot be displayed in a view and it's not applicable to rich text data types.

Computed when composed A formula calculates a value the first time the document is composed. This value is then stored in the document and is never re-calculated. The value cannot be edited by a user and it's not applicable to rich text data types.

Field formulas

You can attach a formula (similar to a macro in a wordprocessor) to any field – normally to validate an entry, change its format or provide a default value. To add a formula, click on the Formula button at the bottom of the Field Definition dialog box.

There are three ways in which a formula can be used – to provide a default value, to translate the user input or to validate the user input. Each way has its own formula window.

Default value

Normally used for basic data, such as the day's date or the user's name, which can be changed but is normally left on the default. Typical entries would be:

@UserName to enter the user's name

@Created to enter the date the document was composed

Input translation

Normally used to convert an entry into a capitalized form or all upper case. For example, to capitalize an entry, use:

@ProperCase(field_1) where field_1 is the name of the field.

Input validation

Normally used to make sure that the input falls between some limits. For example, to make sure that instead of a normal order of up to $1,000, a user doesn't enter a $100,000 order. Normally, the formula used is made up of @If statements:

@If (field_1 > 1000; @Success; @Failure ("Orders aren't normally this big."))

In this example, if the order in field_1 is more than $1000, the validation fails and a message is displayed when the user tries to save the document. If the validation passes, no other action occurs. A validation formula is only calculated when the user tries to save the document. To create a formula:

1. Choose the window; select the Add@Func button to display a list of Notes function commands, highlight one and it's pasted into the window.
2. Now choose the field you want to process by selecting the Add Field button.
3. When you have finished, choose OK. (If you run out of space on the window, select the Zoom In button.)

Field format

If you use a field with time, date, number or keyword data types you can also define the formatting for the field. Click on the Format button in the Field Definition dialog box (*Design ▸ Field Definition*). The format options displayed depend on the data type for the particular field.

Number format

General format suppresses trailing zeros to the right of the decimal point.

Fixed format displays numbers with a fixed number of decimal places specified.

Scientific format displays numbers in exponential format: 1234 is 1.234E+03. Again, specify the number of decimal places.

Currency format displays the value with a currency symbol (specified in Windows) and the fixed number of decimal places.

Percentage check-box multiplies the number by 100 and add a trailing '%' sign, so that 0.75 is shown as 75%.

Parentheses on negative numbers displays negative numbers surrounded by brackets rather than a preceding minus sign.

Punctuated at thousands displays a comma or point at thousand breaks in numbers – set the punctuation in *Tools ▸ Setup ▸ User International*.

Time format

Adjust all times to local zone displays the time relative to the time zone in which the document was created. For example, with this option on a document created at 6.00 PM in London and viewed in New York as 1.00 PM (Eastern time).

Always show time zone will make the previous option clearer by showing the time zone in which the document was created (such as EST for Eastern Standard Time).

Show only when not local cleans up the previous option by only showing the time zone only if the document was created in a different time zone.

Keyword format

If you are entering a list of keywords from which a user can select their entry, you can also use this dialog box to add short-cut keywords (synonyms). For example, to reduce 'DiskDrives' to 'D' add 'D' after the main entry, separated by a vertical bar. Click on the Sort button if you want to arrange the list alphabetically. Once you have entered the list of keywords, you can change the user interface from a standard list to a set of radio buttons or check boxes (under the User Interface pull-down menu).

Hiding fields

Sometimes you might not want a user to see a field – typically, if you are storing an intermediate result in the field. You can easily hide a field from view. First, select the field to hide and choose the *Text ▸ Paragraph* menu option.

At the top, right of the dialog box is a section that describes when the field should be hidden: when reading, editing, printing or copying a form. Each option has an obvious use, except for copying: if set, when a document is copied on to the Clipboard, this field is not copied.

Designing a view

The final main segment of a database is its view. A view lists the documents in a database according to a particular field. All databases must have at least one view, most have several views.

Creating a new view for the documents

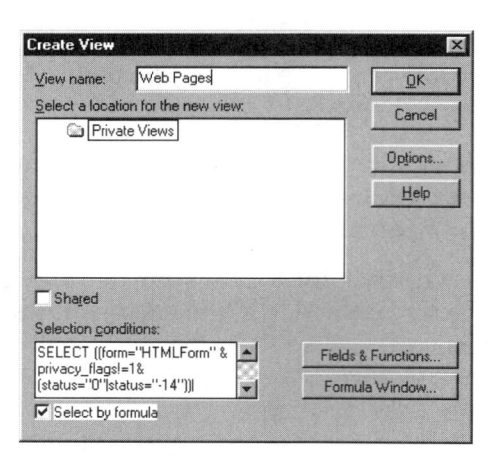

The view is a good way of scanning rapidly through documents. An e-mail database might have three views: documents sorted by date, by sender or by subject. As you can see, views act as convenient indexes for the database and you will need to make sure that you provide enough different views to meet the needs of the users.

Designing a view

The view shown above is from one of the sample databases, the news service, included with Notes. This is a view of documents sorted by date. The sort field is highlighted and ranged to the left. Indented below it are any documents that match the date. The column on the far left of the screen displays an asterisk if the document has not been read, or a tick mark if the user has marked the document.

As a designer, you can define the field to sort on, the columns of information that should be displayed from each document and any actions that a user can do with an entry in a view. The following pages describe how to create a new view and configure its options.

Create a new view

The process of creating and defining a new view follows a similar path to the previous section on forms. If you created the database from an existing database or template, it's likely that you have already inherited a number of views. You can create a new view by copying an existing view or creating a new, blank view. In your workspace, highlight the database you want to edit, select the *Design* ▸ *Views* menu option. The design views dialog box lists the existing views (if any).

Copy a view

To copy an existing view, highlight the view's name and select the New Copy button on the right of the dialog box, a copy is made and you are placed in edit mode.

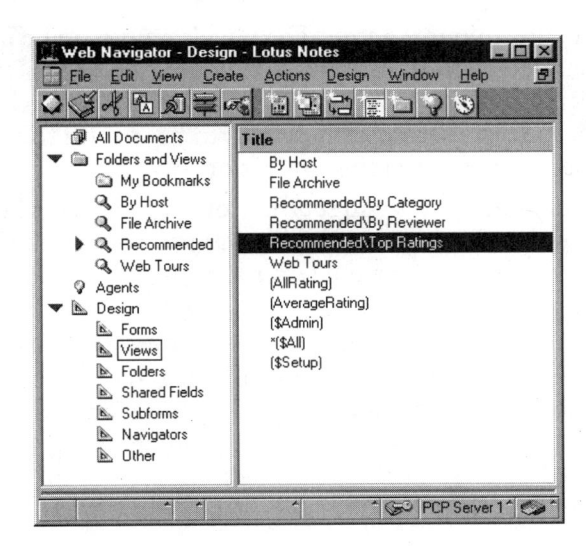

Copying a view

To name the new copy, select *Design ▸ View ▸ Attributes* menu option and save the view. Notes will also allow you to copy views from one database to another using the Copy and Paste buttons at the bottom of the Design Views dialog box. First, move to the database with the existing view, highlight the view and select the Copy button to copy it to the Clipboard. Change to the database where the view is to be added, select *Design ▸ Views* and click on the Paste button – the new view is added to the list. To rename the view, see later in this chapter under the section explaining view attributes.

Add a new view

If you want to add a new, blank view to your database, select the *Design ▸ View* menu option and select the New button. A new, empty view is displayed with just one column pre-defined: labeled '#', this column holds the number of the document in the view.

Configure a view

Once you have created a new view you will want to edit its attributes – how it looks, what it's called and the fields it displays. To access the attribute configuration screen, select the view and, with the view open, select the *Design ▸ View Attributes* menu option. This displays a dialog box that lets you configure most of the properties of a view.

Define a view's name

The first job to do if you have copied a view or created a new view is to give it a meaningful name. The view's name can be up to 32 characters long and can contain spaces, numbers or letters. When choosing a name, remember that Notes will display the list of views in alphabetical order, so try to arrange the names to fit in with this scheme – adding a number at the start of the name is one way.

By default, Notes will set the view's accelerator key to the first character in the view's name. If you want to override this, place an underscore character before the letter that you want to use as an accelerator key.

Just as with forms, Notes lets you use a synonym – one name that's displayed in the View menu and another that's used internally. Separate the two with a vertical bar ('|'); the name on the left is the name that will be displayed. For example, you might enter:

```
By Sender | View2
```

This would display the words By Sender in the View menu, which is more intelligible than the internal name View2.

In some cases, you might want to hide the view's name; do this by enclosing the name in round brackets (the left-hand name if you are using a synonym). This will prevent users seeing the view in the display, but don't rely on it as a security measure since it can be easily avoided: a user has only to create a private view (see below).

Private and shared views

There are two basic types of view: shared views which can be used be two or more users and private views which can only be used by the person who created it. Any user that has at least Reader access to a database can create a private view, which is useful if you want to organize the documents in a particular way.

If a user with Designer access creates a shared view, the view is stored as part of the database. A private view is stored on the local hard disk in the DESKTOP.DSK file. If a user tries to create a view and they don't have at least Designer access, the view is again stored locally in the DESKTOP.DSK file.

The default view

In the bottom left of the Attributes dialog box is a check-box that allows you to define the view as the database's default view. Each database should have a default view which is used to display the documents the first time the database is used. After this, the documents are displayed according to the last view used. Normally, the default view displays all the documents sorted by category, date or author.

To define a default view, select the check-box. The view will be listed with an asterisk beside it in the Views menu option.

No response hierarchy

This check-box, within the Options section at the bottom of the View Attribute screen, describes how the hierarchy of documents is displayed. If you check this option, only the main documents of the same level are displayed. To display the more usual style of view, with response documents listed below the main document and indented to the right, deselect this option. (See *Creating a response hierarchy* later in this chapter for further information on creating and defining a response hierarchy.)

Laying out a view

A view must contain as much information from the document as possible, to make it as useful as possible. Unfortunately, this can easily lead to a cluttered view that's got too many details to digest. Each row of a view will have several columns that show information from the documents or from a category of documents. Try to arrange the design of each row so that the first column is the most important, with details getting less important as the user reads to the right. Try to include some unique field in each row – this could be an invoice number, date or subject field. This will help a user track down and identify the document they want to see. You can include as many columns as you can fit into the width limit of 22.75 inches.

Adding a column

To create a new column, select the *Design ▸ New Column* menu option; this creates a new, blank column which can then be configured using the column definition dialog discussed on the next page.

Copying a column

If you want, you can create a new column by copying an existing column – often the case if you based your database on a template. To copy a column, select *Design ▸ Views* and display the view with the column you want to copy and click on the Edit button. Highlight the column you want to copy and select the *Edit ▸ Copy* menu option. Move to the database or view you want to copy the column to, highlight the column to the right of the position at which you want to insert the copy and choose the *Edit ▸ Paste* command to insert a copy of the column.

Moving a column

To move a column, use a combination of the previous two commands highlight the column, then choose *Edit ▸ Cut*, move to the new position and select *Edit ▸ Paste* (remember, the column is inserted to the left of the position selected).

Delete a column

If you want to delete a column you can do so within the *Design ▸ Views* menu option. From this dialog box, choose the view you want to edit and click on the Edit button; select the column to delete and select *Edit ▸ Clear*.

Configuring columns

Once you have added the columns you want to display within a view, it's time to configure the properties of each column. This lets you set the name of the column, the way it sorts, formats and associated @functions.

Formula to select data for a column

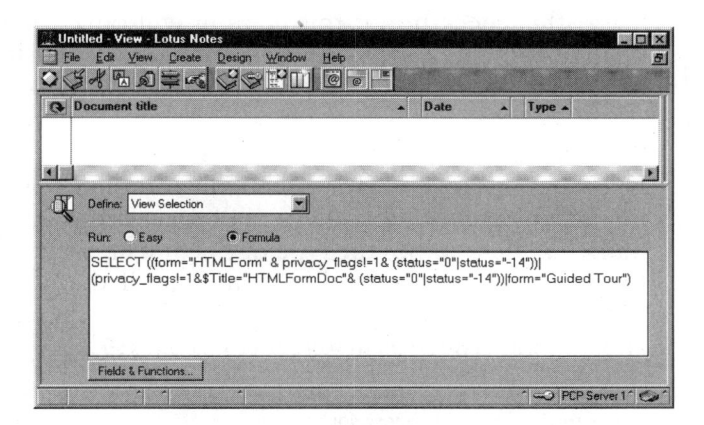

To set the attributes that describe a column you use the Column Definition dialog box. To pop this up, select the column you want to configure and choose the *Design ▸ Column Definition* menu option.

Title:

The title is displayed at the top of the column in the gray bar. It can contain any characters or numbers and there's no real limit to its length if its wider than the column width, Notes will truncate it. It's not necessary to include a title and in many status columns, which are just one or two characters wide, there's no room.

Form__u__la:

Within the scrollable area you can enter a formula that will select the documents that are displayed. For a simple selection, this can be just the field name, such as Subject. If you want to add a more complex formula that combines fields or selects from them, add @-functions. (See the end of this chapter for more details on writing formulas.)

Width ☐ characters

Sets the width of the column in characters. Bear in mind that not all monitors or the resolutions used by different setups will be able to show as many characters across.

Hidden

If this check-box is selected, the column is not displayed – this can be useful if you want to sort on the contents of the column, but not display them.

Responses only

Select this check-box if this column will only contain responses to a main document. A view can only have one column in which this check-box is selected.

Icon

If this check-box is selected then Notes will display one of five predefined icons according to the type of document. You should enter a formula that determines the type of document, which will select the icon to use. For example, to display an icon if the document contains an attachment, use the @-formula 'If' testing on the document type for an attachment, type 5: as in @If(@Attachments;5;0).

Document Type	Description
1	Document
2	Folder
3	Person
4	Group
5	Attachment

List separators

If a field is displayed within a column and the field contains multiple values (see the beginning of this chapter for more on field definitions), you should specify the character that's to be used to separate the values.

Number (button)

The button marked Number allows you to define the format of any numbers that are displayed.

> **General** suppresses trailing zeros to the right of the decimal point.
>
> **Fixed** format displays numbers with a fixed number of decimal places specified.
>
> **Scientific** displays numbers in exponential format. For example, 1,234 becomes 1.234E+03. Again, specify the number of decimal places.

Currency format displays the value with a currency symbol (specified in Windows) and the fixed number of decimal places.

Percentage check-box multiplies the number by 100 and add a trailing '%' sign, so that 0.75 is shown as 75%.

Parentheses on negative numbers displays negative numbers surrounded by brackets rather than a preceding minus sign.

Punctuated at thousands displays a comma or point at thousand breaks in numbers – set the punctuation in *Tools* ▸ *Setup* ▸ *User* ▸ *International*.

Time (button)

If the column contains a field that has time or date information, use the Time button to set the formatting for this information.

Adjust all times to local zone displays the time relative to the time zone in which the document was created. For example, with this option on a document created at 6.00 PM in London and viewed in New York as 1.00 PM (Eastern time).

Always show time zone will make the previous option clearer by showing the time zone in which the document was created (such as EST for Eastern Standard Time).

Show only when not local cleans up the previous option by only showing the time zone only if the document was created in a different time zone.

Sorting (button)

Each view will normally have at least one column on which it sorts the display. Often, the column is the date the document was created (use the @Created command), sometimes the column will be a hidden one (see above under Hidden).

If you set two or more columns to be sorted, Notes will sort according to columns running from left to right. For example, if the first column is date, the second author and third subject and the first two columns are sorted, Notes will arrange the documents according to date, then sort similarly-dated documents according to the author's name. Notes sorts according to the rule: numbers, letters and special characters. Sorting does not differentiate between the case of characters.

Sort You must select this check-box before you can use the following options.

Categorize This check-box tells Notes to group sorted documents according to the heading of this column. For example, if you have an e-mail database, you might want to categorize according to the sender of the mail; this would list the sender's name, then all the mail sent by that person.

Font (button)

Use this button to define the font and typeface used to display the information in this column. Notes pops up a dialog box with a list of all available fonts, and lets you choose attributes (such as bold, italic, underline) together with the point size and color of the text.

Justification (button)

This option allows you to define how the title and contents of the column are displayed.

If you are displaying numbers, you will find it looks neater if you select a monospaced font, such as Courier, and a fixed number of decimal places, then justify to the right – the decimal points will then all align vertically.

Totals (button)

Select this button to create totals for the column – the totals are displayed within the view. Totals are only calculated for main documents, not response documents.

Creating a response hierarchy

At the beginning of this section about views, we mentioned a response hierarchy; we will now explain how to configure a hierarchy. Behind every good hierarchy is a response form, which must be created before you can set up the response hierarchy.

In order to create a response hierarchy for your view, follow these steps:

1. Create a form (see the start of this chapter for more details) and select Response to Document as the form's type in the Attributes box.
2. Deselect the No Response Hierarchy check-box in the View Attribute dialog box, described earlier.
3. Switch back to the view layout screen and create a new column directly to the left of the column holding the main document.

4. Pop up the Design Column Definition dialog box and set the new column's width to one character, and select the Responses Only check-box. Enter a formula that will display the fields from the response document.

Make sure that the selection formula for the main view does include response documents, or you will see nothing.

Navigators

One of the most visible new features of Notes 4.5 is the addition of Navigators. These provide an easy-to-use graphical way for users to select forms and choose documents. You can design your own Navigator, with icons or graphical hotspots to lead users to particular views and documents, or you can use the standard Notes folder icons that can also be displayed in the Navigator pane.

Internet Navigator with graphical hotspots

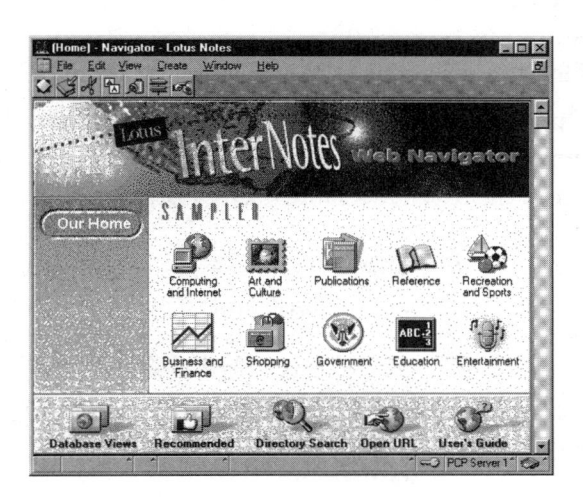

As the designer, you have two ways of creating the icons that are displayed within a Navigator. Firstly, you can draw then by hand using the Notes drawing tools; secondly you can cut and paste from any other graphics application – that lets you use company logos and images to enhance your Navigator. Any graphic object that you include in a Navigator can have actions assigned to it, with the one exception being a background graphic. If you have survived this far without having to carry out any serious programming you can continue in this vein with your design of the Navigators: Notes provides a series of simple actions that you can assign to a Navigator graphic without any programming.

Navigator Actions

From the range of simple actions you can select the following:
- open another navigator
- open a view
- open a folder
- open a link
- assign an @function to the graphical element
- assign a LotusScript program to the element

Creating Navigators

You can create your Navigators in the same way as you create forms: by copying a Navigator from the same database, from another database or by creating your own from scratch.

Copying Navigators

To copy a Navigator from within the same database or from another is a similar process and uses the Windows Clipboard:

1. Open the database and choose *View ▸ Design*.
2. In the Navigator pane, choose the Design-Navigators option.
3. From the list of available Navigators, select the one you want to copy.
4. Choose *Edit ▸ Copy*.
5. Move to the new database and select *Edit ▸ Paste*.

Viewing the Navigators for a database

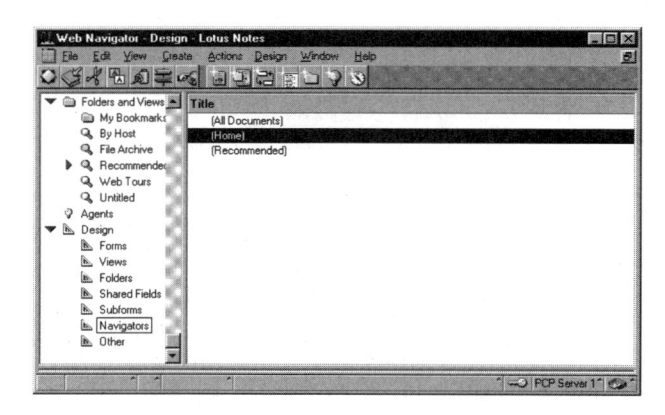

Creating a Navigator from Scratch

If you want to create a Navigator bar from scratch – perhaps you cannot find an existing Navigator that you can use as a template – carry out the following steps:

1. Open the database and choose *Create ▸ Design ▸ Navigator*.
2. Choose *Design ▸ Navigator Properties*.
3. Enter a descriptive name for the Navigator.
4. Click on the new Navigator pane.
5. Use the Create menu to add items to the new Navigator pane.
6. To set the properties of a new item, select the object and choose *Design ▸ Object* Properties.
7. Close and save the Navigator pane.

Creating a new Navigator

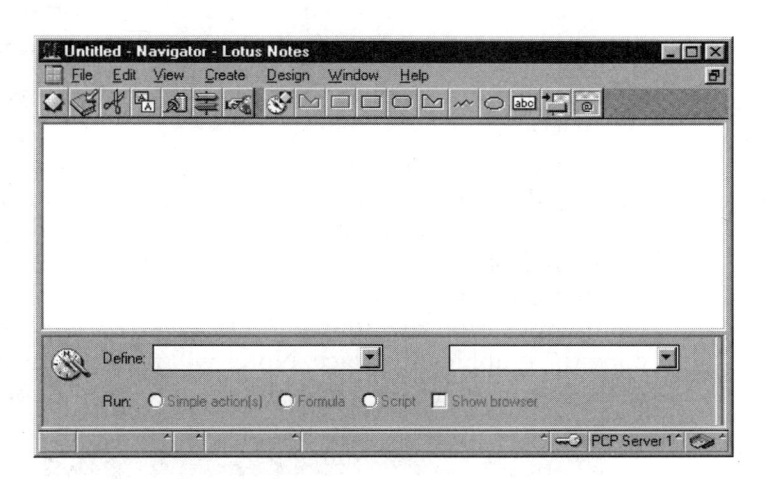

Basic properties for the Navigator

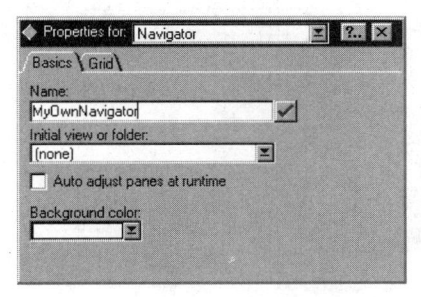

The final touches

There are just a few final touches that you have to make to your database application before you can release it to your users. These include defining an icon that will show up in the user's workspace, writing an About... box that describes what the database does and who developed it and, lastly, a 'using' document that describes how to use the database.

Creating a database icon

To create an icon, carry out the following steps:

1. Select the database and choose the *View ▸ Design* menu option.
2. From the Navigator pane, choose the Design-Other item.
3. Double-click on Icon from the list of 'Other' options.

This pops up a mini application with a grid that you can paint to create an icon.

When you are designing the icon, try to think how it will look in color and mono (for laptop users) – both versions are shown normal size in the bottom right-hand corner of the window. You can always copy an icon from another application or one that you created in another paint package. To do this, select *Edit ▸ Copy* from the other paint application then move to *Design ▸ Icon* and select *Edit ▸ Paste* to copy the graphic into place. Notes will truncate any icon that's too big to fit, so you might need to experiment to get the correct size.

Creating an icon for an element

Writing an About... document

This little document normally carries very basic details about the database – who created it, when and, importantly, what the database was designed to do – just a few lines is enough, although you might want to put in a full mission statement or document the trials and tribulations you encountered on the way!

Editing an 'About...' Document for a database

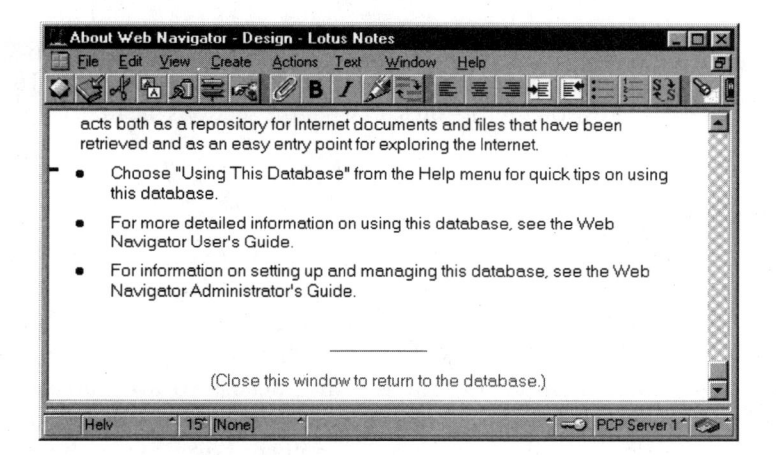

A user will be able to check these points by selecting the *Help ▸ Document ▸ About Database* menu option. To create the About document carry out the following steps:

1. Select the database and choose the *View ▸ Design* menu option.
2. From the Navigator pane, choose the Design-Other item.
3. Double-click on About Database Document from the list of 'Other' options.
4. Type in the text you want to appear in the About document.
5. Check the spelling with *Edit ▸ Check Spelling* and save the document with [Ctrl]+[S].

Writing a Using... document

To complement the About document, it's always a good idea to include user notes that are as comprehensive as possible. These can be conveniently stored as a Using... document and will normally tell a user how to use the basic functions. To create the Using... document carry out the following steps:

1. Select the database and choose the *View ▸ Design* menu option.

2. From the Navigator pane, choose the Design-Other item.
3. Double-click on Using Database Document from the list of 'Other' options.
4. Type in the text you want to appear in the About document; you can also include jumps, hotspots and graphic elements.
5. Check the spelling with *Edit ▸ Check Spelling* and save the document with [Ctrl]+[S].

Tip: If your forms are complex, why not take a screen-shot of the form (using [Alt]+[PrintScreen]) and paste this into the Using... document together with notes on what the sections mean.

Database security

Once you have designed your database, you should begin to think about how you will protect the data stored within it. One of the most useful functions for limiting access to a database is the ACL (Access Control List). This lists the users, servers and groups that you or the database manager has given permission to use the database.

Setting up an Access Control List

To set up or edit an ACL for a database, you must have Manager status for the particular database. Open the database from your workspace and select the *File ▸ Database ▸ Access Control* menu option.

Configuring the access control for a database

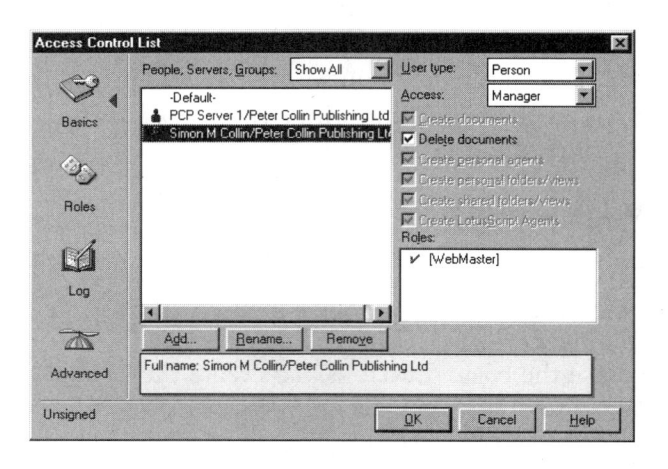

The main scrolling window within the ACL dialog box lists the users, servers and groups and their permitted access to the database. To change the access level of one of the entries, highlight the name and select one of the radio buttons at the bottom of the screen.

If you want to set up access for a number of users, you will find it more convenient to create a group (registered in the public Name & Address book), add the users to the group then manipulate the group in the ACL setup. If a user is a member of several groups, Notes will take the highest access level from the groups. If a user is listed individually by name and appears within a group, Notes will use the individual setting, regardless of whether it offers higher or lower access than the group setting.

Access level	ACL	Design	Edit	Create
Manager	Y	Y	Y	Y
Designer		Y	Y	Y
Editor			Y	Y
Author				Y
Reader				N/A
Depositor				N/A
No access				N/A

Full-text search index

If you want your database to provide the user with the ability to carry out a full-text search, you will first need to create a full-text search index. The advantage of the index is that it means users can carry out searches on the entire contents of a database within seconds. The disadvantage is that the index can be very big – in some cases almost approaching the size of the database itself! Before you add a full-search index, poll your users to see whether they would really need and use the feature, and then check how much free disk space you have remaining on the server.

How the index works

The first time you create the index, Notes will create a subdirectory on the server called 'database.FT' (where 'database' is the name of the database you are indexing). In this is the full-text index file. As documents are added to the database, you will need to regularly re-index the database; each time Notes updates the index, it creates an incremental update index file in this subdirectory. Since all the files in this directory are used for the index, you cannot delete any individual files. If you want to delete the entire contents, you can – but the index will, obviously, no longer work!

When the index is created, Notes examines all the text, date and number fields (including rich-text fields) in each record of the database; it doesn't include bitmaps, attachments or formulas when indexing. The final size of the text that will be indexed tends to be between 25–75% of the size of the database. When generated, the index file itself then takes up between 50–75% of the size of the text. Typically, a 10Mb database would have around 50% text that could be indexed which would generate an index file that's around 4–5Mb in size.

Creating an index

To create an index, make sure that you have Manager or Designer level access in the ACL:

- Highlight the database icon in your workspace, or open the database.
- Select *File ▸ Full Text Search ▸ Create Index* menu option. This displays a dialog box with a range of indexing options for the database – each option will effect the final size of the index.

Options used when creating a full-text database

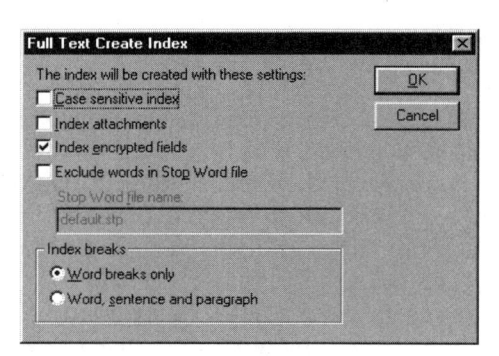

Case-sensitive index

This option creates index entries for each combination of upper and lower case text and adds around 10% to the size of the index file.

Exclude words in Stop word file

If you don't want to index common words, such as 'if', 'and', 'but', etc. you can create a text file, called DEFAULT.STP, that contains the words which should not be indexed. Generally, it's a good idea to remove common short words from the index – you might even want to remove confidential or risky words to prevent anyone searching for a particular entry. Remember, if you stop a word such as 'for', your user's cannot enter a search that reads 'voting for president', they can only enter 'voting' and 'president'. This option reduces the size of the index by around 15–20%.

Index Breaks

This option determines how proximity searching will work. If you select:

> **Word Breaks Only** users cannot restrict a search to one sentence or paragraph.
>
> **Word, Sentence, and Paragraph** allows users to search for words that are all within the same sentence or paragraph.

The first option, Word Breaks Only, generates a smaller index file. The second option adds around 50% to the size of the index file.

Updating the index

As mentioned earlier, when new documents are added to the database, the index will need to be updated. These incremental updates are stored in separate index files within the .FT subdirectory. You can specify how and when the full-text index should be updated. Select the database and choose the *File ▸ Full Text Search ▸ Information* menu option; this displays a dialog box with options to define when the index will be updated.

> **Immediate Update** This will try to update the index as soon as a user quits and closes the database. This could easily tie-up your server if the database is a popular one.
>
> **Hourly Update** The server will update the index every hour.
>
> **Scheduled Update** This option turns to a Program document stored in the public Name & Address file that defines when the update process should occur.
>
> **Daily Update** The update will take place once a day at two am.

Note You can update a full-text index at any time using the server console command, UPDALL. Chapter 8 has more information on server commands).

13

Programming skills

About this chapter

Notes allows the database developer to extend and enhance the capabilities of any form, Agent or database structure using one of the Notes programming methods. In previous chapters I have covered Agents and Simple Actions – the two quickest and easiest ways to get started with Notes programming. In this chapter, I cover the more complex @functions and LotusScript. @functions can be used to add extra functionality to any Notes object, LotusScript is a BASIC-like scripting language that's common to almost all Lotus software products and lets the experienced developer create his own routines and formulas.

Developing applications – the essentials of programming with @-formulas

There are a number of ways you can develop applications within Notes and release 4.5 adds extra options for the more experienced developer. However, once you have created a database the four main ways of adding functionality to the objects are as follows:

Agents: these automated macros let you define actions that are triggered by a time, user or event – covered in detail in Chapter 11.

LotusScript: a powerful, object-oriented scripting language that's similar to BASIC in style. It lets a developer enhance any Notes object. Similar to Microsoft's Visual Basic, LotusScript is Lotus' strategy for all its products and can be used in Notes, Approach, WordPro and 1-2-3.

Navigators: as you'll know from using Notes, Navigators provide an excellent way to display the structure and options of a database to users. Developers can create their own Navigators to enhance any database and make it easier to use.

Simple Action: a new, easy way of creating custom code for Notes. You'll find the development process simpler if you try and use Simple Actions for the initial coding and then enhance the form with scripts.

To make the most of a Notes application, you will need to tackle its programming language. The language is more like a scripting function than a full-blown programming language and you will find that it can dramatically enhance the useful functions of any Notes application – form, view or database.

There's no real structure to the Notes language – just enter the formula line by line and Notes will execute them line by line. The formulas are most commonly used to calculate a value for a field based on other fields, validate data input or to perform a special function.

The @-functions

The functions within the language are prefaced with an '@' symbol. To make life easier for the user, Notes normally includes a button to list the functions in most of the sections where you can enter a script – there's no need to learn them all by heart as in some languages.

The @-functions normally require one or more arguments; these are enclosed within round-brackets '(..)'. If you want to indicate that data is a time or date, enclose it in square brackets '[..]'. Lastly, curly brackets are used to indicate a series or set of data.

For example:

    @LowerCase("Turns this INTO lower case")

or

    @Hour([7:30])

In addition to the functions there are the normal range of operators (+, –, *, \) together with logical AND, OR, and NOT operators and a series of test operators (<, >, =, !=). (See the appendix for the complete list of operators.)

The final part of the scripting language is the data: Notes can use constants, variables and typed data as arguments for most of its functions. For example, if your script has two variables, FirstName, SurName you can use these in a number of ways:

    "Good morning" + FirstName

or

    "Your full login name is" + FirstName + SurName

Evaluation order for expressions

Notes processes functions and operators in a formula in a fairly fixed sequence. Each line is evaluated and processed before execution moves on to the next. This steady progress is only altered if you stop the sequence with an @Return function (normally as a result of an @IF.. statement). There are no GOTO-type statements in Notes.

(See 'Number crunching', on page 253, for the order of evaluating mathematical operators.)

Macros

The @-commands can be used by themselves or as part of a macro. A macro differs slightly from a script in that not only does it carry out some calculation, it then carries out an action based on the calculation. There are a number of different types of macro that should be explained to help understand how they work:

Filter macros

These are normally used to update a selected range of documents – often by a developer who's testing out an application. In order to create a filter macro, you will need at least Designer access to the database.

Execute-once macros

These macros only work within a View – the macros can be accessed by users and are listed under the *Tools ▸ Run* Macros menu option. The macros are normally written by the database's designer who might create a range of special macros for the users.

Search macros

These are similar to a Filter Macro but they can be created by any user with Reader Access. A Search Macro is defined via the full text search bar and works on the range of documents found by the last search. To create a Search Macro, display the Search Bar and click on the down-arrow to display the options.

Button macros

Within a form, you can insert a button that has a macro attached to it. The button macro only operates within or on the current document, but can do a whole range of operations – such as e-mailing the document or processing the fields. To create a Button Macro, you will need Author access to the database: select the *Edit ▸ Insert* Button menu option.

SmartIcon macros

Notes, in common with all Lotus products, uses SmartIcons – a range of icon buttons that carry out a particular function. Any user can create a SmartIcon Macro so that when he clicks on the button, something happens – normally used to speed up access to simple tasks such as spell-checks or cut-and-paste.

Keywords in a formula

Notes has five reserved keywords which can be used in a formula (sometimes, they are added automatically by Notes to your formula). The keywords are:

```
DEFAULT, ENVIRONMENT, FIELD, SELECT, REM
```

These keywords can be entered in either upper or lower case, but Notes will convert them to upper case; they must be at the start of the line.

DEFAULT

This keyword assigns a default value to a field so that if the field does exist, the script should use the field's value; if the field does not exist, the script should continue and use the specified default value in its place.

ENVIRONMENT

This keyword is used to set up an environment variable which is stored in the user's NOTES.INI (or Preferences file on a Mac). The variable is not deleted after being used and any script can then access the variable in the current or future sessions. For example, to set up the variable MaxTimes as an environment variable and assign the string "1" to it:

```
ENVIRONMENT MaxTimes := "1"
```

Future sessions or scripts can then check the status of the variable MaxTimes with the @Environment function:

```
@Environment("MaxTimes")
```

This command and the ENVIRONMENT keyword will only operate on text strings so if you want to use numbers (for example, above, adding each time the form is used) you would have to use the @TextToNumber function to convert the string to a number, add one to it then return. In version 3 of Notes, the ENVIRONMENT keyword was effectively done away with, since the @Environment function has been extended to provide the syntax:

```
@Environment("variable";value)
```

Now, the value is assigned to the variable and stored in the NOTES.INI file all in one operation without the need for the ENVIRONMENT keyword.

FIELD

This keyword is used to assign a value to an existing field in a document or to create a new field in a document. You should not use it for temporary fields. For example, if one of your directors has a stroke of good fortune and so changes his title to President, you could change the Title field in your document to President using:

```
FIELD Title := "President"
```

As it stands, this would also need the SELECT keyword to choose the documents in which the surname matches that of the director. If he was called Mr Johnson and is now to be called President Johnson:

```
SELECT SurName = "Johnson"

FIELD Title := "President"
```

REM

As you might imagine, this keyword lets you add remark lines to a script to make it easier to understand what your program is doing. Enclose any remarks within quotation marks and, if the text needs to run over more than one line, end the line with a semicolon and begin the next line with another REM keyword:

```
REM "This explains that the previous lines were";

REM " used to provide a new search function";
```

It's always a good idea to add as many helpful comments to your scripts as possible – at the time it might be obvious what you are doing, but in a couple of months, when you need to change a line, you might easily be stumped by your clever programming.

SELECT

This keyword lets you identify documents that have a specific value in a field; you would then carry out an operation on the selected documents. For example, if you want to pick out all the documents in which the field Checked is equal to the initials of a user, SC, and change the contents of the field Status in these documents to "Suspended" you would use the following two lines:

```
SELECT Checked = "SC"

FIELD Status := "Suspended"
```

You can also use the SELECT @All function to select all the documents in a database (if you enter just @All in a script, Notes will add the word SELECT before it).

Writing a formula

Notes does, to a greater extent, standardize the way in which you enter a formula. At any point where you could enter a formula, Notes displays a button labeled Formula.... Click on this and you will see a standard dialog box pop up. For example, when in *Design ▸ Forms* mode, highlight a field and select *Design ▸ Field* Definition to pop up the dialog box that gives you access to the field's definition set. At the bottom left of the box is a button labeled Formula... which lets you enter the formula for the field.

You can type in your lines of formula within the main scrolling text panel in the center of the dialog box. Alternatively, let Notes do the hard work for you and use the Add @Func button to scroll through the available commands – you can paste in a command from the list. Similarly, the Add Field button lets you select the field name you want the function to operate on.

Programming examples

String manipulation

The majority of all your Notes formula will be to carry out basic string manipulation. If you enter a string of characters rather than use a variable name, you must enclose the string within double-quotation marks. For example:

```
"Good" + " Morning"
```

will print out the sentence Good Morning

Tip If you want to use double quotation marks within the string, preface them with a backslash:

```
"It'll be a \"great\" day" + "Simon"
```

will display It'll be a "great" day Simon

You can scatter field names or variables within the above examples or use @functions. For example:

```
"Good Morning " + UserName
```

Chapter 13

or

```
"This document was created by " + UserName + "on the " +
@Text(@Created)
```

Converting values to text

This previous example shows the `@Text()` function – which is particularly useful to convert number or values into a text string. In addition, you can add formatting arguments to the `@Text` command to define that the value being converted should be treated as a date or time value or as currency, scientific notation or a percentage.

```
@Text(value)
```

```
@Text(value, "format")
```

Actions and formats for the `@Text()` function

Format	Action	Format	Action
D0	year, month, day	Z2	display time zone
D1	month, day (year if not current)	S0	date
D2	month, day	S1	time
D3	year, month	S2	date & time
T0	hour, min, s	S3	date, time or time today
T1	hour, min	G	significant digits only
Z0	convert to current time zone	F	fixed number of decimal places
Z1	display time zone if not current	S	E notation
C	currency: two decimal places	(	bracket negative numbers
'	comma at thousands	number	define number of decimal places
%	percentage		

You can combine the format codes (number formats must be separated by a comma) within the format string to get the exact format you want. For example, to bracket negative numbers, displayed as currency and punctuated at the thousand mark use:

```
@Text(value, "C,',(")
```

Converting text to a value

Another common task is to convert a text string into a value – for example, to use a series of number characters in a mathematical expression or process a date. To do this, use the `@TextToNumber` and `@TextToTime` functions. For example, to process a text string "234" and add the contents of the field `MarkUp` to it, before displaying it, do the following:

```
@TextToNumber("234") + MarkUp
```

If Notes cannot convert the string, it returns `@ERROR`.

Converting case

To maintain consistency from different operators, it's often safest to convert key fields into a particular case: capitalized, upper or lower case. Notes will do this with any string using the functions:

```
@ProperCase, @UpperCase and @LowerCase. For example:

@ProperCase("john smith")
```

produces `John Smith`.

Number crunching

Notes can carry out simple mathematical operations on any number. Along with the usual +, –, 0…9 digits, numbers can also be specified in scientific notation using the letters 'E' or 'e'.

Operators and their operations

Operator	Operation	Operator	Operation
*	multiply	>=	greater than or equal
<	less than	=	equal
/	divide	!	logical NOT
>	greater than	*	permuted equal
+	addition	&	logical AND
<=	less than or equal	<>	not equal
–	subtract	|	logical OR
!=	not equal		

The divisions above represent the order in which Notes processes operators. To change the order, simply enclose the operation in brackets. Permuted operators is the name given to any of the mathematical (not logical) operators above that works on two sets of numbers, carrying out the operation on each number of one set with each of the numbers in turn of the second set. To define a permuted operator, prefix the operator with an asterisk.

Time and dates

Times and dates are important in any Notes database: to tell Notes that a value is a time or date, you must enclose it within square brackets '[..]'. If you are displaying a time or date, see the previous section on using the formatting options in the @Text function.

There are a few functions that you will use regularly:

@Accessed() returns the time and date of the last access

@Created() returns the time and date of the document's creation

@Date() today's time and date as a time-date value

@Day() today's time and date as a number

You can convert number values into a time-date format using the @Time function. This accepts the year, month, day, hour, minute and second as digits and returns an equivalent time-date value.

Programming with LotusScript

One of the most powerful features for the developer is the inclusion of LotusScript within Notes 4.5. This structured, object-oriented language is similar to BASIC and is common to many of the Lotus Windows applications, including WordPro and Approach. Just about every object and action within Notes can be assigned a script, which can carry out simple instructions or can process complex functions.

Scripts are entered using the script editor which is displayed in a pane beneath the object to which the script is assigned. Notes compiles scripts in two phases: part of the compilation occurs as you enter the script commands – which might throw up errors – and the final compilation occurs when you save the script – which will throw up any other errors in your code. Notes includes a debug window that lets you place breakpoints (where the script stops so that you can examine registers and code values) and lets you step through the program one line at a time. For developers who have used Microsoft's Visual Basic development tool, the LotusScript language will be very familiar.

Through LotusScript subroutines, a developer can locate, open, update and search a database on a local or remote server. The LotusScript language also provides a set of tools that interfaces with any ODBC (open database connectivity) database – ODBC drivers are available for most common database applications including Access, Paradox and dBase. Finally, LotusScript can be used to process individual documents in all sorts of ways – from a simple update to a full retrieval.

The LotusScript language is very rich with hundreds of individual commands. It would take a book the size of this one to describe the language elements and how to use them. Since LotusScript is a common language with other Lotus products there are plenty of books that describe how to program effectively in LotusScript. For this chapter, I have included a number of example scripts that are specific to Notes and will provide a good basis from which you can experiment.

Example 1: creating a new document in a database

To create a new document in a database, you need to open the database, create a new document and set the required fields to their values before saving the entire structure.

```
Sub Initialize

    Dim session As New NotesSession
    Dim db As NotesDatabase
    Dim view As NotesView
    Dim doc As NotesDocument
    Set db = session.CurrentDatabase
    Set doc = New NotesDocument(db)
    doc.From = session.UserName
    doc.Subject = "Simon Collin"
    doc.Office = "London Sales"
    doc.Client = "Lotus"
    doc.Body = "sample body text"
    Call doc.Save(True, False)

End Sub
```

This subroutine starts by opening the current database and assigning it the ID 'db'. It then creates a new document with the handle 'doc' and fills in some of the document fields. Lastly, it saves the new document.

Example 2: deleting documents

This example will search through a database and remove any document that contains the word 'expire'.

Sub Initialize

```
Dim session As New NotesSession
Dim db As NotesDatabase
Set db = session.CurrentDatabase
Call db.UpdateFTIndex(True)
Set dc = db.FTSearch("expire",0)

For j = 1 to dc.Count

    Set doc = dc.GetNthdocument(j)
    Call doc.Remove(True)

Next
```

End Sub

Example 3: links to documents

The following example scans the open database for documents and records a link (a DocLink) in a new document. This summary document is then sent to the Directors of the company. As you will see, the subroutine uses the Notes newsletter feature to gather the doclinks and then extracts the subject field as the one line within the summary document.

Sub Initialize

```
Dim session As New NotesSession
Dim db As NotesDatabase
Dim db as NotesDocumentCollection
Dim news As NotesNewsletter
Dim doc As NotesDocument
Set db = session.CurrentDatabase
Call db.UpdateFTIndex(True)
Set dc = db.FTSearch("Acme", 0)
Set news = New NotesNewsletter(dc)
news.SubjectItemName = "Subject"
news.DoSubject = True
Set doc = news.FormatMsgWithDoclinks(db)
Call doc.Send(True, "Director")
```

End Sub

14
Setting up Notes

About this chapter

Once you have installed Notes onto the server, the next task is to set up and configure your Notes server. The main task will be to install and set up the new Notes users. This chapter shows you how to add new users, together with shortcuts to speed up the process and make it easier to manage if you have tens of users to add to add to the system. Later in the chapter, you'll see how to set up server interconnections to other servers and other mail systems. Security settings are also covered to ensure that your system is secure and your data safe from unauthorized break-ins.

Setting up users

Setting up new users is a two-part process: the first section, registering the new users, is carried out on the server and generates a user ID and Person document for each new user in the public Name & Address book. The second part is done at the user's workstation and involves installing the workstation software and retrieving the certified ID file (generated at the server) – this certified ID file gives the user access to Notes.

Registering new users

There are two options when registering new users at the server. If you have just one or two new users, it's quicker and more convenient to use the manual registration with its on-screen dialog box to enter the user's name and personal details. If you are setting up a lot of users you might find it easier to use Notes' text-file function that generates user IDs from a text file of user names and personal details. This latter option is ideal if you are setting up a new Notes server and you have a list of user names in a text file – which you would typically generate from an existing network operating system's user list (such as Novell NetWare's Bindery).

The Administration screen allows new users to be registered

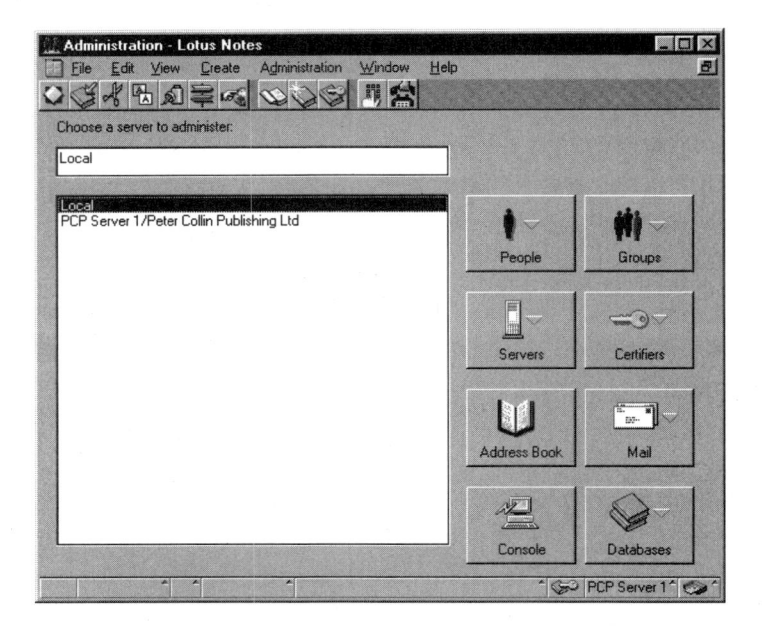

Setting up users

Manual user registration

To register a single or just a few users, it's often more convenient to use Notes' on-screen forms. Select the *File ▸ Tools ▸ Server Administration* menu option. Click on People, choose Register Person.

Registering a single new user

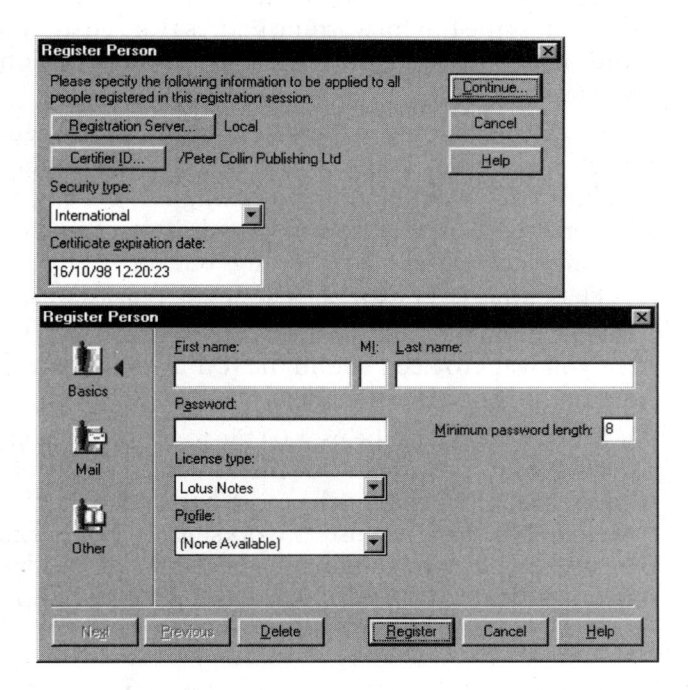

You are asked to confirm that you have purchased a workstation license for this user – if so, press OK to continue. You will be asked to enter the administrator's password.

The next screen is a registration form for the new user in which you can enter their name, password and mail information. Each of the name fields for the user can be up to 79 characters long and can include spaces and dashes to ensure each user has a unique name. When you register a new user, you should enter a password for them – it can be up to 31 characters long and is case sensitive.

Note If you are working with several Notes servers, it's wise to use one as the certifier server. If you are registering new users on a different server to the one that will issue the certifier ID, click on Registration Server and select the server that will carry out the certification.

Chapter 14

To setup the e-mail file for the user, click on Mail. Notes gives you the option to choose the type of electronic mail system for the new user. Normally, the default option of Notes Mail is fine, but you may already have a company-wide e-mail system or install another e-mail application. If you are using Lotus cc:Mail or any other VIM-compatible software, enter the full forwarding address for the user. If you are using any other mail software you should set the mail option to 'none' for the time being.

By default, Notes will create a Person document for this user and attach a certified ID file to the entry in the public Name & Address book. If you're not planning on using this system, or you want to save the certified ID file on to a floppy disk you can change this default by clicking on the Other User Settings button.

The Other User Settings dialog box gives you two extra descriptive fields, Comment and Location into which you can add any extra text that you want to keep within the ID file – such as a company identification number or office number.

If you don't want the user ID file to be stored as an attachment to the user's Person document but instead want to generate an ID file on a floppy disk, then change the radio button labeled Store User ID. When you load Notes on to a user's workstation, Notes expects the user ID to be saved as an attachment in the Name & Address book; you can equally input the ID file if you've stored it on a floppy disk, but it's more convenient to stick to the attachment method.

> **Tip** Within this User Setting screen is the option to define the minimum length of password. You should set this to a reasonable length, typically eight to ten characters long. (The user can change his password at any time, but cannot change the minimum length requirement.)

If you have a couple of users to register, you move on to the next user by clicking on the Next button. This pops up another user registration form; you can shuttle backwards and forwards between the forms until you have finished entering details for all the users. At this point, click on the Register button to start the registration process (this process will take a couple of minutes for each user).

During the registration, your workstation is at its most vulnerable: don't leave it for a coffee break until the process has finished, or an intruder could easily break into the system.

Automatic user registration from a text file

When registering lots of users – typically when first setting up Notes – it's easier and quicker to use Notes' automatic registration from user details stored in a text file rather than repeatedly using the entry form described above. This is particular convenient if you already have a list of your user names stored in a text file; network operating systems such as Novell NetWare and Microsoft Windows NT can generate a list of user names from their user databases.

To create a text file of user information, start your text editor (which must be able to output to a plain ASCII file). Each user's information is stored on one line with the elements on the line separated by semicolons. The format for each user's entry on one line is:

```
LastName; [FirstName]; [MiddleInitial]; [OrganizationalUnit];
[Password]; [ID File Directory]; [ID File Name]; [HomeServerName];
[MailFileName]; [Location]; [Comment]; [ForwardingAddress]
```

The first field, LastName and the Password field are the only two fields that are required for each user. All the others are optional. If you skip a field, leave it blank but keep the semicolons in; you can remove any trailing semicolons from the end of a line.

For example, a typical entry in a registration text file might look like this:

```
Jennings; Simon;;;password1
Jones; Michael;;;password2
Smith; Andrew;;;password3
```

Once you have edited your text file of user information, you can feed it into the registration program. Select the *File ▶ Tools ▶ Server Administration*. Now choose the *People ▶ Register* option from the File menu. You will be prompted to check that you have bought enough workstation licenses. Enter your Administration password and select OK.

Like the Manual Registration method, automatic registration from a file can either generate a certified ID file and attach it to the newly created Person document in the Name & Address book, or can create a separate ID file stored on a floppy disk.

When you select the Register button, Notes will start to process the contents of the file. If it doesn't understand any entry it will skip to the next. The registration process will take a couple of minutes per user, so be ready for a long wait if you are registering a lot of users.

Security

Your Notes server holds all your data and databases and as a central store it needs to be well protected against potential unauthorized users – malicious or careless. Notes has a series of security measures built in that help ensure only authorized users use the system and that data is secure.

User security

The most obvious threat to your Notes server is from an unauthorized user breaking in from a workstation and accessing a database. To counter this, Notes employs User ID files. Every authorized user and server in a Notes network has a User ID. The ID file contains just enough information so that Notes can recognize the authenticity of the user, but not enough to give full access to Notes. In addition to the User ID, you need to enter your user password.

The User ID file

A User ID file contains the name of the user, the Notes license number for the user, keys for encryption of the user's mail and, lastly, a certificate from a certifier ID. This last chunk of data is added to the User ID file by the administrator during user registration; the administrator has one master certifier ID file with which he stamps all User ID files to prove that they are authentic – like an official stamp on your passport or driving license.

When a user tries to log into Notes, his workstation sends the user's ID file to Notes and waits for Notes to check the authenticity of the file. Once the ID file is deemed to be authentic, Notes asks for the user's password. When this is entered correctly, the user has access to Notes.

User passwords

In addition to the User ID, you should ensure that all users have a password. This is an optional switch in the user registration form; if you don't require your users to have a password, you're leaving Notes wide open for abuse from unauthorized users.

You are strongly recommended to force all users to use a password. To make it secure, a password should be at least eight characters long, with a maximum of 31 characters. Try to point out to user that obvious words, such as the user's name, wife's name or nickname are too obvious. The best passwords against an educated guess from a hacker are phrases or odd combinations of letters and numbers – although a phrase is easier to remember!

Remote user security

One security risk that may be of concern to you is the use of public telephone lines by any remote users. If a remote user logs in via a modem link, all your Notes data is being transferred across an insecure telephone link. Passwords are the exception, since these are encrypted by Notes before being sent for validation at the server.

In order to maintain a secure system, you can set up Notes so that data transmitted or received from a remote user is encrypted. This will slow down the rate of data transfer a little, but unless your users are using very fast modems, in which case there may be a short delay, your users will not notice any difference.

If you decide to encrypt the data to and from a remote user, you must do so for the port rather than the individual user. Select the *File ▸ Tools ▸ User Preferences* menu option, select Ports and highlight the COM1 port – you can now select the Encrypt Network Data check box.

Note   You can also use this feature to encrypt all network transmissions over your LAN by highlighting the LAN0 port and selecting the Encrypt Network Data check box. This is only really useful if parts of your network cabling are accessible by the public, or you are very concerned by security – encrypting all network traffic will slow down the response of both the server and workstation.

Mail security

If you send a mail message to another user, you would normally prefer it if no one else read the message – as welcome as an inquisitive neighbor opening all your mail! In fact, there's little chance of other users being able to read your mail, unless they can access your workstation (see later for details of secure screen-savers and passwords).

However, when you send your mail message, the text is stored in readable form on the server in the mail database. If you have a particularly sensitive message, or if you are worried that someone has the technical expertise to 'listen in' with a network probe, you should encrypt your mail messages.

When you send a mail message you have the option to encrypt the message. This uses an algorithm built into Notes and should offer good enough protection for most cases. The recipient doesn't realize that the message was encrypted, since Notes will automatically detect this and decrypt it when it's displayed.

Tip   If you want all your users to always have their mail messages encrypted, you can configure this within NOTES.INI. Add the line:

```
SecureMail=1
```

to the INI file on each workstation and their outgoing mail will be encrypted.

Database security

Once a user gains access to the Notes network, they can be stopped from accessing your database by ACLs. An ACL (Access Control List) can be attached to any database and lists the users, servers and groups that the database manager has permitted to use the database.

A database is protected by its ACL

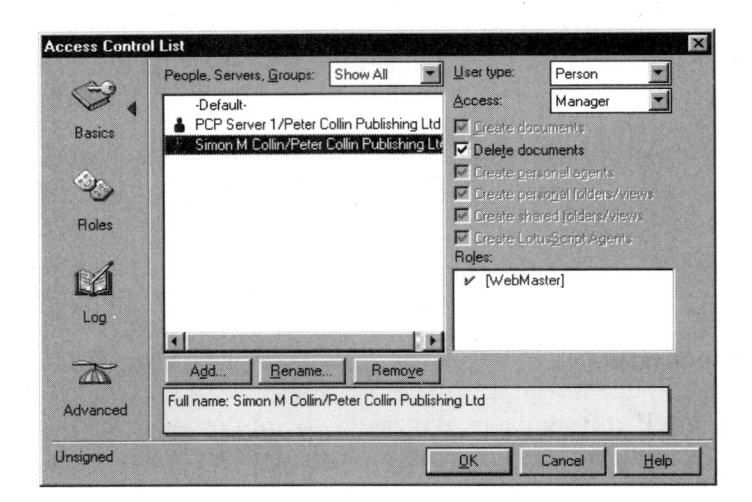

To set up or edit an ACL for a database, you must have Manager status for the particular database. Open the database from your workspace and select the *File ▸ Database ▸ Access Control* menu option.

The main scrolling window within the ACL dialog box lists the users, servers and groups and their permitted access to the database. To change the access level of one of the entries, highlight the name and select one of the radio buttons at the bottom of the screen. If you want to set up access for a number of users, you will find it more convenient to create a group (registered in the public Name & Address book), add the users to the group then manipulate the group in the ACL setup. If a user is a member of several groups, Notes will take the highest access level from the groups. If a user is listed individually by name and appears within a group, then Notes will use the individual setting, regardless of whether it offers higher or lower access than the group setting.

Table of ACL settings and rights

Access level	ACL	Design	Edit	Create
Manager	Y	Y	Y	Y
Designer		Y	Y	Y
Editor			Y	Y
Author				Y
Reader				N/A
Depositor				N/A
No Access				N/A

Using encryption in a database

Rather like mail encryption, described above, it's possible for the database designer to improve the security of a database by encrypting either the entire document within a database or, a more sensible option, encrypting just particular sensitive fields within the document template.

Server security

There are three main threats to your server: a user accidentally switching off the server, someone typing in commands at the server console prompt, lastly the possibility that someone loads 'rogue' or infected software on to the server.

The first measure is, if at all possible, to keep your Notes server in a separate locked room together with your network servers. If this isn't possible – if you're using the Windows-server version of Notes and using the PC as both a server and workstation – then you will need to take extra precautions to ensure its security.

Stopping access to the server

The first threat is a purely practical one, but it's one that happens often enough to make it worth protecting against. Someone could easily switch off the server PC; this normally happens accidentally, but the problems it causes are still the same. It won't do any lasting damage, but it could corrupt user data and, if the system administrator is not present, could shut down an office for a few hours. The simplest solution is to fit a power-switch lock and an uninterruptible power supply (UPS).

The power switch lock will prevent anyone being able to physically switch off the power with the server PC's power switch. The user could still flick the switch at the main electricity socket, but this would be protected by the UPS. A UPS monitors the main supply and, if it drops, will provide mains electricity for a few hours from a bank of batteries.

The network operating system running under Notes (either OS/2, Novell NetWare or Windows NT) can monitor a UPS and, if it switches in, will send an urgent mail message to the network administrator that the server is running on batteries.

Password protecting the server

From the server, you can carry out maintenance and administration tasks both of Notes and of the network operating system running under it. At the file server console, you have more power than from a workstation and a Machiavelian user could easily wreck havoc with your data. The aim, therefore, is to make it as difficult as possible for all except the administrator from gaining access to the command prompt at the console.

Server access lists

In the same way that a database has an ACL associated with it, it's possible to add an access control list to a server. This access list defines which users, servers or groups can use a server or the ports of a server.

In addition to the security levels described above, Notes provides another level of security that requires a password to be entered at the command prompt before it will respond to any other command. The SET SECURE Notes command locks the server console until the correct password is entered. To establish this security level, type:

```
SET SECURE password
```

Once this is in force, no other Notes applications can run on the server machine. If you share the Notes server as a workstation, the workstation can't be used while SET SECURE is on. In the Windows-server version of Notes, this means that one PC cannot be shared as a server and workstation. In addition, LOAD, TELL and SET CONFIG commands won't work until the correct password is entered. To clear the security, type the correct password.

Network operating system security

In addition to the security guards provided by Notes, it's worth remembering the functions available under the network operating system that's running under Notes. If Notes is running on a Novell NetWare server, the main status screen and management utility is called MONITOR. It's an NLM (NetWare Loadable Module) program so first you will have to load it by typing LOAD MONITOR at the NetWare system prompt. From within MONITOR, you can force users off the network, re-assign memory and resources and control the basic working methods of the LAN. You can also lock the server from within MONITOR. From the Available Options menu, choose the Lock File Server Console option. You will be prompted to type in a password. Once you have entered the password, the server console is locked; NetWare will ignore any commands typed from the keyboard until you enter the correct password. Obviously, don't forget the password once you have locked the console.

Microsoft's LAN Manager runs under the OS/2 operating system. As a multitasking operating system, OS/2 lets you switch to the main program manager and start a new session or window. There's no way of preventing this, and indeed sometimes it can be a help when troubleshooting your LAN to have workstation and server software running on the same machine. LAN Manager does lock its areas of disk and requires a password before you can access its management utilities.

For network operating systems that offer a remote console utility, giving full control of the server from a workstation (like NetWare's Remote Console utility), you will need to ensure that security rights in its directory prevent anyone but the supervisor from running it.

If you are running the Windows version of Notes, you should disable its function to switch between the tasks (using [Alt]+[Tab]). This feature can be disabled to cut down on the risk of switching to the Notes console screen, but it should be combined with the Notes SET SECURE feature.

In addition, Windows cannot lock areas of its disk, so the PC running a Windows version of the Notes server is vulnerable to users copying or deleting files or databases from the server. Again, if the server is not being used as a workstation, one safe (but drastic) method would be to delete the File Manager utility icon from the Windows screen.

You should also remove the DOS icon, which gives a user access to the hard disk and DOS's COPY command. Windows for Workgroups provides a number of functions that let you configure the Windows shell so that users have a limited range of operations and cannot run other programs from within Windows. Again, if you are not planning to use the PC as a workstation, you should try to minimize any threat from users gaining access to the PC's disk.

Using Windows security features

One way that users can get into problems is if they have a free run of their workstation system software. For example, if you can keep your users out of DOS and in Windows, you will have greater control of their environment and will lessen the chance that they might delete an important file. Windows allows the administrator to limit the actions of a user under Windows.

Security for workstations running Windows 3.1x

Within PROGMAN.INI is a section labeled [Restrictions] that lets a supervisor limit the potentially dangerous uses of the Windows Program Manager. There are a number of settings that give you great control over the choice of actions open to a user.

1. NoRun set to 1 will disable the *File ▸ Run* menu command, preventing users running any applications that aren't already on their desktop. Setting this to 0 or leaving it blank will enable the Run option.
2. NoClose set to 1 will disable the Exit option from the File menu. This effectively stops any user from exiting Windows and running around the DOS system. It will also prevent you exiting by disabling the [Alt]+[F4] action and double-clicking on the top-left hand corner of Program Manager.
3. NoSaveSettings set to 1 will prevent a user from saving their desktop settings – any of their re-arranged icon or group placings – on exiting Windows. If you want to keep your Windows screens looking the same on startup, set this option to 1.
4. NoFileMenu set to 1 will completely disable the options within the File menu. Remember, even with this set a user can still exit using [Alt]+[F4] unless NoClose is set.
5. EditLevel defines the level of control users have over their desktops.

A quick summary of the five levels is shown in the table on the next page.

Level	Comment
0	imposes no restrictions
1	prevents a user from deleting, creating or changing parameters of groups
2	adds to level 1 by preventing the creation, editing or deletion of items within a group
3	adds to level 2 by disabling the Properties dialog box
4	prevents users changing anything except moving icons around the screen

By setting these restrictions you can minimize the chance of a user getting into trouble and cut the calls to your help desk.

Security for workstations running Windows 95

If you are running Windows 95, you have far greater control over the configuration users see. There are two main ways of controlling the user's environment: System Policies and User Profiles. System Policies are far more powerful in that they allow the network supervisor to control access to various programs, applets and commands within Windows 95 – so preventing users from doing things that might wreck the computer's setup. In addition, System Policies can also be used to define user settings by changing the User Policies (to do this, the User Policies feature needs to be enabled).

For example, you can use System Policies to prevent a user running a particular application – such as starting an MS-DOS session, restricting access to the Control Panel or customizing the Desktop. Because System Policies are a fairly complex and major subject, Microsoft has included a set of template System Policies that you can use, or you can always define your own.

Before you use System Policies, you need to install the Editor – although it might seem tempting to make changes to the Registry using a text editor, do not! It's not like the old INI files, and Windows will become corrupted if you do not use the Editor. To install the System Policy Editor, insert the distribution CD-ROM and start the *Add/Remove Programs* icon in the Control Panel. Click on the Windows Setup page tag and click on the Have Disk button. Select Browse and point to the \ADMIN\APPTOOLS\POLEDIT folder on the CD-ROM. Click OK and the System Policy Editor will be added to the options that can be installed. Select it and click on Install.

Once you have installed the System Policy Editor, you'll notice that no entry is made in the Start button menu, so to run the System Policy Editor click on Start\Run and enter POLEDIT at the command line. You can then create a shortcut to the program for convenience.

You can use the Editor in two ways: either to directly edit the Registry or to create a Policy that can then be run to make changes to the Registry. (Note that you can edit either the local Registry or a Registry on a remote computer.) If you directly edit the Registry, any changes will be reflected immediately. If you create a Policy, this will only take effect when the specified user logs in and the Policy is downloaded.

> ### Three states of Registry options
> When you are editing the Registry or editing a System Policy, you must be aware that each Registry option has three possible states: on, off and greyed. Although the options look like a normal check box, you actually cycle through these three states as you click on the check box. It's very important to make sure that you are using the right state for the check box, or you could easily wipe out the user's Registry settings.
>
> - **Checked** – this state, with a tick in the box, mans the policy for the option will be used and the user's Registry changed accordingly.
> - **Unchecked** – this state, an empty box, means the policy is not implemented and any existing setting is cleared from the user's Registry.
> - **Greyed** – this state, a grey box, means that no changes are made to the Registry.

Creating a New User Policy

To create a new policy for a user, start the Policy Editor and select the *Edit ▸ Add User* menu item. Type in the name of the user that you want to add and a new user icon appears in the main Editor window. It's the same process to add a new Computer icon and policy: choose the *Edit ▸ Add Computer* menu item.

You can now edit the individual sections of the policy by double-clicking on the icon and scanning through the tree structure.

There are so many different Policy settings that I cannot cover them all in this book. However, the descriptions you'll see in the section tree structures are very clear and backed up by on-line help. As an example, here is a way of defining how to set the preferred NetWare logon server for a computer using a System Policy:

Create a new Computer policy using the *Edit ▸ Add Computer* menu item. Double-click on the Computer icon and move down through the tree structure to the Network options. Open this view by clicking on the word Network and move to the tree branch labeled Microsoft Client for NetWare Networks. Double click on this line and it will expand to show the various options. If you check the first option, Preferred Server, you can specify the name of the NetWare server that the computer will use for its primary log in.

Blocking server software access

If an intruder is more capable and persistent, or simply unlucky, he might try and load a disk with a virus or a badly-written utility on to the server. In practice, viruses are rare especially if you take reasonable precautions, such as an automatic scan that runs when you boot up each workstation.

Viruses under NetWare or OS/2 are virtually unknown. More likely is a problem from a badly written application, perhaps one written in-house and poorly tested. For an intruder to load an NLM or VAP on to a NetWare server, they would have to be an experienced NetWare programmer – it's not a trivial job writing a NetWare application. With LAN Manager running under OS/2, it's easier to recompile a utility to run under OS/2, but if it tries to interfere in another processes memory or disk space, OS/2 will stop it.

A more likely scenario is that someone will load an untested NLM or utility on to the server in good faith. The utility then crashes and brings the server down with it. Under OS/2 it is very difficult for one process to interfere with another, so it's more robust in these situations than NetWare is. Loading an untested or unapproved utility NLM or VAP on to a NetWare server could, easily, crash the entire server. The reason is because NetWare allows NLMs to run in ring zero of memory – an unprotected and unsupervised mode that offers the highest performance but greatest risk. The solution is to again lock the server console using NetWare's MONITOR or fit disk drive locks.

Intruder prevention

User accounts and passwords

Network security has two important roles to play. The first is to make sure that your company's data is safe from intruders. The second is to provide a real sense of security to users so that they are not afraid to save their private or personal data on to the network server. These are the principal aims of network security. But there's also a secondary aim: to minimize the entire effort that's required from users and supervisors. If maintaining security becomes a drudge or a nuisance, it will be dropped and your LAN will be wide open to intruders or accidental damage.

All network operating systems provide some form of data security, from basic password protection to data encryption and government-approved status. There are two basic types of network file security:

Share-level security associates a password with a shared drive, directory or single file. You can limit the read/write capabilities assigned to the password. This level of security is normally used by DOS-based LANs making it easy to move the shared resources. The disadvantage is keeping track of all the passwords. It's easy for security to be breached and security would be a real headache since one password would be known to all the users of the drive, directory or file. Simple peer-to-peer networks use this level of security. Share-level security is cumbersome for large networks and not very flexible (it's hard to limit what a particular user can and cannot do). But it is quick and easy to set up and so ideal for small networks where security is not a big issue.

User-level security moves the password protection to each user. A network administrator would set up groups that have rights to particular areas of a drive and individual users are assigned to groups. Each user logs in with their login name and a password. Once cleared, the user has access to the LAN according to the security definitions in the groups he belongs to. The supervisor can plan the network and ensure that security is not compromised by forcing regular changes of each user's password. Since they only have to remember one password, there own, security is tighter.

Notes and most high-end network operating systems implements a user-level security system that offers a supervisor the greatest control and power when designing a secure LAN. It is, initially, an effort to define the groups, hierarchies and user-levels, but you will be in control. Before you start to create users or define the rights of groups and managers, it's worth spending time drawing the hierarchies and departmental divisions within your company.

The users

Every person that is registered in the Notes Name & Address Book has an associated account. Every user has limited access to the system – only the administrator has unrestricted access to the whole system. The user's entry in the Name & Address Book defines their rights to use different databases and their ability to add or change data within documents.

Passwords are a necessary part of logging into any network. To most office workers, they are also a nuisance. It's worth enforcing password protection since this is the single most effective deterrent against casual intruders. In NetWare, the supervisor can specify the minimum number of characters for a password and set a renewal date. Typically, it's worth setting a minimum password length of six characters and a renewal date once a month. There are utilities available that will check that passwords are not too obvious – for example a user's surname.

Remember that if you start to enforce password changes too often, users will get fed up and will jeopardize the security with passwords like 'PASS1', followed next week by 'PASS2' and so on. One tip to deter users from telling each other their passwords or from writing them on the corner of the monitor is self-protection. Create a home directory for each user, to which only they have access. This will mean the users will start to save their personal data in this directory and will become sticklers for security to protect their own data.

Improving security

The software controls discussed will help considerably in providing a secure Notes network. These will help protect especially against accidental and innocent users damaging data. A lockable power switch and UPS will protect the server from someone pulling out the power cord, and password protection will stop casual or inexperienced users.

One problem that is not addressed by any of the recommendations mentioned is a fundamental problem with most network hardware. The worst offender is Ethernet, the most popular transmission method with over 60% of the installed base, uses a bus-based topology in which every message passes through every workstation. The same problem exists with Token Ring and, often, also with 10-Base-T. If a user is determined enough, they can install monitoring software that will display any text from any user that's sent over the network.

However, it's worth pointing out that the hacker would need considerable network knowledge and so this is only a problem if you are dealing with very sensitive material.

Every piece of confidential data you view on your PC's monitor, or type in, passes through every workstation's network adapter card. Normally, only the server and your workstation recognize the ID and read off the data. Any intruder with a network probe or monitor can view every packet of data that's carried over the cable. There's rarely any data encryption, so you can view exactly what's being sent around the network.

If you are worried about this threat, there are a number of solutions. Passwords are not sent as plain text, they are encrypted before they are transmitted from the workstation to the server, but the rest of the traffic is not encrypted. LAN Manager and some other network operating systems have an option to encrypt all workstation traffic, which will provide a very secure LAN, but will slow down performance (admittedly, this performance drop is only by a few per cent and won't be noticed by most users).

An alternative option is open if your network is wired using a star-topology with a hub in the center. A number of hub vendors sell secure hubs that will limit the traffic between the relevant workstations instead of a general transmission to all workstation.

The second problem that's often overlooked is the risk when a user walks away from their PC for a coffee or lunch break. Very few users can be bothered to log out for a short break. But then, the data on their local machine and a link to the network is open to any passing intruder.

It's worth investing in software protection: if your users are running Microsoft's Windows, it comes bundled with a screen-saver that will clear the screen after a pre-defined number of minutes of inactivity. To continue using the PC, you have to enter a password. It's easy to get around this, for example, by leaving Windows, but it's a good deterrent against opportunists.

If you are using DOS workstations, Novell DOS 7 includes a DOS-based screen-saver with password attached, and for Macintosh users System 7 includes password-protection on its screen-saver.

Setting up international support

With its role as a company-wide information management system, a lot of users will want to use Notes in an international environment. This means setting up Notes for different languages and different time zones.

Language support

There are parts of Notes that can be configured to use different languages, and parts that must always stay in one language. The language for servers within a domain must be the same: this is because the public Name & Address book, which replicates between servers in a domain must be consistent. In practice, the language of the public Name & Address book is set as the language of the first server. If your first server is set up with US English then the public Name & Address book will be in US English.

Unlike the language used across the domain, each individual server can be set up with its own language. The server's language determines the style used to display dates, time, the sort order, mail system, and the language for the help database and formulas.

The final part of the system, the workstation, can adopt any language, and it's here that the flexibility is required by users. The workstation's language defines the words displayed for the menu system, the user's personal Name & Address book and the spell-check dictionary. All these features are accessed through the Notes workstation's International page: *File ▸ Tools ▸ User Preferences ▸ International*.

Defining the international look of your database

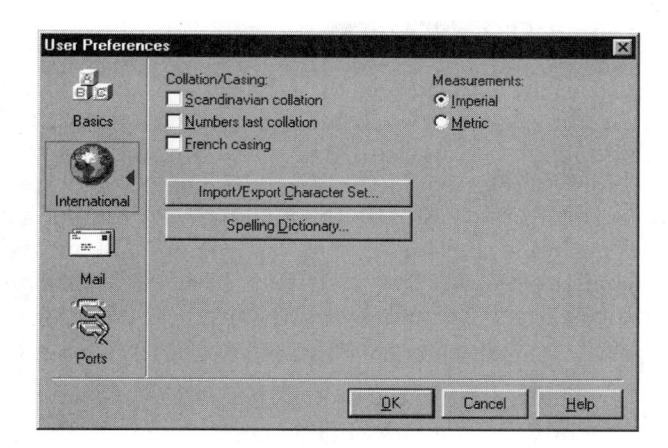

If you design a database and want to use it in a number of different languages, you can translate the descriptive words displayed on screen without losing any data; make sure that you don't change the names of the field labels or element labels, otherwise you will run into problems when trying to access the data.

Notes, like several other Lotus products, uses the Lotus Multibyte Character Set (LMBCS) standard; this means that it can display a very wide range of character sets and alphabets. To set up the workstation's language, you need to revert to DOS commands: the country code, keyboard table, local codepage and multinational codepage. These settings are all configured within the workstation's AUTOEXEC.BAT and CONFIG.SYS files.

Time zone support

There should be few problems with time zones, since most users will only see their own time zones. Notes uses an internal clock based on Greenwich Mean Time (GMT); this lets it order documents from different time zones within a single view without getting thoroughly confused!

If you have a multi-time zone installation, each server can have its local time setup within its Location document. To edit this document, open the Public Address Book, open the Location document and press [Ctrl]+[E] to switch to Edit mode. You can now change the location for your server.

If a user creates a document, it will have a time/date stamp that shows the server's local time.

Configuring the user's workspace

Each user's workspace, their Notes Desktop, can be configured and customized so that on installation, each workstation has the same icons and menu options. This will make training and troubleshooting a lot easier! All the settings that describe a user's workspace are stored in the file DESKTOP.DSK. The simplest way of creating a custom workspace for all your users is to copy the default, blank workspace from the installation disks into your C:/NOTES directory and tailor this. The process is very straightforward:

1. Make a copy of your DESKTOP.DSK file (called MYDESK.DSK); make a copy of the Notes installation disks.
2. Copy the default, blank DESKTOP.DSK file from the Notes installation disk to your NOTES subdirectory.
3. Start Notes on your workstation.
4. Add database icons and change the palette and layout of the desktop.
5. Exit Notes.
6. Copy the new, customized DESKTOP.DSK from your workstation back on to the installation disks.
7. Install Notes on to the workstations: as you install the software, each user will have the customized DSK file.
8. Copy your original DSK file back from MYDESK to DESKTOP.DSK.

This gives you the opportunity to configure user's workstations as they are installed. Another method is to send the updated or customized desktop files to the user's workstation as the log in to the network operating system. For example, if you are running Novell NetWare, you could copy a new, updated DESKTOP.DSK file from the server to each workstation using the Login script. Always remember to thoroughly test the desktop before copying it to each user and keep regular backups in case of any problems.

15
Domino Server

Introduction

Lotus Notes provides an excellent system to distribute information throughout your company. It does not stop there. Almost every major company is linked to the Internet or is considering setting up an intranet. In many situations, the information that you use and update for use within the company could also be very useful to your customers and potential customers.

Up until now the traditional way of publishing information onto either an intranet or the Internet has been to create Web pages using an authoring tool. This produces rather static pages that need to be updated regularly to keep the user's attention. The alternative is to link a database to the Internet and allow visitors to your Web site to interrogate the database and view the results. But what a lot of effort: you need to install a Web server platform – with software and hardware – configure a link between the server and your database server, setup a special translation utility that formats the information for a Web page and, finally, setup firewalls to ensure that no one can break into your system.

Lotus Domino 1.5 makes Web publishing and database publishing easy! Domino is a Web server application that works closely with Notes to allow you to publish any Notes application directly onto the Web. A visitor can interact with the Web page and retrieve information from the underlying Notes database. Domino does all the conversion to and from Notes database formats to the HTML coding system used for Web pages. If your Web pages need sprucing up, Domino also supports a wide range of standard enhancements including ActiveX and Java applets, Javascript, CGI and Perl scripts and more. The software provides a secure environment and ties in with the ACL settings for a database together with the Address book (Web users can even be listed in the Address book to control access).

Best of all is the news that Lotus Domino is available free of charge – for the moment. Once you've filled in a simple registration form, you can download a version from the Lotus Web site (www.lotus.com). Officially, Domino is included in the price of your Lotus Notes 4.5 product – when you download Domino you are not obtaining a trial version, this is the full shipping version.

Domino and InterNotes

InterNotes is a Web publishing tool that currently ships with Lotus Notes 4.5. The software provides links for Notes users to the Internet and lets a designer create static Web pages which can be published on the Internet. Domino, on the other hand, creates dynamic Web pages as they are requested using the information in an existing Notes database. With Domino, there's no need to do any extra HTML programming, but you can if you want – to enhance a page or include links, forms, scripts or applets.

Some sites could work well with the InterNotes package, especially if you do not want to publish your information in an interactive form. Other sites are ideal for Domino – where a visitor can search through an existing database and receive an interactive response. Advanced Web sites could support both InterNotes and Domino, perhaps with Domino supplying the enhanced service or a search function to backup the static pages published with InterNotes.

The Domino system

Lotus Domino provides a full Web server using the HTTP protocol providing documents to Web clients. The Web pages are created using HTML with support for extensions included in HTML 3.2 – unlike a static Web page, Domino creates the HTML code on-the-fly when a user requests a page. Domino supports a wide range of scripting and applet standards, together with several common authentication and security systems.

Here is a brief summary of the main features of Domino 1.5:

- Full HTTP server.
- Support for HTML 3.2.
- Support for Java and ActiveX applets.
- Support for Javascript.

- Support for CGI and Perl scripts.
- Access to any Notes database.
- Links to the ACL of a database for field-level access control.
- Access control via Notes' Name & Address book.
- Support for Secure Sockets (SSL) for authentication and encryption.
- Converts all Notes database elements direct to HTML.
- Support for image maps and forms.
- Support for standard URLs to database items or HTML files.
- Built-in search function.

How it works

Domino Server works beside your Lotus Notes 4.x server software on the same server. Once you have installed and configured the software (see later) Domino is easy to start – using either a command line or automatic execution. Most of the time you can forget about Domino, since it works in the background managing the process involved when users want to view a Web document.

The core of Domino works in a similar way to many other Web server applications; the main feature being its HTTP server. HTTP (Hypertext Transfer Protocol) is a standard protocol that allows clients to access Web pages either over an intranet or the Internet. Without this function, users with a Web browser would not be able to access any of the Web pages created by Domino. When a user types in the address for the Web page he or she wants to access, they normally write it in the format `http://www.lotus.com` which tells the Web browser that the document is stored on an HTTP server. Most browsers let you enter the address for the Web page (called the URL) without the prefix `http://`. It's worth noting that most browsers support FTP calls to remote servers if you enter the full FTP address instead of the Web page – for example:

`ftp://ftp.lotus.com`

The Domino HTTP server runs the whole time looking for requests for Web documents. These requests arrive when a user points their browser to the full address for the Web document. This full address is called the URL (Uniform Resource Locator) and is a standard way of locating files, pages and servers over the Internet.

The Domino HTTP server will look at each URL that it receives and determine whether the URL points to a static HTML file that is stored on the server or if it refers to information stored in a Notes database. When the URL points to an HTML file, Domino simply opens the file and sends the data (the HTML codes) from the file back to the Web client. If, however, the request is for information stored in a Notes database then Domino steps up a gear.

To retrieve information from a Notes database, Domino opens the database, extracts the data and formats it according to your rules (see later in this chapter). This process of formatting the data is done on-the-fly and converts the Notes visual objects such as navigators, links, information, buttons *etc.* into HTML code. For example, a link to another document is converted as a standard HTML instruction that includes the URL to the document. In some cases, URLs will directly access Notes functionality (either because the Web client knows how to control the Domino system or, normally, due to generated URLs in a database that's been translated to HTML). For example, the URL:

`http://www.xyz.com/welcome.nsf?OpenDatabase`

will open the `welcome.nsf` database stored on the Domino server at XYZ's offices. Note that these direct instructions are limited by the security system you setup (see later) and do not provide a loophole for hackers.

System requirements

Domino Web Server 1.5 currently requires the same system requirements as your Lotus Notes release 4.*x* server software but you should make sure that the server has at least 64Mb of RAM and 1Gb of hard disk storage available. However, you will need extra network connections (if you do not already have these in place) to provide links to the Internet. The primary requirement is for a network that uses TCP/IP in addition to any other network protocol you might currently use on your LAN. In practice this means installing the TCP/IP protocol on the Notes server and ensuring that the server has a link to your office network (for an intranet) or an Internet service provider that supports the TCP/IP protocol.

If you are using Domino internally to drive an intranet, you do not need to install any communications hardware and your site will be secure and relatively simple to setup. If you plan to use Domino to drive a Web site that's accessible to any user on the Internet then you will need to discuss with your Internet service provider (ISP) the best way to connect to their system. A cheap option is to use a dial-up modem link, but this is slow and expensive in telephone calls for a busy site (a faster option is to use an ISDN link). However, the best solution for a large Web site is to install a leased line direct to the ISP. Various connection options are discussed below.

Dial-up modem

Cheap, and all ISPs support this, but your server needs to dial up the ISP. Unfortunately, there are high running costs and phone bills once you have a semi-permanent link.

Dial-back modem

Slightly more expensive, this uses a dedicated modem at the ISP that calls your server when any user tries to access your server. However, this can result in slow access-time for the user.

Dial-back ISDN

A faster, more expensive, solution that creates a near-instant link from the ISP to your server on demand. The problem is that you still have to pay telephone charges.

Leased line

This provides a permanent link between you and the ISP with no connect charges. However, the supplier will charge several thousand dollars per quarter for rental and the ISP will also charge you a higher rental.

Installing and running Domino

Once you have downloaded the Domino software (currently a 3Mb file stored on the Lotus server at http://domino.lotus.com) you can install the software. This is very simple as Domino copies itself to the existing Notes program folder and installs graphic and help files in the existing Notes data folder.

With Domino installed, you can start the Domino server by entering the following command at the Notes console (either directly or using the console command utility in the Administrator's screen):

```
load http
```

To ensure that Domino is always running, you should edit the NOTES.INI file to add Domino as a startup task for the Notes server. Edit the NOTES.INI file with a text editor and add ", http" at the end of the SeverTasks line. For example:

```
ServerTasks=Replica, Router, http
```

You can stop the Domino server at any time by entering the following command from the Notes console screen:

```
tell http quit
```

TIP   If you want to check how Domino is performing or to view its statistics, enter the following command at the Notes server console:

```
show stat domino
```

Configuring Domino

With Domino installed and running you can now turn your attention to the way in which you configure the server to provide a complete Web site. Each Web site has a home page (in a static Web site this would be called INDEX.HTM) that provides an introduction to your company together with links to other Web pages. For your home page you could either create a separate HTML file or use an existing About document, database document, or view.

Before you design your Web site, you make sure that all your databases are protected against possible intruders. Set the ACL for each database to either prevent a user viewing the database or to allow a user access. This setting is in the *Access Control List ▸ Advanced* section under the 'Maximum Internet browser access' section.

With the home page defined and the databases protected, you can define the way in which your Domino server will interact with the Internet. Open the Server document from the Public Address Book and open the HTTP Server section. There are basic fields that you should configure and these are described below.

- **TCP/IP port number**

    Defines the port that is used to transfer information between the Web client and server – set this to 80, the standard for browsers. Try not to set a port number other than 80 – it complicates life for the users. Note that if you really do want a port other than 80, ensure that you enter a number above 1024 because all the addresses below this value are reserved for TCP/IP applications.

- **TCP/IP port status**

    Enable this setting to allow non authenticated (non SSL) connections to your server.

- **DNS Lookup**

    If this is enabled, Domino will ask the Web client for their host DNS address. Although this adds a little to the processing time you will find it very useful to have the full text DNS address included in the visitor access logs for your server rather than the IP address of the visitor. It makes life much easier when reading and analyzing access logs.

- **Host name**

    This is the domain name of your host. If you are publishing on the Internet you will need to register a domain name either via your ISP or directly with the InterNIC organization (`www.internic.net`). Once registered, the domain host name will translate a simple name such as `www.xyz.com` to the server's full IP address such as 123.123.111.222. If you are publishing on an intranet, you can use any host name.

- **Home URL**

    The default name that is used by Domino if a user does not provide the full URL. For example, if you set the Home URL to `http://www.xyz.com` this will be added as a prefix if a user enters `/index.html` without a full URL.

- **Default Home Page**

    Enter the name of the HTML file that should be used as the home page – normally called `index.htm` and stored in the default Domino HTML folder.

- **HTML directory**

    The name of the folder which holds static HTML files that will be used by Domino.

- CGI directory

  The name of the folder that contains any CGI programs that will be used.

Domino runs an HTTP server with a simple setup document

```
Basics
TCP/IP port number:     80

TCP/IP port status:     Enabled
SSL port number:        443
SSL port status:        Enabled
Host name:
DNS lookup:             Disabled
Default home page:      default.htm
Maximum active          40
 threads:
Minimum active          20
 threads:
```

The user's view of Domino

When a user accesses your Web site, he or she will see the home page that you have created. If you have not created (or specified in the Server document) a home page, the user can only access Web pages by entering their full URL. It's well worth spending some time on a neat, attractive home page even if you are setting up a site for an internal intranet.

If there's no home page, or if you have allowed users to access the Notes databases (by setting the "Allow HTTP clients to browse databases" option in the server document) then a user can see a tree view of the databases stored on the server by entering the command:

    server/?Open

from his browser's URL field. Each database on the server is listed as a hypertext link that points to the databases on your server.

One of the simplest ways of setting up a home page is to design an About document for each database (or for one central database) that contains links to views, forms and documents. Choose the *File ▸ Database ▸ Properties* menu, click the Launch tab and select "On Database Open: Open 'About Database' Document." This will ensure that the About document will be displayed automatically whenever any user opens the database, giving them a guide to the contents.

Web users can, if authorized, view all Notes databases on your server and so access Notes remotely

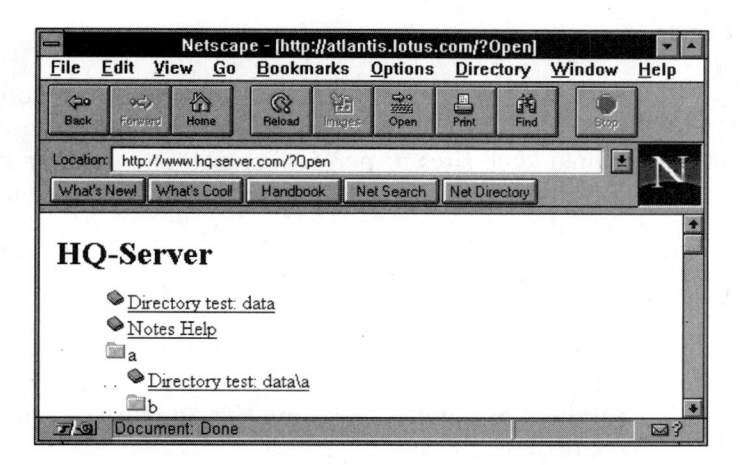

Programming with Domino

One of the most powerful features of Domino is that it lets you add extra functionality to your Web pages by inserting program objects or commands directly into the Web page. For any Notes application designers this provides one of the easiest way to create sophisticated, interesting Web pages – without having to struggle with HTML or scripting tools. However, once you have exhausted the functionality of the Notes @-set you can turn to a range of standard scripting tools to add features to you site. In addition to the @-set of commands native to Notes, Lotus Domino supports the following programming options.

CGI scripts

CGI scripts are the mainstay of many complex Web sites, allowing you to access system functions including Perl scripts. For many traditional Web sites, CGI scripts provide just about the only way to implement simple search functions, mail programs and buttons. With the Notes @-set of commands, you will probably find that you need never touch CGI. For examples of CGI scripts, look on the following Web site:

    http://domino.lotus.com

Perl scripts

Perl is a scripting language that lets you create complex applications that can run from any Perl interpreter. Perl scripts are often used on traditional Web sites to perform search and counter functions. Domino supports any standard Perl program which should be stored in the cgi-bin folder.

Java

Java must be one of the most popular ways of authoring applets for Web pages. You can create a Java applet using any of the commercial compilers available. The applet is downloaded automatically by the Web browser.

Javascript, VBScript

Domino supports any standard Javascript or VBScript instructions that are included in HTML documents (these provide extra functionality without the bother of compiling a Java applet). Javascript or VBScript files are normally accessed as a passthru HTML command or stored in an $$HTMLHead field.

@functions, @commands

The main way of adding extra functions to your Web page is to use the @functions and @commands supported by Notes. These are covered in depth in this book.

LotusScript

Domino supports LotusScript under certain circumstances within the NotesSession class.

Creating image maps

One of the ways of getting away from a plain text interface to your Web pages is to use an image map. This is a graphic image that has areas defined with URLs attached to each area. A user points to an area of the image and clicks to jump to the URL. It's easy to use and, with Domino, reasonably easy to implement.

The way in which you create an image map in Domino is to design a navigator and define regions that jump to particular URLs. When a user accesses the Web page, Domino will automatically convert the navigator to an image map. In order to get this feature to work you need to use the *Create ▸ Graphic Background* command (not a simple *Edit ▸ Paste*) to setup a graphic image in a navigator.

Creating links

Within a standard traditional Web page you can create a hypertext link to any other page, file or section of the page using the `A HREF` HTML command. Within Domino, the system is slightly different and is similar to the way in which you would add a link within any Notes database.

To provide a simple link you can use the *Edit ▸ Copy As Link* menu command which places an icon on the Web page – with an associated hypertext jump if a user clicks on the link. Alternatively, you can create an action hotspot using an @command formula or the `@URLOpen` formula to setup the link. To provide a link to any other Web page you could use a passthru HTML command. Lastly, you can create an extra function in an action bar that is displayed on the Web page and links to a database view.

Text searching

A powerful feature to add to any Web site is a search function. For an intranet this duplicates the role of Notes itself, but for the Internet it allows any user to search a database for information.

Domino allows you to add full-text search functions to your Web site with little effort

In a traditional Web site hosted by an ISP, you rely on the functions provided by the ISP. For a traditional Web server run with standard server software you need to install a special search add-on function (or a Perl script). Under Domino it is simple to add a full-text search feature that lets a user search any database.

To add text searching, first ensure that the database has a full-text index then add a link to a view or which gives the user access to the Notes search dialog box.

Security

One of the most important factors you must consider when designing your Web site is the security of the site. You must provide all the security blocks necessary to prevent an intruder from getting into your network and Notes system. In a standard Web server system you would install a firewall or you would ensure that there is a physical break between the Web server and the rest of the network (perhaps by using a router or protocol block).

Domino can protect your network and databases using a range of security measures

With the Domino/Notes system the Web server runs closely with your data store (Notes) so you must make sure that there are plenty of security checks. There are two levels at which you can limit user access:

- Using ACLs associated with all Notes databases.
- Using the Address Book to limit identified users.

Once a user has been identified and logged in, you can use the SSL authentication and encryption system supported by Domino that lets users transmit sensitive data across the public Internet.

To setup the security for your Domino site, make sure that you create specific Person documents for any Web user who will need to be verified. This is fine if you only want your site to be accessed by official users, but is a problem when dealing with the general public. To handle anonymous users you could setup SSL (Secure Sockets Layer) using the server document on the server. Alternatively, for a more open feel you could setup password security for databases, forms or views. You do not have to worry about passthru problems since the current edition of Domino does not allow Web clients to access other Notes servers using passthru.

A quick way of forcing a login screen to ensure that a user is recognized is to append &Login to the URL linking to the document – this will display an authentication dialog screen and prevent any unauthorized access.

Protecting your databases with the ACL

The main way in which Notes protects a database is via its associated access control list (ACL) that defines who can access the database and lists the tasks that a user can carry out (see earlier in this book for full details on the ACL). The access levels set up in the ACL are identical in limitations to the levels that apply for any standard Notes database.

Glossary

10Base-T: A cabling and connection standard used to carry Ethernet signals. 10Base-T is the offspring of the generic Ethernet specification which defines data transmission of 10Mbits per second using 802.3 data packets over twisted pair cable with telephone-style RJ-45 connectors. Unlike ThinWire Ethernet, 10Base-T has a physical star topology that makes it more robust and more secure than its predecessor. However, it needs a central hub.

Access list: List of authorized users or groups that are allowed to use the resource – normally either a server or database (called ACLs).

ACL (Access Control List): List maintained by the database manager that contains a list of users that can access the database together with their rights – from read-only to full manager.

Action bar: A non-scrolling region above a view that can be configured by the database designer to show buttons, icons or other navigational aids.

Agent: A new term (in Notes 4) for a macro that allows designers to add automation to a form, database or view. The macros can run at particular times of day and can look for documents that match a rule.

API: Application-Programming Interface; standard set of commands that control an application. The application in this case would normally be a low-level product such as the mail server software or the operating system.

Attachment: File linked to an e-mail message, and sent at the same time. The file can be any file such as a document, spreadsheet or application file. This is different from OLE in which Windows objects (such as a graphic or clipboard of text) can be inserted into the rich text field of a document.

Authentication: Method of determining whether a message or user ID file is authentic.

Bridge: An interconnection device that can connect LANs at the data link level allowing similar LANs using different transmission methods, for example Ethernet or Token Ring, to talk. Bridges are able to read and filter the data packets and frames employed by the protocol and use the addresses to decide whether or not to pass a packet.

Brouter: Brouters combine the functions of bridges and routers in connecting two LANs. A brouter will route data packets if the protocol is known and bridge them if the protocol is unknown.

Bus: One of the simplest network topologies in which a single length of cable connects all network devices. It has a definite start and end – contrasting with a ring or star topology. Thin and Thick-wire Ethernet use a bus topology. Bus networks are easy to implement, but one break in the wire brings the whole network down. Star topology networks (such as 10Base-T) avoid this problem using one central connection point – the hub – with lots of short wires to each node.

Certification Log: Record stored by Notes listing who and what was certified at what time.

Certified ID: An ID file that has been correctly authenticated by an administrator using his certifier ID.

Certifier ID: The original ID file that is used to electronically 'stamp' every authorized user or server of the Notes network.

Client: Technically, the network workstation that communicates with a server or an e-mail address. In the case of Notes, it's the user accessing the central Notes Server application from his or her Desktop program.

Client–server: A computing system consisting of networked 'clients' which request information and a central 'server' which stores data and manages shared information and resources. Client–server software, or architectures, are trying to reduce the amount of data traffic flowing over the wires between clients and server. It does this by processing data at the server as well as simply retrieving it. For example, a client PC with a simple front-end application asks the server to find all contacts in New York. The server trawls through the database and only returns the correct matches. The alternative is for the client to request the entire database to be sent which it then searches. The difference is subtle, but this is the new design on which server-based SQL databases work. The result being that the network is not stressed so heavily. The only caveat being that the server does more by having to run an application in parallel with the NOS. Notes works as a very efficient client–server application to minimize traffic as much as possible.

Connection Document: Document within the Public Name & Address Book that defines how and when the server should contact another Notes server to exchange mail or data.

Dead mail: Mail that has not been properly delivered (and which often indicates a problem with a mail router). Any dead mail will be listed when you issue the SHOW TASKS server command.

Document: One entry or record within a database. The document can contain fields for data together with buttons and graphics. Within the Public Name & Address Book database, each document describes an object such as a user, server or connection.

Domain: A group of Notes servers that share the same Public Name & Address book. Domains are a convenient way of cutting down on management chores and improving security.

Encryption: Method of scrambling the contents of a mail message or file so that only the intended recipient can read it. Your Notes workstation will normally de-crypt messages automatically as they are received.

Ethernet: One of the earliest networking architectures which normally refers to transmission of packets of data at 10 Mbits/second over co-axial cable with BNC connectors. It defines how the packets of data are formed, using IEEE standard 802.3; variations include the 10Base-T standard which uses twisted-pair cabling and various proprietary high-speed networks.

Fixup: Notes server utility that checks through a database to see if it has been corrupted and attempts to fix any problems it finds.

Folder: An element in a Navigator that can contain documents. The Navigator window is normally on the left of the screen and shows the Folders in a tree-type layout.

Gateway: High-level interconnection device which passes packets of data from one type of networking system, computer or application to another by converting the protocols and format of the packets used.

Gateway (e-mail): Interface between different e-mail systems; gateways convert protocols to connect dissimilar networks.

ID file: User ID that proves that a user has been correctly registered with Notes. The ID file is an encrypted number that has been correctly 'electronically' stamped by the certifier ID. A user cannot log in nor use Notes without a certified ID file.

ISP (Internet Service Provider):

ISO (OSI reference model): The Open Standards Interconnect (OSI) definition was published by the International Standards Organization (ISO) in 1977. It describes seven layers of network function from the lowest layer (physical), which deals with physical connections such as the wires, connectors and electrical signals; to the highest layer (application), which provides the user interface to the lower levels. OSI offers guidelines for developers enabling them to design networks and related products which can talk, regardless of their make and use.

LotusScript: Programming script language included with Notes 4.5 that allows programmers to carry out complex tasks that would be very difficult using @functions. LotusScript also provides external database access using ODBC drivers.

Mail-enabled application: A normal application from which it is possible to send mail without specifically calling up your e-mail package. Lotus is mail-enabling new releases of its Windows packages to automatically call up cc:Mail; WinMail supplies macros to mail-enable standard applications.

MAPI: Microsoft's open Mail Application Programming Interface.

MHS: Message Handling Service, Netware's store-and-forward message transfer mechanism. Some packages use this as the message transfer system (BeyondMail, WinMail); others can access it through a gateway.

Mapping: Linking a directory path to a local drive letter, enabling a user to log directly on to a server's network drive without having to select volumes, directories and files individually.

Message Transfer Agent (MTA): A type of gateway that extends Notes to provide access to another type of mail system. For example, if you want to link Notes with your mainframe-based mail system you would add the correct MTA package to link the two.

Name & Address Book: – see Public Name & Address Book.

Naming Services: An important development within the last couple of years, spurred on by the importance of WANs. It simply dictates that within a network, each node has a unique address and name and any server or workstation can reach and communicate with any other. NetWare 4.0, DECnet and Vines employ global naming services.

Navigator: A window on the left side of the database layout that provides links to important sections of the database or provides icons to allow a user to switch view. For example, the Navigator could be designed to show folders that represent an outline structure of the database, or could include icons for each type of sort order for the documents.

NetBIOS: Network Basic Input/Output System (NetBIOS) is a low-level software interface that lets applications talk to network hardware. If a network is NetBIOS compatible, it will respond in the same way to the set of NetBIOS commands, accessed from DOS by the Int 5Ch interrupt. NetBIOS was the de facto standard, thanks to a lack of international standards, but its limitations and age now make it almost redundant.

Network server: The central computer that runs your network operating system that controls access to the network and provides the main shared file storage location. If you have a medium number of users to support, you could install Notes on to your existing network server to share resources; for large installations, Notes would run on its own dedicated server connected to the network.

Notes sever: Computer on which the Notes Server application runs. This can be the same machine as the network server or can be a dedicated computer that is only running Notes Server. This machine also provides the main store for the databases. One Notes server can be connected to others either by a network link or remote dial-up link to allow data to be exchanged during mail exchange or database replication.

NotesFlow: Set of functions that makes it easier to create programs or databases that implement work-flow to pass documents between users for authorization or between programs.

Notes/FX 2.0: Feature of Notes that allows actions within a Notes form field to be available to OLE 2 objects.

Packet: The basic unit of data sent over the network during intercommunication. A packet includes the address of the sending and receiving stations, error control information and check procedures, and, finally, the information itself.

Pane: A separate, scrolling window that displays part of a view of a database or document. When a database is opened, the window splits into panes that show the Navigator, Action bar, and document.

Passthru: Notes 4 includes this feature that lets two servers or a workstation and a server communicate via a third Passthru server. For example, if one server only supports NetBIOS and another only supports TCP/IP, the two can communicate via a Passthru server that supports both protocols. It's often used with remote workstations to allow them to dial into a Passthru server that then gives them access to any Notes server on the network - without having to dial each server individually.

Protocol: Rules covering format and timing of messages on a network.

Public Name & Address Book: Address book that contains the names and their mail address or access route of all the objects that the server recognizes including users and other servers. To add a user, you add a new User Document within this address book. In addition to the Public Name & Address Book, each user can have a separate personal Name & Address book which lists a subset of users they contact frequently. See also Domain.

Remote client: User accessing mail without being connected to the mail server's local network. The user can be elsewhere in a WAN, or accessing the mail system via a modem link.

Replication: Main method by which Notes distributes data and ensures that the data across a network of Notes servers is up to date. Replication happens at preset times according to the schedule in the Server Document; this defines when one Notes server will contact another and exchange updates to the documents within databases and transfer any mail.

Route (mail): Software routine that filters out mail messages addressed to a user on a different Notes server and transfers them during a replication or mail connection.

Router: An interconnection device similar to a bridge but operating at a higher level within the OSI reference model. Routers detect protocols rather than the data they carry and use the destination address to work out the best route for the packet through a complex network. Typically used within WANs, intelligent routers can select whether to use telephone links, LANs, or particular shortcuts through a network.

Schedule: Timetable set up by the Notes supervisor to define when an action will take place. This is normally used to define when one server will call another and replicate the databases and exchange mail.

Server document: A document within the Public Name & Address Book that defines the basic properties of a server – such as its name and domain.

SMTP: Simple Mail Transfer Protocol – Internet protocol for e-mail transfer.

Store-and-forward: Method of transferring mail by moving copies of the messages, rather than pointers to the messages on the server. MHS and X.400 are store-and-forward systems.

TCP/IP: Transmission Control Protocol / Internet Protocol (TCP/IP) is a set of communications protocols developed by the US Department of Defense (DOD), originally for use in military applications. TCP/IP bundles and unbundles sent and received data into packets, manages packet transmission and checks for errors across networks. Originally found binding Unix networks together, its flexibility and portability are making it a de facto standard for LANs and WANs.

User document: A Document within the Public Name & Address Book that defines a user on a Notes server. The document includes their rights, name, home server and any restrictions.

View: A way of looking at a series of documents in a database. For example, in a contact sales database one view would show contacts that are due to be telephoned today and another that shows contacts which have generated sales.

VIM: Vendor-Independent Messaging – the common API set established by IBM, Borland, Novell and Apple, and built into OS/2 2.0. This system is used by Notes Mail to send messages within Notes and to Lotus cc:Mail.

WAN: Wide area network. Multiple small, linked local area networks or a network with multiple servers linked together using public telephone circuits, leased lines or high-speed bridges.

Workspace: Environment in which a user can use Notes on his or her workstation. The Workspace consists of several pages on to which you can add large icon buttons that give access to a particular Notes database. SmartIcons give one-click access to common functions and pull-down menus allow access to more advanced functions.

X.400: CCITT standard: application layer OSI mail transfer method.

Appendix A: @-functions

A – C

@Abs(number)
Returns the unsigned, absolute value of **number**.

@Accessed
Returns the time and date when the document was last accessed

@Adjust(time-date; year; month; day; hour; minute; second)
Adjusts the time-date value that's specified by the amount in the following arguments. For example, to increase a value **Date** by one month you could use the function:

@Adjust(Date; 0; 1; 0; 0; 0;0)

@All
Selects all documents in a database to show in a view. This should be used with the SELECT command as in SELECT @All.

@AttachmentLengths
Returns a list of the size of each attachment linked to the current document. This size might be slightly wrong, because Notes tries to calculate the size the file would take on disk if uncompressed from its compressed form as an attachment.

@Attachments
Returns the number of attached files linked to the current document.

@Author
Returns a list of all the users that have saved documents within the database – the 'authors' of the database's material. Note that servers, which might have provided material through replication, are not included in this list.

@Begins("string"; "substring")
Returns a TRUE value of 'I' if the contents of "substring" is stored at the beginning of "string". Returns FALSE, '0' if it is not. The function is case-sensitive.

@Char(number)
Converts a code number into a single-character string. The code number refers to the IBM code page 850 range of characters.

@Command([command]; options;..)
This function will execute a Notes command – any of the standard menu commands can be run using this.

@Contains("string"; "substring")
Returns a TRUE value of 'I' if the contents of "substring" are stored anywhere within "string". Returns FALSE, 0 if it is not. The function is case-sensitive.

@Created
Returns the time-date variable when the current document was created.

D – F

@Date(year;month;day)

@Date(year;month;day;hour;minute;second)

@Date(time-date)

> Converts the numbers into a time-date format and returns this as a value. This can also work with time-date variables to return their contents.

@Day(time-date)

> Returns the day of the month from the time-date variable. Can also use secondary functions, such as @Now, to return today's date.

@DbColumn("class": "NoCache"; "database"; "view"; column)

> Returns a list of values stored as a column in a database (either the current or another database). Be careful, this command can return a large amount of data – up to 64Kb as a list.

@DbLookup("class": "NoCache"; "database"; "view"; "key"; "field")

> This function looks through a specified view and retrieves all the documents that contain the "key" value within their first column of the view.

@DbManager

> Returns a list of the names of the users who have manager access to the current database.

@DbName

> Returns the name of the current database and the current Notes server. These items are returned as a single line with each element separated by a semicolon.

@DbTitle

> Returns the title of the current database.

@DDEExecute(ID; "command")

> Sends the command string, "command" to the DDE application that's pointed to by the ID. Up to 10 DDE applications can be running concurrently. The ID is provided by the DDEInitiate function. You must finish a DDE application using the DDETerminate function.

@DDEInitiate("application"; "topic")

> This function starts a DDE application, returning an ID number that can be then used within other @DDE functions. You must finish a DDE application using the DDETerminate function.

@DDEPoke(ID; "location"; "data")

> Inserts data into a DDE application, specified by the ID, at the location pointed to. If the data is correctly inserted into the application, this function will return TRUE.

@DDETerminate(ID)

> Terminates the current conversation with the DDE application pointed to by the ID. You can only have 10 conversations running, so be sure to terminate all those you have finished.

@DeleteDocument

> Deletes the current document.

@DeleteField

> Deletes the current field.

@Do(expr1; expr2; expr_n)

> Evaluates the list of expressions from left to right and returns the value of the last expression.

@DocChildren

> Returns the number of documents or categories that are children to the current document (this normally means the responses to a document).

@DocDescendants

> Returns the total number of entries – both documents and subcategories – within a view.

@DocLength

Returns the approximate size of a document, normally rounded to the nearest 64 bytes.

@DocLevel

Returns the level of the current document or category.

@DocNumber

Returns the entry number of an entry within a view.

@DocParentNumber

Returns the entry number of the parent of an entry within a view.

@DocSiblings

Returns the total number of entries at the same level as an entry within a view.

@Elements(list)

Returns the number of values within a list.

@Ends("string"; "substring")

Returns a TRUE value of 'I' if the contents of **"substring"** is stored at the end of **"string"**. Returns FALSE, '0' if it is not. The function is case sensitive.

@Environment("variable")

This function can set or return the current setting of a variable within the NOTES.INI file.

@Error

This function will generate an error within an expression and is used for testing.

@Exp(number)

Returns the result of e raised to the power **number**.

@Explode(string)

Returns a list of the elements within a text string.

@Failure(string)

Whenever a user input doesn't pass a validation test, the **string** in this function is displayed.

@False

Returns the logical FALSE function, '0'.

G – I

@Hour(time-date)

Returns the hour of the month from the **time-date** variable.

@If(condition1; action1...condition99; action99; else_action)

Evaluates the list of conditions and carries out the associated action if the condition is TRUE. If none of the conditions are TRUE then the **else_action** is performed.

@Implode(textlist, separator)

Converts a list into a string made up of the list's elements separated by the specified character.

@Integer(numberlist)

This function truncates the last numbers in a number list to the nearest integer.

@IsAvailable(fieldname)

Returns TRUE if the **fieldname** exists within the document.

@IsCategory

Returns a value if any item within a view is defined as a category.

@IsDocBeingLoaded

Returns TRUE if the document is currently being loaded into memory ready to be displayed.

@IsDocBeingMailed

Returns TRUE if the document is being mailed.

@IsDocBeingRecalculated

Returns TRUE if the document is being recalculated.

@IsDocBeingSaved

Returns TRUE if the document is being saved.

@IsError(value)

If the value is an @Error value, this function will return TRUE.

@IsExpandable

Returns the character '+' if the string is expandable, '–' if it is not.

@IsMember(string; stringlist)

This function returns TRUE if the string is one of the elements within the list. If both arguments are lists, returns TRUE if all the elements are contained in each.

@IsNewDoc

Returns TRUE if the document has not yet been saved to disk.

@IsNotMember(string; stringlist)

Returns TRUE if the element string is not contained within the stringlist.

@IsNumber(value)

Returns TRUE if the value is a number or a number list.

@IsResponseDoc

Returns TRUE if the document is a response document (a document that was created using the Compose Response... menu option).

@IsText(value)

Returns TRUE if the value is a text string or a text string list.

@IsTime(value)

Returns TRUE if the value is a time-date or a time-date list.

@IsUnavailable(field)

Returns TRUE if the field does not exist within a document

K – M

@Keywords(stringlist1; stringlist2)

Returns any matching items from stringlist1 and stringlist2.

@Left(string; number)

Returns the 'n'-most characters of the string starting at the left of the string.

@Left(string1; string2)

Returns all the characters of string1 before string2 is matched.

@LeftBack(string; number)

Counts, from the left, through number characters of string and returns these as a string.

@LeftBack(string1; string2)

Returns all the characters of string1 before string2 is matched.

@Length(textlist)

Returns the length of each string within a list of text strings.

@Ln(number)

Returns the natural log of the number.

@Log(number)

Returns the common log of the number.

@LowerCase(string)

Converts any uppercase characters into lowercase ones.

@MailDbName

Returns the name of the user's current Notes server and mail database, returned as one item with the two elements separated by a semicolon.

@MailSend

Sends the current document as a mail message to the user specified within the document's SendTo field (there must be a field named SendTo).

@MailSend("sendto"; "copyto"; "blindcopyto"; "subject"; "remark"; "bodyfield"; flags)

Sends the current document as a mail message to the user specified in the arguments of the function.

@Matches(string; pattern)

Returns TRUE if the **string** contains the **pattern** of characters. The pattern can contain wildcards.

@Max(number1; number2)

Returns the largest of the two numbers.

@Member(value; stringlist)

Returns FALSE if the **value** is not an element within the list. Returns the position of the value in the list if it is an element of the list.

@Middle("string"; offset; numberchars)

Returns **numberchars** characters after counting in **offset** characters from the left of the **string**.

@MiddleBack("string"; "separator"; number)

Searches through the **string** until it finds the **separator** character, then returns **number** characters to the right of the separator.

@Min(number1; number2)

Returns the smallest of the two numbers.

@Minute(time-date)

Returns the number of minutes of the **time-date** argument.

@Modified

Returns a time-date value that states when the document was last edited and saved.

@Modulo(number1; number2)

Returns the remainder of the operation dividing **number1** by **number2**.

@Month(time-date)

Returns the number of the month of the value. Can also use @Now within this function to find the number of today's month.

N – P

@Name([action]; name)

Carries out an **action** (such as abbreviate or expand) on a distinguished **name**.

@NewLine

Inserts a newline character (ASCII 13h) into a text string.

@No

Returns the logical value FALSE, '0'.

@Now

Returns the current time-date.

@Password(string)

Encodes the string as an unreadable list of numbers. Useful to translate a password field into an encoded form.

@Platform

Returns the name of the platform that Notes is running on (such as Windows/16, OS/2v1, Macintosh).

@Power(base, exponent)

Returns the calculation of **base** raised to the power of **exponent**.

@Prompt(style; title; prompt; default; choices)

Displays a dialogue box with the characteristics defined in the arguments and returns the user's response as a text string.

@ProperCase(string)

Capitalizes each of the words within the **string**.

Q – S

@Repeat(string; number)

Repeats the **string** by **number** of times.

@Replace("sourcelist"; "fromlist"; "tolist")

Searches through the string **sourcelist** and replaces all occurrences of **fromlist** with the values in **tolist**.

@Responses

Returns the number of responses to the document that are listed in the current view.

@Return(value)

Stops execution of a formula and returns the **value**.

@Right(string; number)

Returns the **number** rightmost characters within the **string**.

@Right(string1; string2)

Returns all the characters of **string1** that are to the right of the first match with **string2**.

@RightBack(string; number)

Returns the **number** characters, working from the right of the **string**.

@RightBack(string1; string2)

Returns all the characters of **string1**, working from the right, until it matches **string2**.

@Round(number)

Rounds the number to the nearest whole number.

@Round(number1; number2)

Rounds the **number1** to the nearest multiple of **number2**.

@Second(time-date)

Returns the seconds value from the **time-date**.

@Select(number; value1; value2..)

Returns the value that is the **number** in the list. If **number** is greater than the number of elements in the list, returns the last element.

@Set("variable"; value)

Sets the (temporary) **variable** to the **value**.

@SetEnvironment("variable"; value)

Sets the named environment **variable** within the NOTES.INI file to the **value**.

@SetField("fieldname"; value)

Sets the field to the value.

@Soundex(string)

Returns the special Soundex code for this **string**. Used in the Name & Address book.

@Subset(list; number)

Returns the first **number** of items within the **list**.

@Success

Returns logical TRUE, '1'.

T – V

@Text(value)

Converts a **value** to a string.

@TextToNumber(string)

Converts a text **string** to a numerical value (if possible).

@TextToTime(string)

Converts a text **string** to a time-date value (if possible).

@Time(hour; minute; second)

Returns the time-date value built up from the various elements.

@Today

Returns today's date.

@Tomorrow

Returns the time-date value of tomorrow.

@Trim(string)

This function will remove any leading or trailing spaces from a string or blank elements from a **string** list.

@True

Returns logical TRUE, '1'.

@Unavailable

Returns UNAVAILABLE if you want to make a field not available.

@Unique(textlist)

Removes any duplicate entries from the list.

@UpperCase(string)

Converts all lower case characters to uppercase.

@UserName

Returns the user's name.

@UserPrivileges

Returns a list that contains the user's current privileges (returned as the position of the privilege within the list rather than the name of the privilege itself).

@ViewTitle

Returns the name of the current view.

W – Z

@Weekday(time-date)

Returns the day of the week of the **time-date** value (as a number with 1=Sunday, 7=Saturday).

@Word(string; separator; number)

Returns the **number** word within the **string** (where a word is defined as characters with a **separator** character on each side).

@Year(time-date)

Returns the year of the **time-date** value.

@Yes

Returns logical TRUE, '1'.

@Yesterday

Returns the time-date value for yesterday.

Appendix B: NOTES.INI variables

Allow_Access_[portname] = name

Defines the users, servers or groups that can access a server's port (**portname** is the name defined in the Port Setup dialogue box). If the entry has an asterisk, this means everyone in the Name & Address book; an asterisk followed by a view name means everyone in this particular view; an asterisk followed by a slash and a certifier's name means everyone certified by this certifier.

Background_Filter_Day = day and time

When the Chronos program will run its weekly macros on the server.

Background_Filter_Hour = day and time

When the Chronos program will run its daily macros on the server.

Default_Index_Lifetime_Days = days

Function that will delete indexes associated with a particular view after the specified number of days. This helps to save space on the server. It is overridden by the setting in the Design View Attributes box of a database which has the same effect.

Deny_Access_[portname] = name

Defines the users, servers or groups that cannot access a server's port (portname is the name defined in the Port Setup dialog box). If the entry has an asterisk, this means everyone in the Name & Address book; an asterisk followed by a view name means everyone in this particular view; an asterisk followed by a slash and a certifier's name means everyone certified by this certifier.

Desktop = filename

Name of an alternative workspace configuration file. Normally, Notes will try and load DESKTOP.DSK from the local workstation's disk drive. Most useful if you need to maintain multiple configurations on your computer, for training or for different users.

Domain = name

Name of the domain to which this server belongs (or the domain of the user's home server).

DST = 1

(Daylight Savings Time) If this is set to 1 the server or workstation will observe DST which has the same effect as choosing this option from the Time Zone Location Setup dialog box.

Fixup = value

Defines the type of database fixup actions that are carried out when the server is first started up. Values are:

0 – scan all databases and delete corrupt documents

2 – scan all databases, even if they were properly closed, and delete corrupt documents

4 – as per 2 but scans each individual document

These values can be added together, for example: 6 carries out the functions of 2 and 4.

FT_Max_Instances = words

Maximum size of a document within a database that can be indexed. By default this is set to 100,000 words. When using full-text indexing, the memory required is around ten times the value specified in this setting.

KeyFile = filename

Filename and path that points to the Notes ID file.

Log = value

Defines the options for any log file that is to be kept. There are five values each separated by commas; these are:

i) log file name

ii) selection of following options (added together):

1 – log to console

2 – force fixup when opening log file

4 – full document scan

iii) not used

iv) age of log file in days before it is deleted

v) size of log text as number of events

Example:

Log = LOG.NSF, 1, 0, 14, 10000

Log_Replication = 1

If set to 1 then the start and finish actions of a replication are saved as part of the log file and shown on the server console.

Log_Sessions = 1

If set to 1 then the individual sessions are saved as part of the log file and displayed on the server console.

MailEncryptIncoming = 1

If set to 1 this forces all mail by all users to be encrypted. If this option is not set, users can encrypt their own mail using the encrypt check box in the compose dialogue or by setting the Encrypt Incoming Mail option within their Person document in the Name & Address book.

MailLowPriorityTime = time

Defines period of the day when the server will call other servers to exchange mail if there is only low priority mail in the queue. Normally, this would be between midnight and 6.00am, but can be set as required. Note: you must enter a time range, not just a single time, and it's specified in 24-hour clock.

MainTimeout = days

Period of time, in days, before Notes returns undelivered mail to the sender. If there's no setting, this is taken as one day.

Memory_Quota = size

Maximum size of the Windows swap file that Notes can allocate as virtual memory. Minimum value is 4Mb, without any setting Notes will try and use all available memory.

MinNewMailPoll = minutes

Defines how often the workstation software will poll the server to check if there is any new mail for the user. Normally set at 15 minutes. If you reduce this setting, you will increase the network traffic and could reduce response time of the network as well as providing more load for the Notes server, slowing its performance.

Names = filenames

Lists the **filenames** of the Name & Address books (without their NSF extension) that are searched by Notes when trying to verify the correct address of a mail message. The first filename must be called NAMES, thereafter you can list other filenames. Workstations will search through all the filenames listed, but a server will only look for other servers or group names within the first Address Book (NAMES) which therefore must contain all user, group and server names. (Maximum length of line is 256 characters.)

NIF_Pool_Size = number

Defines the maximum amount of memory set aside to be used as short-term memory to store index and data about views currently in use. For workstations, the default setting of 1Kb should be sufficient, but for servers you might need to increase this to support large numbers of users or concurrent views. (Maximum size: 64Kb.)

NoDesignMenu = 1

If set to 1 this removes the Design menu from the Notes workplace. This means that a user cannot create their own private views.

NoExternalApps = 1

If set to 1 this prevents certain functions under Windows and certain external Notes functions on the workstation to prevent the chance of viruses crashing the workstation. Prevents the following features:

Windows:

OLE, DDE, DIP

Notes:

@Command, @DBLookup and @DBColumn (for Non-Notes drivers),

@MailSend, @DDExx, Launching file attachments

NoForce_Activity_Logging = 1

If set to 1 this will prevent the Catalog function from automatically setting every database on the server to Record Activity mode, which would add 64Kb to the size of each database.

NoMailMenu = 1

If set to 1 this will remove the Mail menu from the Notes workplace. This means users cannot send Notes mail – this option would normally be used if you have another, external mail package.

NoMouse = 1

If set to 1 this will disable the workstation's mouse.

NSF_Buffer_Pool_Size = size

Defines the amount of memory used as a buffer to cache I/O operations when indexing a database. You might need to adjust this setting to provide the best performance which is not too small to be effective and not too large to cause Windows to swap. (Default setting is 2Mb.)

PhoneLog = number

Defines which phone calls made by the server are recorded to the Notes log file. The possible values of the number are:

0 – don't log phone calls

1 – log all calls except when the number was busy

2 – log all phone calls

SecureMail = 1

If set to 1 this option will automatically add security features to all mail sent: all mail is signed and encrypted. Additionally, the sign and encrypt check box options are not displayed to the user.

Server_Console_Password = password

This setting works with the SET SECURE command on the server to provide a server password.

ServerKeyFileName = UserIDfilename

If you are running the Windows server and Windows workstation program on the same PC and need to log in to the workstation as a particular user rather than as the supervisor, you can specify the ID file that you want to use here.

Server_Session_Timeout = minutes

Defines the amount of time of user inactivity before the server will disconnect either a remote dial-in user or a LAN user. Normally, this is set to 15minutes. For dial-in users, XPC

ServerTasks = tasks

has its own timeout variable that, if shorter, will override this setting.

ServerTasks = tasks

Defines the tasks that load automatically and run when the server starts up and continue to run until the server is shut down. The default setting starts Replica, Router and Update utilities, but you can add other server-based utilities — although each will increase the load on the server.

ServerTasksAt<time> = taskname

Defines a schedule for server maintenance tasks and when they are run. Normally, the following tasks are run at these specified times:

Database Catalog and Design 1.00am
Views in all databases updates at 2.00am
Database statistics in log files updated at 5.00am

You can specify your own schedule using the `ServerTasksAtn` command where **n** is the time in the 24-hour clock. For example, to set the Views to update at 3.00am instead of 2.00, you would enter the following line:

ServerTasksAt3 = UpdAll

Update_No_Fulltext = 1

If set to 1 this will prevent any full-text search from being updated during an UPDALL utility process.

Update_Suppression_limit = number

If set, this will override the setting in the `Update_Suppression_Time` variable if more than a certain number of duplicate requests to update an index are received.

Update_Suppression_Time = minutes

Defines the delay between updating the views and the full text index of a database.

Index

Symbols

@All 250
@Environment 249
@Hour 247
@LowerCase 247
@URLGetHeader 192
@URLHistory 192
@URLOpen 192

A-C

Access control level
   and remote access 102
   and replication 115
Access Control List (ACL)
   Agent creation 199
   creating 240–1
   database security 264
   Domino Server 279, 281, 284, 290
   field and form design 219
   settings and rights 265
Activity log (database use) 137–8
ActiveX – see *Domino Server*
Administration (of administrator) 156
   adding new 157
   leaves company 157
Administration (of server) 147
   backups 52, 151

backup strategy 152
full backup 152
incremental backups 153
media rotation 153–4
disk mirroring 52
restoring 152
timing 153
database FIXUP 149–51
dead mail 148–9
Remote Server Console 149, 159–60
server access lists 158
server commands
   BROADCAST 160
   DROP 160
   EXIT 160
   HELP 160
   LOAD 160
   PULL 161
   PUSH 161
   QUIT 161
   REPLICATE 161–2
   ROUTE 162
   SET SECURE 162
   SHOW CONFIGURATION 163
   SHOW DIRECTORY 163
   SHOW DISKSPACE 163
   SHOW MEMORY 163
   SHOW PORT 163–4
   SHOW SCHEDULE 164
   SHOW SESSIONS 164
   SHOW STATISTICS 164
   SHOW TASKS 148, 164
   SHOW TRANSACTIONS 164
   SHOW USERS 164
   TELL 164

server log
    activity recording 154–5
    LOG.NSF 154
    viewing 155–6

Administration (of users) 140
    changing a user's ID 144
    changing a user's name 142–3
        via mail 142
    editing the Person Document 144–5
    groups and users 146
    recovering ID or password 145
    user leaves the company 141

Aging 134–5

Agents 4, 198, 207
    actions available 200
    configuring 199
    creating 39–40, 198
    database FIXUP 151
    document selection 201
    Internotes Refresh Agent 188–89
    triggering 200
    update Web pages 188
    vacation example 201–2

Apple Macintosh
    connectivity issues 81
    workstations 72–3

AppleTalk
    and NetWare-4 80–1
    and Notes for Windows NT 81
    platform connectivity issues 81

Applications (designing)
    About… Document 239
    Agents and actions 207
    database creation 207–8
        by copying 210
        new, blank database 208
        using a template 209
    database elements
        document 206
        field 206
        folders 206
        form 205
        view 206

database icon 238
database security 240
fields
    creating and defining 219–23
    field format 224–5
    field formulae 223–4
    hiding fields 226
form creation 210
    copying a form 212
    form types 215
    inheriting changes 212–13
    new, blank form 213
    setting attributes 214
form design 215
    adding graphics 218
    adding text 217
    design guidelines 216
forms
    setting default 215
full-text search index 241
    creating 242
Navigators 235–6
    creating 236–7
programming – see *Programming*
types of database 204
    approvals 205
    broadcast 204
    discussion 205
    reference 204
Using… Document 239
view
    configuring 228–9
    creating 227–8
    designing 226
    designing/configuring columns 230–1, 233
    response hierarchy 234–5

Approvals database 205
ATM (backbone) 78
Attachments 33
    changing user ID with 143
    document links 36
    files 33
        compressing 34
        options for recipient 34
    files and RTF fields 33–4

Notes documents 35
OLE and RTF fields 35

Backbone connecting servers 78
Backups
    server – see *Administration (server)*
Bandwidth
    increasing effective 77 – see also *Network traffic*
Banyan VINES 76
Bridges 58
BROADCAST 160
Broadcast database 204
Bus
    EISA 48
    ISA 47
    mastering 48, 55–6
    MCA 48
    PCI 48, 56
Button 172

CATALOG.NSF 133
Certifier Documents 124
Certified ID 142
Certifier ID 97
Certifier server 259
CGI 281 – see also *Domino Server*
    file directory (Domino Server) 286
    scripts (Domino Server) 287
Character Set (LMBCS) 275
Client–server model 77
Compressing
    e-mail attachments 175
CompuServe 182
Connecting platforms 80
    Macintoshes 81
    NetBIOS 81
    OS/2 platforms 82
    PCs to multiple LANs 82
Connection Documents 96, 123
    controlling replication and routing 109–11

creating 112
mail routing 118

D–F

Database
    access using icons 19
    access via menu 19
    adding documents 29
    backups
        restoring 152
    categories for organization 25–6
    copying to laptop 101
    document navigation 25
    how to use 21
    navigators 40
    opening 20
    replication – see *Replication*
    viewing
        documents 24
        panes and windows 24
    viewing (panes and windows) 22
Database administration 132
    activity log 137–8
    aging 134–5
    compacting 139–40
        LOAD COMPACT 140
    data directories
        directory pointers 132–3
    database files
        cataloging (CATALOG.NSF) 133
        creating a library 133
    database FIXUP utility 149–51
    database pointers 133
    database statistics 137
    monitoring database use 135–7
        user activity 136
        user transactions 136
    monitoring replication 138
    removing old documents 134
    replication history 138–9

Index

Database applications – see *Applications (designing)*
Database exchange 86–7, 99, 100
Database pointers 133
Database replication – see *Replication*
DBLIB4.NTF 133
DEFAULT.STP 31
Destination server 90
Directory pointers 132
Directory services 123
Discussion database 205
Documents
    adding to a database 29
    attachments 33
    checking for unread 37–8
    mode
        edit 28–9
        read-only 28–9
    navigation 25
        hotspots, buttons and URLs 27
        symbols and data status 26
    types
        About… Document 239
        Certifier Document 124
        Connection Document 123
        Domain Document 124
        Group Document 124
        Mail-in Document 124
        Person Document 123
        Program Document 124
        Server Document 123
        Using… Document 239
Domain Documents 124
Domains
    defined 124
    domain name vs. server name 127
    managing multiple 126
    setting up 125–6
    types of (compared) 125
Domino Server
    ACL 281
    ActiveX 279–80
    CGI 279, 281
        CGI files 286
    configuring 284
    database publishing 279
    database security (ACL) 284
    FTP 281
    hardware requirements 282
    home page 286
        'About' documents 286
        creation 284
        setting default 285
        URL for 285
    HTML generation 279, 282
        automatic 280
        from Notes databases 282
        version 3.2 280
    HTTP
        protocol 280
        server 281
    installing Domino Server 283
    Internet 281
        service provider 283
    and InterNotes 280
    intranet 281
    Java 279–80
    Javascript 280
    and NOTES.INI 284
    Notes databases (linking to) 282
    obtaining (via download) 280, 283
    performance statistics 284
    Perl 279, 281
    quitting ('`tell http quit`' console command) 284
    security issues 290
        ACLs 290
        Person documents 290
        Secure Sockets Layer (SSL) 290
    starting ('`load http`' console command) 284
    TCP/IP 282
        port settings 285
    text-search functions 289
    Web publishing 279
    Web-page programming 287
        CGI scripts 287

Index

    creating links 289
    image maps 288
    Java 288
    LotusScript 288
    Perl 288
DROP 160

Edit mode
  switching to 28–9
EISA 47, 48
E-mail 13 – see also *Mail*
  addressing the message 170
  attachments 174
    compared to import 175
    compressing 175
    files 16
    OLE 174
    receiving 175
  checking from another computer 176–7
  configuring remote access 98–9
  dead mail 148
  fax gateway 181
  finding address 15
  front-ends 178
  gateways to other systems 178
  Hold Mail 98
  Internet 182
  mail standards 178
  MAPI 179–80
  Memo 14
    To, CC, BCC and Subject 14, 15
  message
    creation 169
    delivery options 17, 18, 173–4
    encryption 174
    message priority 18
    receipt report 18
    security 176
    signing 176
  message features
    button 172
    link hotspot 172
    table 171
    text popup 172

  Mood Stamps 16
  postbox folder structure 169
  remote users 97–8
  routing
    connection document 118
    control and connection documents 109–11
    controlling 109
    defined 109
    scheduling 119
    setting up 117
  RTF (Rich Text Field) 15
  saving messages 17
  sending to a list of named users 15
  sending to other systems 179
  standards
    MAPI 179
    Novell MHS 179
    PROFS 180
    SMTP 181
    X.400 and X.500 180
  To:, CC:, BCC: 170–1
Encryption
  and security 263
  in a database 265
  of e-mail 176
ENVIRONMENT 249
Ethernet
  bandwidth 77
EXIT 160

Fax
  gateway for e-mail 181
  Lotus Fax Server 181
  providing 60
FDDI 77
FIELD 249–50
Fields (defining)
  form design 219–23
  format 224–5
  formulas 223–4
  hiding fields 226
Firewall 195
FIXUP 149, 150
  NAMES.NSF 151

NOTES.INI values 150
PULL and REPLICA 150
Formula
  writing 251
Forwarding address 141
FTP
  and Domino Server 281
Full-text search 31
  Domino Server 289

G-I

Group
  creating new 146
  editing 147
Group Documents 124
Groupware 2

HELP 160
Help icon 12
Hold Mail
  and remote access 98
Hotspot – see *Document navigation*
HTML 192 – see also *Domino Server*

Icon editor 12
Index
  and searches 31
Interactive connection 86, 104
International support 274–5
  time zones 276
Internet 3, 42
  access 189
    controlling 190
  Domino Server 194, 281
  e-mail 182
  HTML 192
  Internet service provider (ISP) 283
  InterNIC organization 285
  InterNotes
    configuring 188
    and Domino Server 280
    Gopher function 187
    obtaining 186
    Refresh Agent 188–9
  InterNotes News 194
  Lotus Domino 186
  security 194
    firewall 195
    isolated LAN security 195
    protocol security 195
  updating Web pages 188
  Web Navigator 190
    @-commands for 192
    editing home page 191–92
    setting up 187
  Web Publisher 192
  www.lotus.com/inews/ 192
  www.lotus.com/inotes 186
InterNIC organization
  registering domains 285
InterNotes – see *Internet*
Intranet – see *Domino Server*
IPX.COM 79
IPX/SPX protocol 65
  and Windows NT 67
ISA 48
ISDN 61–2

J-L

Java 288 – see also *Domino Server*
Javascript 280

Languages
  character sets 275
  international support 274
LANs – see also *Network*
  connecting PCs to multiple 82
Laptop computer
  copying database to 101
Link hotspot 172

LOAD 160
LOAD MONITOR 267
LOG.NSF 151, 154–5
   protocol activity 83
Lotus Domino 186
LotusScript – see also *Programming*
   and Domino Server 288

M–O

Macros 247
Mail – see also *E-mail*
   MAIL.BOX 98
   MAIL.NSF 151
   Notes.ini and SecureMail 264
   security of 263
Mail-in Documents 124
MAPI 179–80
MCA 47
MDM files 93–4
Memo 14
Modem 60
   fault debugging 94
   (of) remote access workstation 95
   TEMPLATE.MDM file 95
Mood Stamp 16, 174

Name & Address database (personal)
   items stored in 129
   using nicknames 129
Name & Address database (public)
   8 document types 123–4
   directory services 123
   managing multiple 124, 126
      multiple books per server 126–7
      one book per server 126
   NAMES.NSF 122
   on user's workspace 128
   two types 122
Name and Address book

   and remote access 96–7
NAMES.NSF 121–2, 126, 151
   and FIXUP 151
Navigators 40–1, 206, 235–7
   creating image maps 288
   home page 191
NDIS 79
NetBEUI 67, 79
NetBIOS 67, 78
   and connecting platforms 81
NetWare 65, 67, 70, 79
   connecting to 80
   poor integration with NT 67
   prior to 4.0, a warning 70
   versions 3.12, 4.01 or 4.1 68
NetWare 4
   linking platforms 80
   Macintosh support 81
Network 46
   adapter card 55
      bus mastering 56
      DMA 56
      PCI local bus 56
      programmed I/O 56
      shared memory 55
   bandwidth
      Ethernet 77
   client–server
      model 77
      setup 46
   configurations for Notes server 46
   connectivity issues 56–7
      fax–modem 60
      hardware 57
      ISDN 61–2
      modems 60
      repeaters 57
      software 56, 57
      WANs 59
   network name vs. domain name 127
   Notes traffic 76
   peer-to-peer 46
   protocols 78
      activity – Log.NSF 83

Index

AppleTalk 78
Banyan VINES 78
NetBEUI 79
NetBIOS 78
Novell SPX/SPX II 79
TCP/IP 79
shells 79
Windows-95 80
traffic
(and) client–server model 77
solutions to 77–8
wide-area network 59
Nicknames 129
Notes
starting 6
Notes server
3 ways of running 46
architecture 47
bus 47–8
disk cacheing 50–1
disk controller 49
how much RAM? 49
processor 48
backup hardware 51 – see also *Administration (server)*
disk mirroring 52
siting 52
dedicated server 47
hardware requirements 47
and OS/2 64
software requirements 64–5
making the choice 70
Novell NetWare 4.1 68–9
OS/2 65–6
under Window-95 66
Unix 69, 70
Windows NT 67
where to place it? 51
NOTES.INI
and Domino Server 284
setting environment variables 249
setting values in (SET CONFIGURATION) 162
Novell MHS 179

Novell NetWare 4.1 68–9
Novell ODI 79
Novell SPX/SPX II 79

ODI
connecting to multiple LANs 82
OLE
attachments 35, 174
On-line discussions 29
OS/2 1, 2, 65
and workstations 72
compatibility 66
connectivity issues 82
Notes network configurations 46
Notes network support 76
protocols supported 66
setup 66

P-R

Page tags
configuring 10
Passthru server
connection document 96
replication 114
setting up 89
destination server 90
workstations 91
Password 262
intruder prevention 271
protection (server) 266
recovering forgotten 145
and remote users 97
PCI 47–8 – see also *Network adapter* and *Bus*
Perl 281
scripts 288
Person Document 123
editing 144–5
Printing 36–7

318

PROFS 180
Program Documents 124
Programming 245 – see also
Applications (designing)
    @All 250
    @Environment 249
    @functions 246
    @Hour 247
    @LowerCase 247
    formula writing 251
    LotusScript 254
        examples 255–6
    Macros 247
        Button 248
        Execute-once 248
        Filter 248
        Search 248
        SmartIcon 248
    number crunching 253
    reserved keywords
        DEFAULT, ENVIRONMENT, FIELD, SELECT, REM 248
    string manipulation 251
        @Text(@Created) 252
    time and dates 254
Protocol activity
    Log.NSF 83
PULL 161
    and FIXUP 150
PUSH 161

Query Builder 32
QUIT 161

RAID disk arrays 52
Read-only mode 28–9
Record locking
    database replication 109
Reference database 204
Registering
    new users 258
Registry

Windows 95 options 270
REM 250
Remote access 86
    connection document 96
    database exchange 86–7, 99, 100
        configuring replication 101–2
        dialing the server 103
    e-mail 97–8
        configuring 98–9
        Hold Mail 98
    interactive connection 86, 104
    modem configuration 93–4
    Name and Address Book 96–7
    Replicator Page 103
    server configuration
        serial port 92
    server requirements 92
    setting up 87
    workstation
        configuration 94
        modem setup 95
        requirements 92
        serial port 95
Remote Server Console 159
Remote user – see also *Remote access*
    registering 97
    security issues 263
Repeaters 57
REPLICA
    and FIXUP 150
REPLICATE 161–2
Replicate Access Control 100
Replication
    control
        access control levels 115
        connection documents 109–11
    creating a connection document 112
    databases and mail messages 109
    databases on remote servers 113–14
    defined 108
    deleting old documents 134
    individual database settings 115–16
    monitoring 116, 138

Index

passthru server 114
problems with 109
and remote access 101–103
replication history 138–9
Replicator Page 103
Replicator Workpage 87
rules governing 114
scheduling 112–13, 119
setting up 111
Replicator Page 103
Replicator Workpage 87
Reserved keywords 248
  DEFAULT 249
  ENVIRONMENT 249
  FIELD 249, 250
  REM 250
  SELECT 250
Restoring
  a backed-up database 152
ROUTE 162
Routers 58
RTF field (Rich Text Field) 15
  and OLE object attachments 35
  formatting text 41

S-U

Schedule
  mail routing 119
  replication 112–13, 119
SCSI 49
  backup hardware 51
Search
  AND, OR and NOT operators 32
  DEFAULT.STP 31
  documents for text 29
    extended searches 30
  full-text 32
    creating index 31
  highlighting successful search 33

Secure Sockets Layer (SSL)
  Domino Server 290
Security 262
  data encryption 263
  databases 240
    encryption 265
    (via ACLs) 264
  Domino Server 290
  firewall 195
  improving 273
  Internet 194
  intruder prevention 271
  mail 176, 263–64
  network file
    share-level and user-level 272
  network operating system
    LOAD MONITOR 267
  passwords 262
  remote user issues 263
  Secure Sockets Layer (SSL) 290
  server 265
    access lists 266
    password 266
  user security 262
    user leaves the company 141
  Windows 3.1x 268
  Windows-95 269
    editing System Policies 269
    User Policy (creating new) 270
SELECT 250
  and FIELD 250
Serial port
  of remote access server 92, 94
  of remote access workstation 95–6
Server access lists 158
Server Document 123
  adding an administrator 158
  server access list 159
Server log (LOG.NSF) 154
SET SECURE 162
SET STATISTICS 163

320

Index

Setting up
   international support 274–5
      time zones 276
   users 258
      certifier server 259
      registering new 258
      security and user ID 262
      user registration (automatic – via text file) 261
      user registration (manual) 260
SHOW CONFIGURATION 163
SHOW DIRECTORY 163
SHOW DISKSPACE 163
SHOW MEMORY 163
SHOW PORT 163–4
SHOW SCHEDULE 164
SHOW SESSIONS 164
SHOW STATISTICS 164
SHOW TASKS 164
SHOW TRANSACTIONS 164
SHOW USERS 164
Signing
   e-mail message 176
SmartIcon bar
   for document navigation 25
SmartStatus bar 8
SMTP 181
Starting Notes
   StartUp folder 6
System Policies 269
   editing 269–70

TCP/IP 65, 79
   and connecting platforms 80
   Domino Server 282
   port settings
      and Domino Server 285
TELL 164
TEMP.NSF 145
TEMPLATE.MDM 95
Time zones 276
Tracking database 205

Uninterruptible power supply (UPS) 53
   UPS power ratings 54
Unix 69, 70
   and workstations 72
Unread documents 37–8
URL – see also *Internet*
   creating links (Domino Server) 289
   hotspots 27
   image maps 288
User groups 130
User ID 260
   backup ID disk
      creating 177
      using to log on 177
   changing 143–4
   changing via mail 142
   for remote mail-checking 176
   recovering forgotten 145
   and security 262
User Policy
   creating 270
User Profile 269

V–Z

Vacation Agent 201–2
Views (designing) 226
VIM 180

Web site – see also *Internet* and *Domino Server*
   Domino Server:
      http://domino.lotus.com 283
   InterNIC (www.internic.net) 285
   InterNotes 4
   Lotus (http://www.lotus.com) 28, 280
Web publishing – see also *Domino Server*
   InterNotes 279–80
Web.NSF 188
White space

Index

database compacting 139
Wide-area networks 59
Windows-95 1, 46
   multiple protocol stacks 80
   and Notes Server 66
   workstations 71–3
Windows NT 46, 66
   NetWare integration 67
   Notes Server 67
Workspace
   setting preferences 129
Workstation
   configuring for passthru 91

hardware requirements 54
   Macintosh workstations 55
   PC workstations 55
remote access 94–5
software requirements 71
   Apple Macintosh 72–3
   OS/2 72
   Unix 72
   Windows 3.1 71
   Windows 95/NT 71–2
World Wide Web (WWW) – see *Internet*

X.400 and X.500 180

Also from Digital Press:

Microsoft Exchange Server: Planning, Design, and Implementation
by Tony Redmond

Microsoft Exchange Server is for people interested in deploying Microsoft's electronic messaging and groupware server in the distributed environments commonly encountered in large corporations.

1996   450 pp   pb   ISBN: 1-55558-162-5   DEC Part No. EY-U042E-DP $34.95

Migrating to the Intranet and Microsoft Exchange
by Randall J. Covill

This book provides critical information for information system managers concerned with providing information and network infrastructure especially for Exchange, enterprise-wide mail systems and the Intranet.

March 1997   250pp   pb   ISBN: 1-55558-172-2   DEC Part No. EY-V420E-DP $29.95

Intranet Development: An IS/IT Manager's Guide
by Judith Hall and James Keenan

Intranet Development: An IS/IT Manager's Guide follows the development of Intranets within a range of companies by using step-by-step case studies. The stages of Intranet development documented in these various businesses can be broadly applied to all organizations setting up Intranets of their own.

March 1997   350pp   pb   ISBN: 1-55558-171-4   DEC Part No. EY-V427E-DP $29.95

Electronic Mail: A Practical Guide
by Simon Collin

A practical guide/source book of tips and ideas for experienced system managers together with all the information to help someone who's just been landed with the project of installing E-Mail. The content covers choosing and installing E-Mail for small peer-to-peer LANs to client server models to WANs.

1995   350 pp   pb   ISBN: 0-7506-2112-5   DEC Part No. EY-T859E-DP $29.95

**Available from all good booksellers or in case of difficulty call:
1-800-366-2665 in the U.S. or +44 1865 310366 in Europe.**